THE 356 PORSCHE

A RESTORER'S GUIDE
TO AUTHENTICITY

NEW REVISED EDITION

DR. B. JOHNSON

Copyright © 1990, 1992, 1997
Brett Johnson

ISBN 0-929758-16-1

All rights reserved. No part of this publication may be reproduced,
stored in a retrieval system, or transmitted, in any form or by any means,
electronic, mechanical, photocopying, recording or otherwise,
without prior written permission of the publisher.

Published by Beeman Jorgensen, Inc.
7510 Allisonville Road, Suite 115, Indianapolis, IN 46250 U.S.A.

Printed and bound in the United States of America
Cover design and photography by Llew Kinst, Cupertino, California

First Printing, October 1997

Contents

Acknowledgments iv
Introduction v
Background vi
The Models 1
Inner Body and Chassis 9
Exterior Body Panels 19
Exterior Trim 45
Luggage Compartment 77
Interior 87

Appendicies

    Color Charts 134
    Chassis Number Chart 143
    Spotter's Guide 150

Index 152

Acknowledgments

I am grateful to the following "experts" for supplying informational literature and for proof reading this text for technical accuracy, spelling, grammar etc. Without the help of these people, the following text would have been considerably less thorough and correct: Bruce Baker, Frank Barrett - *Toad Hall Motorbooks,* Bill Block - *Block's Books*, Don Fowler, Julie Johnson, Llew Kinst, Theresa Mason, Dale Miller, Richard Miller, Brad Ripley - *NLA Limited,* Ron Roland - *Roland Automotive*, Cole Scrogham, Vic Skirmants - *356 Enterprises,* Mark Turczyn and Don Zingg.

Without the following photographers and photogenic models, I can assure you that this book would not be particularly useful. Due to the number of photos it was not practical to credit individual photos, but these 356 enthusiasts and their vehicles are: Shep Adkins - '64 coupe, Mike Allen - '65 coupe, Bill Altaffer - '57 Speedster, Arthur Arakelian - '64 cabriolet, Jack Arct - '62 Carrera 2 coupe, Alan Bambina - '62 Karmann Hardtop, Otto Bargezi - '52 coupe, Jim Barrington - '52, '53 & '54 coupes, Fred Bernardo - '63 & '64 coupe, '63 cabriolet, Jim Billig - '60 Roadster, Tom Birch - '51 cabriolet, Barnett Black - '59 coupe, Patty Block - '65 cabriolet, Simon Bowery - '50 coupe, Bill Brown - '57 Carrera Speedster, Dave Busteed - '54 cabriolet, Charles Coker - '60 Super 90 GT coupe & '63 Carrera 2 coupe, Scott Coverly - '64 coupe, Richard Cowan - '62 coupe, Stephen Craig - '58 Speedster, Ken Daugherty - various, Dave Derossett - '58 cabriolet, James Dix - '60 Roadster, Steve Douglas - '58 Speedster, '58, '59 & '60 coupes, Bill Durland - '64 SC GT, Erling Falck - '57 coupe, George Field, '57 Speedster, Don Fowler - '58 Speedster, Denny Frick - '65 cabriolet, Bill Garvey - '65 coupe, Jack Gosnell - '58 Speedster, Kent Fujikawa - '59 coupe, Jack Griffin - '55 Speedster, Tom Grunnah - '57 Speedster, Gene Gully - '64 coupe, Shelley & Fred Harper - '61 cabriolet, Dale Hawley - '64 coupe, Victor Ingram - '55 coupe, Bob Jernigan - '53 coupe, Del Johnston - '56 coupe, John Kent - '64 coupe, Llew Kinst - various, Ed Kollar - '52 coupe, Tom Lovelace - '56 Speedster, Ted Lyman - '56 cabriolet, Jerry Manna - '57 coupe, Michael Marino - '65 coupe, John Markle - '63 coupe, Diane McWilliams - '58 cabriolet, Gary Meyer - '60 Roadster, Jack Miles - '63 coupe, Dale Miller - '58 Speedster, Richard Miller - '54 coupe & '54 Speedster, Dale Moody - '58 Convertible D, Bill Moore - '63 cabriolet, Steve Moore - '61 Karmann Hardtop, Tony Murad - '59 Convertible D & '64 coupe, Nestor Negron - '59 GT Speedster, Tom Niedernhofer - '51 cabriolet, William Noroski - '58 coupe, Fred Otjen - '58 Speedster & '63 coupe, Paul Parouse - '60 Roadster, John Paterek - '52 America Roadster, Bill Perrone - '61 Roadster, Orr Potebnya - '57 Speedster, Wayne Potter - '64 cabriolet, Jerry Purtell - '63 coupe, Bill Rienecke - '62 Roadster, Denny Robertson - '60 coupe, Frank Scheller - '55 coupe, Bob Schmitt - '55 Speedster & '58 coupe, Phillip Schudmak - '51 coupe & '51 cabriolet, Mark Scorgie - '58 coupe, Cole Scrogham - various, Tom Scott - '51 cabriolet & '52 coupe, Bud Shank - '63 coupe, Tony Singer - '58 Speedster & '65 cabriolet, Stephen Speidel - '64 coupe, Bob Stonerock - '65 coupe & '65 cabriolet, John Summer - '56 Speedster, Victor Triana - '64 coupe, Tom Tuccillo - '59 cabriolet, Mark Turczyn - various, Bob Vinson - '63 cabriolet, Keith Vollenweider - '60 Roadster, Joe Vomund - '60 Roadster and Randall Waldron - '56 coupe, Marshall West - '51 coupe, Kenneth Wunsche - '56 coupe & '62 Karmann Hardtop, Greg Young - '57 Speedster, Don Zingg - '54 Speedster.

Finally, I would like to thank Dick Ferrer for his original illustrations.

Introduction

There are a number of books that detail the Porsche factory's history. They include fascinating tales of the personalities present and politics involved during the development of the world's finest automobile. While most are entertaining to read, they are generally lacking to some degree in accurate descriptions of the various models of 356 and the changes made over the years. This book, which originated as a collection of articles printed in the *356 Registry,* seeks to be what the other books are not: an accurate guide to the authenticity of the 356 Porsche.

There once was a popular misconception that each 356 Porsche was a unique, hand-built masterpiece. At any given time during assembly, the story continued, capricious workers would pluck odd-ball or obsolete parts from bins along the line, wantonly installing them at random. This was apparently done to confound future generations of concours judges and competitors alike. Fortunately, this just was not so.

With few exceptions, 356 Porsches were constructed on assembly lines with detail changes occurring on a sequential basis. This is not to say that cars were assembled in numeric order. In fact, virtually all cars were built out of sequence. Because of this, the use of chassis numbers to identify part changes in this text should be interpreted as relative rather than absolute. Changes were often not associated with model or year breaks and may not have occurred at precisely the same time among various coachbuilders. However it is the rule, not the exception, that up to a certain point, things were one way. At that point, a change was made and all cars subsequently assembled featured the update.

The earliest cars seem to have more than their share of peculiarities. Many were likely due to the small size of Porsche at that time and the rapid evolution of the 356 in the first few years. Later cars show remarkable consistency. Occasional cars with unusual features do turn up, but dealer and owner modifications account for the vast majority.

The publication of the first edition of this book in 1987 was a starting point. This third edition has clarified additional information, filled in several of the blanks and dispelled some more of the myths. As with previous versions, this book serves as a guide to those restoring damaged or incomplete 356 Porsches and is a valuable reference for the concours participant and enthusiast with acquisition in mind.

356 Registry members have "kept the faith" in a world of look-alike cars designed for the average driver. The continued input from these enthusiasts has made this revised edition possible. Those interested in the organization should write to: The 356 Registry, 27244 Ryan Road, Warren, Michigan 48092.

Brett Johnson

Background

Porsche Part Numbers

Porsche part numbers come in two basic formats. Early part numbers have eight digits in three groups separated by periods (NNN.NN.NNN); later numbers, which commenced during 1955, have eleven digits and appeared in four groups (NNN.NNN.NNN.NN).

The first group of three numbers in both the eight-digit and eleven-digit series represents the car type, engine type, or gearbox type. The second group of numbers within the series is a further defining of the part into a category. For example, in the number NNN.559.NNN.NN, the 559 represents an external trim part. The third group of numbers with the series, again is further definition. With sided pieces the third group denotes left or right; an odd number is left and an even number is right.

As a rule of thumb, when looking at the last two numbers in the eleven digit type part numbers, 00 is generally found on the original parts. As this part is amended the number increases. For parts found only on open models these numbers are often 40 or occasionally 20. When the 356B was introduced the last two numbers were often 05 if a change had occurred. The number 06 is frequently observed on parts found on T 6 bodied cars with 07 on parts changed on the 356C model.

Tools Of The Trade

Frequently, in the following discussion, there are references to the parts manuals or parts books. Six of these were published during the seventeen years of 356 production:

```
1953   356
1955   356
1957   356A with 1959 Additions
T-5    356B
T-6    356B
       356C
```

The other relevant factory publications used were accessory books, color charts, and of course, the chassis number list. The latter was reworked somewhat from the original Porsche supplied document.

There are also occasional references to the "owner's survey." This survey was actually a culmination of several questionnaires printed through the 1980's in the *356 Registry* magazine. Due to the assistance of the enthusiastic membership many questions have been answered and mysteries solved.

Chapter 1

The Models

For the purpose of limiting the material covered to less than encyclopedic dimensions, the vehicles described within are those models that were standard production cars. These were steel bodied vehicles with integral steel chassis. They were produced from model year 1950 through 1965 (ten cabriolets were built in 1966). The major divisions were as follows:

Model	Model Years
356	1950 - 1955
356A	1956 - 1959
356B T5	1960 - 1961
356B T6	1962 - 1963
356C	1964 - 1966

Model years bear some relation to calendar years, but they start sooner. A car built in October of 1958, for example, is generally a 1959 model. Model years generally start in September or October of the previous year. During this time frame Porsche's model years started as early as July and as late as February. Another peculiar feature about model years that is especially true of older Porsches is that the production year, model year, and the year on the car's registration may all be different. In the fifties and early sixties Porsches did not enjoy their current popularity; for this reason they did not always sell immediately when they arrived at a dealership. Since they did not change much from year to year and every other person didn't own one, they had a tendency to "become newer" at model year changing time. Thus, you may find 356As titled as 1960 or 1961.

When in doubt, go by the chassis number list. The one found on pages 143 - 149 is the most accurate chassis number list around. It does not agree 100% with the one provided by the Porsche factory and is substantially more detailed. I am grateful to Olaf Lang at Porsche AG and Marco Marinello for their time and effort researching this important area.

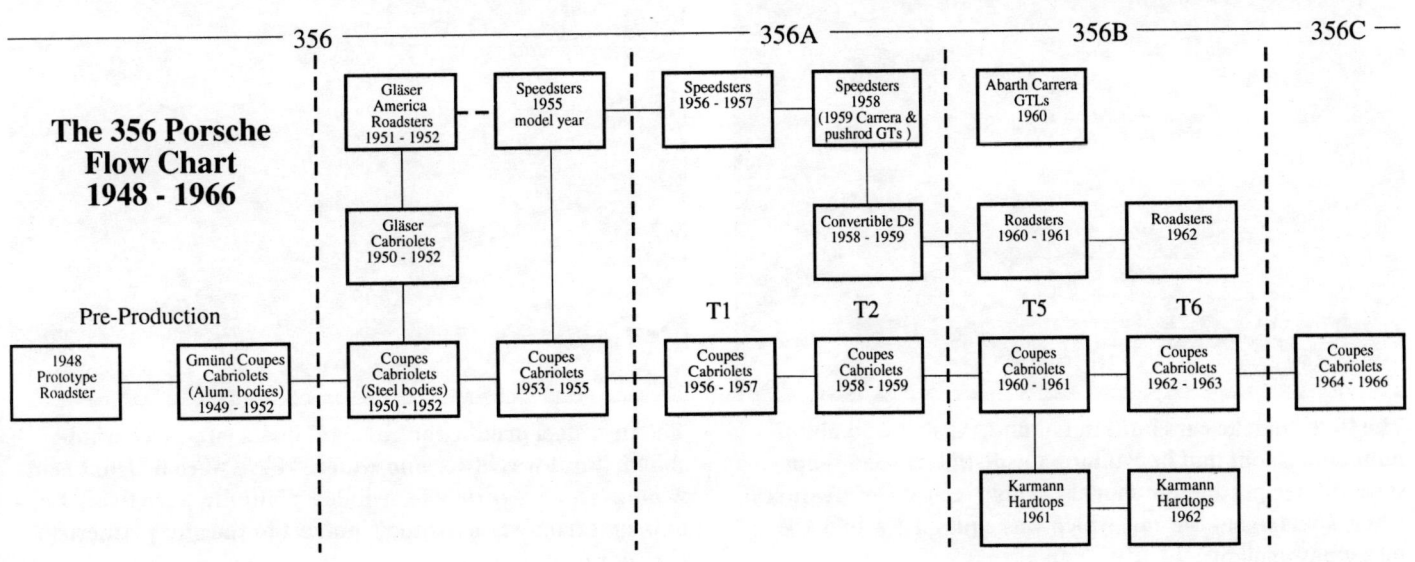

The 356 Porsche Flow Chart 1948 - 1966

356

The steel bodied 356 came in two basic body styles: the coupe and the cabriolet. Both had two doors, rear-mounted air-cooled engines, and sixteen inch wheels. The painted steel dashboard was reminiscent of many American cars of the forties and fifties. Bodies were built by Reutter, a Stuttgart coachbuilder, which was absorbed by the Porsche factory in 1964. Some early cabriolet bodies were built by the coachbuilder, Gläser, located north of Munich.

Both styles had a distinct aerodynamic appearance. Their narrow wheels, rear lever shocks, low horsepower engines, and non-synchronized gearboxes made them challenging to drive... challenging enough that with the exception of the wheels, all of these systems received major changes with the first three years of production.

Major changes occurred primarily with the introduction of a new model. The first few years are a bit confusing but they are as follows:

1950: These coupes and cabriolets correspond to the first order of bodies from Porsche to Reutter. Their chassis numbers have four digits starting with the number 5. Production ceased mid-March 1951.

Model 51: For the second order of bodies, Porsche had decided to assign a different series of five digit numbers for coupes and cabriolets. Gläser cabriolets began with 103 or 104 and Reutter cabriolets 100 or 101. No significant changes occurred at the introduction of this model which was constructed from mid-March 1951 through February 1952.

Model 52: The Model 52 was distinguished from earlier cars with its one-piece "bent" windshield. They also had slightly larger hood handles with a hole and deep faced gauges with green and red graphics. They were produced only from March through September 1952. The final Gläser cabriolets were Model 52s.

1953: The 1953 model was produced from October 1952 through March 1954. Externally the bumpers were modified to the versions used through the end of 356A production. Side-by-side "beehive" tail lights replaced the verticle arrangement used previously. Front signal lights were directly below the headlights. A Porsche crest adorned the horn button of the new steering wheel. The 519 gearbox with Porsche synchromesh and 11" aluminum brake drums were major advances.

1954: April through October 1954 was the abreviated 1954 model year. The main visual differences were the horn grilles up front, the first fuel gauges and the dashboard knobs which were no longer of VW origin.

1955: The new front hood handle was much larger and featured an enameled Porsche crest. The three-piece case Porsche engine replaced the two-piece modified VW unit used previously. The low priced Speedster was introduced slightly prior to the 1955 model year which commenced in November 1954. It was produced for the American market and featured a low removeable windshield, light-weight removable soft top, and side curtains. Coupe and cabriolet models destined for the American market were given side scripts with the name Continental.

The first Porsche cars built in Gmünd, Austria had aluminum bodies, but had in common the distinctive 356 shape seen in later production models. This "record car" features wheel spats to aid the car, which was equipped with a VW-based powerplant.

The first steel production cars still had a two-piece windshield, but it was lower and wider. There were no front vent windows and rear quarter windows initially were fixed. Lack of bright trim was a distinct contrast to the glitzy American cars of the period.

This Model 51 coupe shows lack of rear window bright trim and initial rear light arrangement.

The Model 52 featured a one-piece "bent" winshield, with bright aluminum trim and a larger front hood handle.

Model 52 Reutter cabriolet with U.S. spec. "export" bumpers with aluminum bumper guards.

Separate bumpers for all models were present on 1953 models and the turn signals were directly below the headlights.

The Speedster was introduced as a 1955 model. Note side trim and side-by-side beehive tail lights.

By late 1955 rocker panel moldings were added to coupes and cabriolets, giving a dressier look.

356A

Coupe, cabriolet, and Speedster models were continued from the 356. This body style was referred to internally at Porsche as the T 1 which stood for Technical Program 1. External changes were minor. A curved windshield for the coupe and cabriolet replaced the "bent" version used on the 356. 4 1/2 x 15" wheels replaced the 3 1/4 x 16". Other major changes included a more modern looking dashboard with a padded vinyl top and a larger displacement (1600cc) engine.

The T 2 body change came mid-year 1957. The main visible changes were in the doors. All three models featured a lower positioned striker plate mounted by three screws (earlier cars' were mounted by five). Cabriolets also featured a modified rear cowling which allowed a new optional hardtop to be fitted. Front vent windows were also featured for the first time on cabriolets. Prior to the T 2 change two other outward modifications occurred: teardrop taillights replaced beehive units and U.S. market cars had chrome-plated tubular overrider bars on the bumpers.

During the 1958 model year the Speedster was replaced by the Convertible D. The "D" stood for Drauz, the coachbuilder. The Convertible D had a taller windshield with chrome-plated frame and roll-up side windows replaced the side curtains of the Speedster.

1956 U.S. spec. coupe with early taillight arrangement and single rear bumper overrider tube

Early 1956 cabriolet with European side script. Until the 1958 model year cabriolets had no vent windows.

356A Speedsters looked similar to their predecessors, except for the 15" diameter wheels and shorter flat rocker panels.

The 1958 model year T 2 cabriolet could be supplied with an optional removeable hardtop.

T 2 cabriolets featured movable vent windows. Note also crested hubcaps and exhaust-through-the-guards.

Split rear overrider tubes were added to U.S. spec. bumpers in March 1957 when teardrop tail lights appeared.

The Convertible D was natural progression from the Speedster. An obvious improvement was roll up windows.

Coupe with high overrider tube on front bumper, only used in 1959.

1959 GT Speedster with flat bumper trim, Spyder mirror and six-louvered rear lid.

356B

Coupe and cabriolet body styles remained and the Convertible D was replaced by the Roadster. The 356B T 5 body was totally new (the T 3 and T 4 models did not make it beyond the design phase). While it closely resembled its predecessor, both front and rear end sheet metal was totally redesigned. The main visible change consisted of larger, higher bumpers. The headlights were also raised and a larger chrome-plated hood handle was present. Coupes also got front vent windows. The interior was also face lifted with a new steering wheel and column. The rear seating area was also modified. Mechanically, there were many changes, including new brake drums and upgraded gearbox.

In 1961 another model was introduced: the Karmann Hardtop. It was basically a cabriolet body with a hardtop welded in place. It was built by Karmann, a German coachbuilder. Roadster production was moved from Drauz to D'Ieteren in Belgium.

The 1962 model year brought with it the final body change, the T 6. The front lid was squared off and the fuel filler moved to the top of the right front fender. Windshield and back glass were enlarged on the coupe. From the rear, an obvious difference was the addition of the second vent grille on the rear lid.

The Roadster and Karmann Hardtop were discontinued during 1962. Karmann began producing coupes, sharing this task with Reutter.

T 5 356B front featured rounded hood, upper and lower grilles and raised headlights and bumpers.

The T 5 356B had a single rear grille, raised bumper and different reflector placement than the 356A.

The Karmann Hardtop was built in 1961 and 1962. From the side it appeared to be a cabriolet with hardtop welded in place.

T 6 356B front featured squared hood and a external fuel filler on the right front fender.

The T 6 coupe featured a larger dual-vented rear lid and larger rear window.

The T 5 356B cabriolet; only the earliest cars featured front Porsche scripts.

The T 5 Roadster was a logical progression from the 356A Convertible D.

This 356B Carrera 2 used the Porsche designed annular disc brakes. Note also the rear skirt below the valance.

356C

Coupe and cabriolet models were the only body styles available. The only visible change externally, aside from the model designation on the rear, was the slightly different wheel and hubcap necessitated by the new four wheel disc brakes.

The interior featured a slightly redesigned dashboard, but was otherwise similar to earlier models. The most significant mechanical advance was the disc brakes; other improvements were made, however, including the most powerful pushrod Porsche engine ever produced: the SC at 95 hp.

356C Carrera 2 used standard Ate disc brakes. They had front mounted oil coolers and no upper horn grilles.

The 356C coupe was nearly identical to the T 6 356B. Only the disc brake wheels give it away from this angle

356C cabriolet with enameled hubcap crests.

356C coupe from the rear with optional Leitz luggage rack.

356SC cabriolet with soft top folded, high reflectors and aftermarket tail pipe extensions.

Chapter 2

Inner Body and Chassis

Inner Nose and Battery Compartment

All non-removable parts of the 356 body (fenders, top etc.), were load bearing parts of the chassis. The definition of chassis used for our puposes excludes all external body panels and consists of only the lower and inner structural elements.

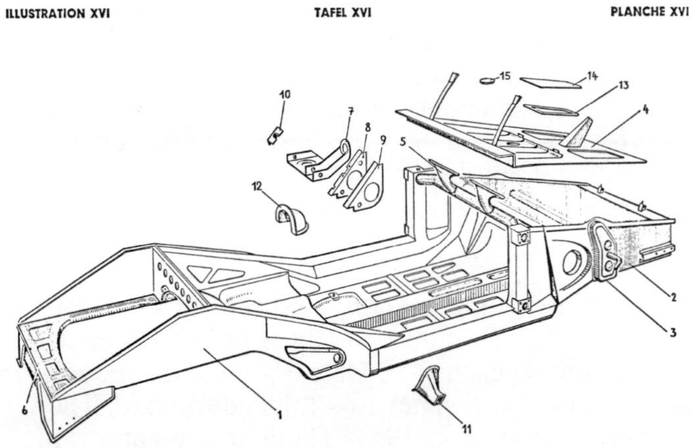

Comparing illustration 16 of the 1953 parts book with illustrations 25 and 26 of the 1955 book reveals a few subtle changes in the inner nose area. In the early car the spare tire was horizontal in front of the fuel tank. The luggage compartment floor had an aluminum cover over the battery area. Note also the lack of jack supports on the nose panel.

Illustration 16, 1953 Parts Book

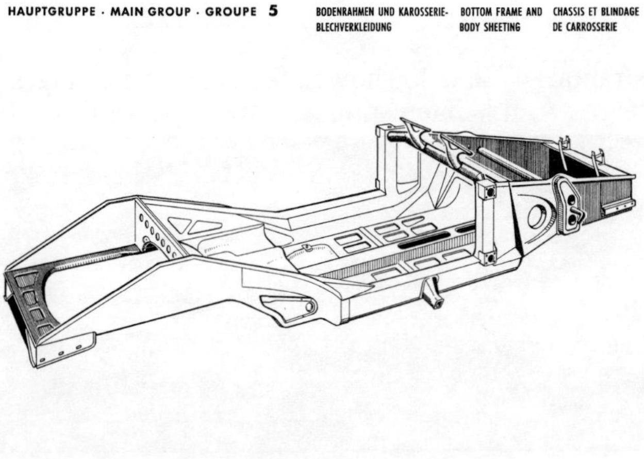

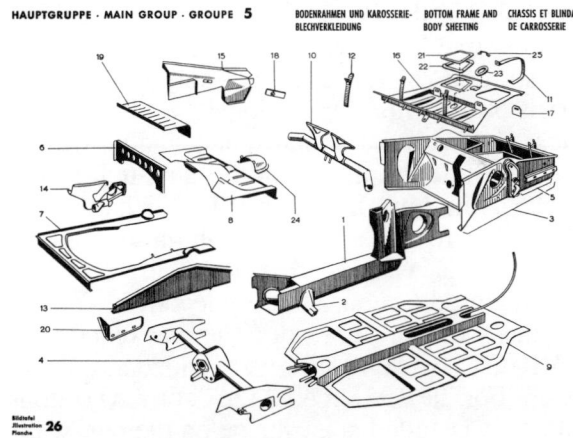

Illustration 26, 1955 Parts Book

Illustration 25, 1955 Parts Book

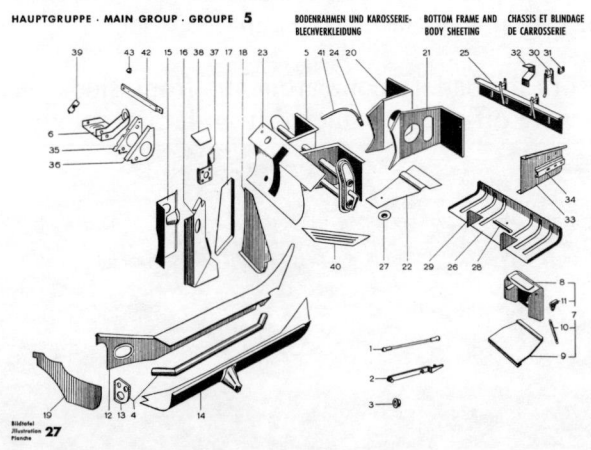

Illustration 27, 1955 Parts Book

9

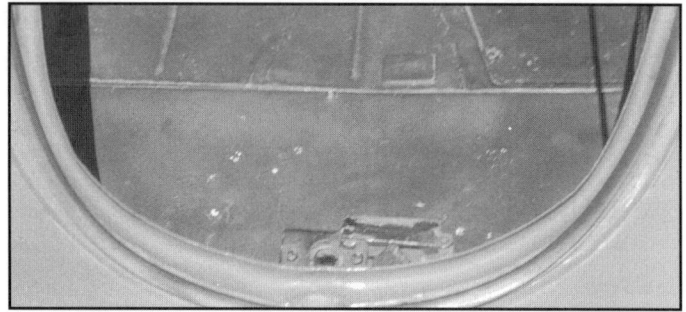

Early luggage compartment with aluminum panel which covered the battery area.

Front of luggage compartment showing the hood latch and bracket that held the jack. To the upper right is one of the two brackets which aligned the vertical-mounted spare.

Model 52 coupe with central battery and "horn" for mounting tire.

1953 car without "horn" had two brackets on the lower back wall of the battery area and outward facing impressions.

Determining exactly when the tire became vertically mounted is our first encounter with conflicting information provided in the Porsche parts books. The 1955 book lists only one luggage compartment floor (number 16, illustration 26) for all coupes and cabriolets from chassis 5001. This was obviously not the case. The earliest cars with horizontal spares had no way to secure the wheel. It simply lay on the carpeted floor. The Model 52 cars built from June of 1952 had a mounting "horn" for the spare. The aluminum battery compartment cover was not present on these cars which also featured a central battery location. They were previously on the right side. The brackets to hold the VIGOT (Bilstein) jack were added at this time as well. For the 1953 model the "horn" was gone and a bracket was added at each side on the rear wall to angle the wheel (now more vertically placed) and a central bracket through which a leather (or cloth see page 82) strap was placed to secure the wheel.

The rest of the battery compartment – front, sides, and floor – were officially unaltered from 1950 through 1955. Actually, the front wall was changed when the horns were moved from the horn "pockets" in the inner nose to the fender braces. This occurred in May 1952 with the introduction of the Model 52. Coupe, cabriolet and Speedsters all shared this common chassis section. The battery compartment floor was not shown anywhere in the 1953 book but turns up in illustration 27 of the 1955 book. It was basically flat with strengthening ribs; toward the front it rolled up with a 1.5" radius.

Another interesting area on pre-1956 356s was the rear of the battery compartment, which had a circular indentation on each side. On early cars, the indentation faced back; on later cars it faced forward. The change occurred mid-1951. There are exceptions to this, with some early 1951 cars having outward facing impressions. On coupes 5215 and 5276 (1950) no impressions exist.

Illustrations 47 and 48 showed the extensive changes of the 356A. It is interesting that it was possible to

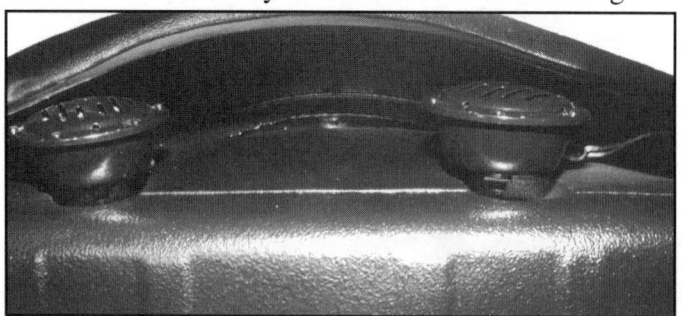

Early nose with horn pockets (from bottom)

Early battery floor from the bottom; note central drain

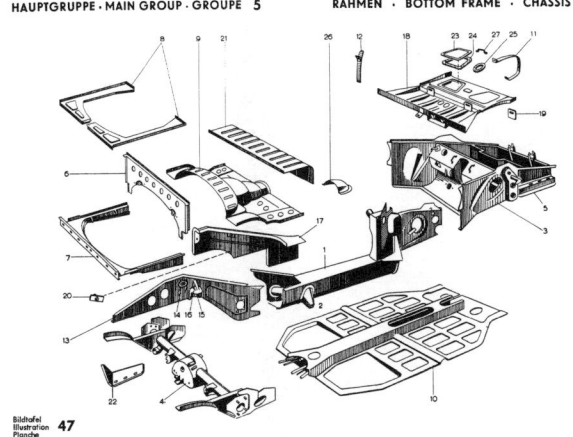

Illustration 47, 356A Parts Book

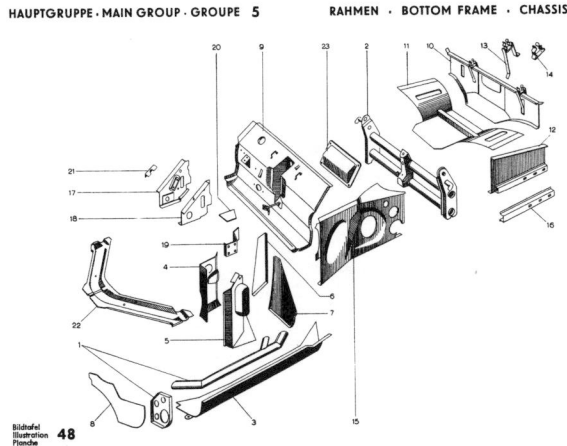

Illustration 48, 356A Parts Book

obtain only major chassis sections for the 356, but after the advent of the 356A, many smaller pieces were made available, perhaps due to customer demand. One thing readily apparent in illustration 48 is that the battery floor (number 11) lacked a center rib. This was true in 1956 356As, but by early 1957 the rib appeared. When the rib was added was not noted in the 356A parts book, which listed only one part number. Information provided by 356 Registry members narrows the gap:

	Speedster
Flat	83378
Rib	83498

This places the change in early 1957. An interesting difference on 1959 GT Speedster 84935 (6-volt) was that the battery floor was 25mm wider than the standard floor.

The towing hook was added with the introduction of the T 2 model. Interestingly, it was not illustrated in the 356A parts book. There seems to be a correlation with appearance of the battery floor rib, but the rib was there first. Use of the towing hook for its intended purpose is not a good idea.

Early 356A battery floor without central rib

T 5 356B battery floor was similar to the 356A, but its leading edge was straight.

Late 356A battery floor with central rib

Bottom of T 5 battery floor showing location of towing hook

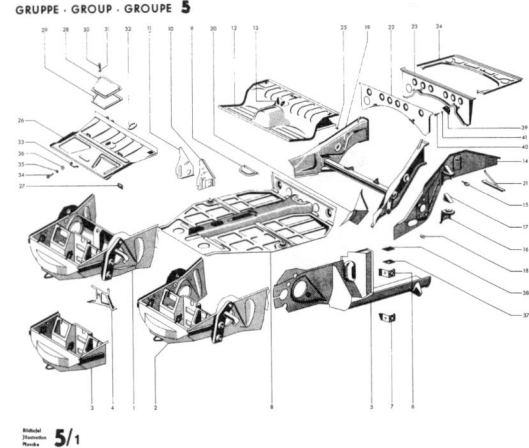

Illustration 5/1, 356B Parts Book

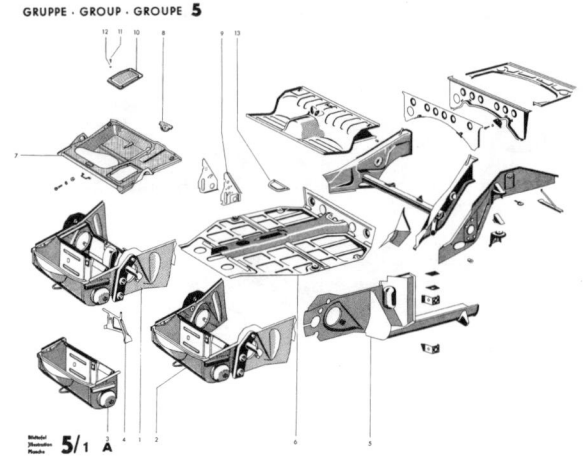

Illustration 5/1A, T 6 Parts Book

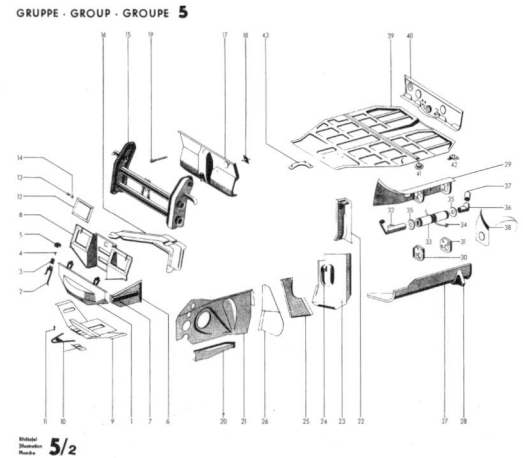

Illustration 5/2, 356B Parts Book

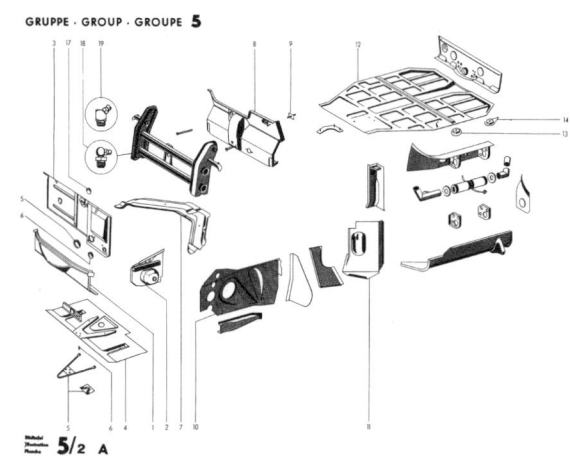

Illustration 5/2A, T 6 Parts Book

The T 5 356B front chassis was similar to the 356A in general conformation. In illustration 5/2, changes can be noted in front and side walls. A change in bumper channels occurred at the same time as the change in bumpers and bumper brackets on the 356B. The 356B's basic battery floor area was very similar to the 356A's, the only difference being its straight leading edge compared to the butterfly appearance of the 356A.

The T 6 battery compartment floor

The T 6 356B was significantly different in this area. Illustration 5/2A showed the battery position and substantially altered sheet metal. The battery was put on the passenger's side of the car presumably for better weight distribution, since right-hand-drive versions had the battery on the left. A small hollowed-out compartment in the left battery compartment side wall accommodated the optional gasoline heater. A change in the inside tow hook mount plate occurred, although the actual hook was unaltered. There were no changes in this area for the 356C.

Inner Nose, Upper Panels

The upper sheet metal of the luggage compartment was shown in illustration 17 of the 1953 parts book and in illustration 28 of the 1955 book . The drawings seem identical except for a change in the mounting of the gas tank from a bolted mount at the bottom of the tank to straps encircling the tank. The early tank was also narrower, so the depression in which it was located was consequently smaller than for the later tank. The change occurred at the 1953 model year. The part numbers given in the 1955 book match those of the 356A book, indicating that there were no changes here between 1950 and 1959.

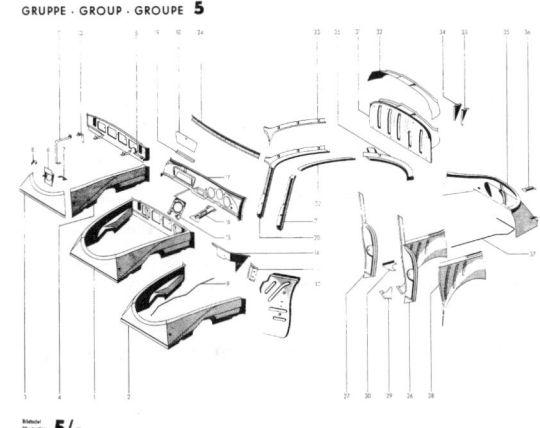

Illustration 5/3, 356B Parts Book

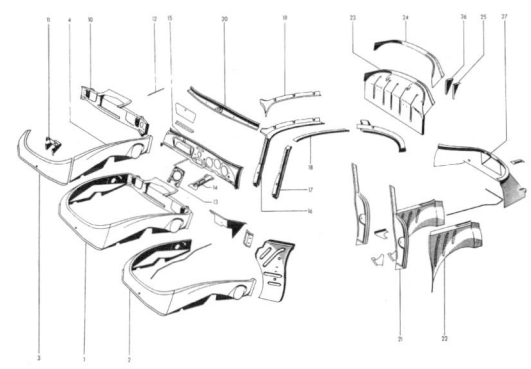

Illustration 5/3A, T 6 Parts Book

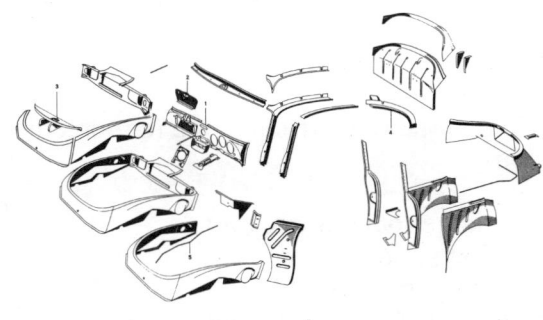

Illustration 5/3C, 356C Parts Book

Illustration 5/3 showed the substantial changes that occurred for the T 5 356B. Another change for the T 6 accommodated the new front hood and gas tank. The only change for the 356C was the addition of a modified latch plate shown in figure 5/3C.

Front Fender Brace

The front fender brace served a triple function: it acted as a conduit to convey wiring for headlight and horn, it supported the horn, and it supported the fender and nose. Prior to the introduction of the Model 52, horns were recessed into the front of the forward wall of the battery compartment.

The first style brace was used on coupes 5001-11778 and cabriolets 5015-15050 (through Model 52), the second on coupes 11779-52029 and cabriolets 15051-60549 (1953 models), and the final variety from coupe 52030 and cabriolet 60550 (from the 1954 model). This last type was used through the duration of the 356 and 356A. All styles were similar in appearance. The first had no horn bracket since the horns were located on the nose panel. The second had a brace, initially bolted and later welded, which angled back and attached to the chassis around the torsion bar area. The horn mounting plate was welded to the leading edge of the brace. The final variety had a rectangular pressed steel horn bracket welded to the trailing edge of the brace.

Early fender bracket without horn mounting

Second type of bracket with bolted-on rear-angled bracket

This fender bracket was used on late 356s and all 356As

Fender brace on T 5 356B

The T 6 fender brace

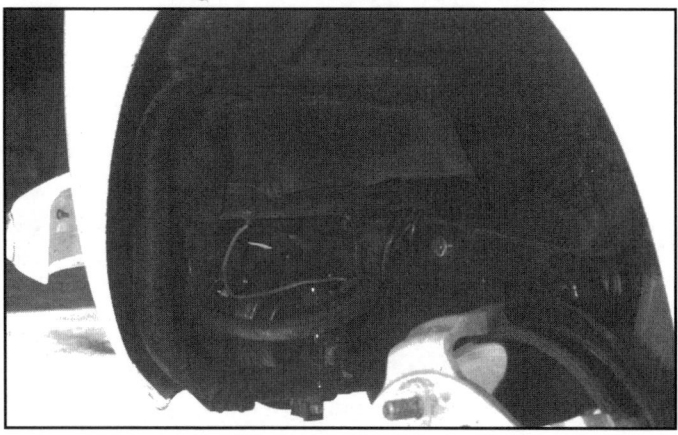

Carrera 2 tubular fender brace

The fender brace was changed for the 356B to accommodate the revised coachwork. Its appearance was similar, but the horn bracket was welded to the leading edge of the brace. The T 6 brace changed again due to the revised battery compartment wall. The difference between the the T 5 and T 6 braces can be seen by the angle of the lower outside part of the brace. Carrera 2 models had a tubular brace, with tabs at the top to mount oil coolers. The horns were attached to the lower part of the tube by clamps.

Front Chassis

The area from the front suspension torsion bar tubes back to the main floor section had one substantial change when the 356A was introduced. Illustration 27 (page 9) of the 1955 parts book showed the area around the torsion tubes to be much different from the later style in illustration 48 (page 11) of the 356A book. From this point, changes in this area were minimal. The 356B parts book stated that 356A side panels were interchangeable. A change was noted for the T 6 model for fuel tank mounting and fender mounted filler.

The 356A and T 5 356B diagonal member (number 16, illustration 5/2, page 12) was identical. This piece replaced the box section of the 356. The T 6 356B and 356C versions differed only by a large round hole on the right side, for grease fitting access.

This chassis area was particularly critical due to the propensity for rust. The front struts and diagonal member were particularly important to structural integrity of the 356. The strut (number 20, Illustration 5/2, page 12), was used from mid-1956 but is not illustrated in the 356A parts book.

Front Closing Panels

This piece, seen by looking rearward into the front wheel arch, was generally regarded as the troublemaker which trapped water, mud, and salt, causing exterior rust at the rear of the front fender. Only one change occurred according to the parts book, that being at the introduction of the 356B. The basic shape was unaltered from the early model, with minor contour changes toward the inner surface near the top being the only difference.

At least four variations existed in the reinforcement impressions:

1950 - four large round impressions
1951 - two long impressions
1956 - five long impressions
1958 - four long and two small impressions

There were some subtle variations in angle and length of the impressions. The small impressions in the 1958 and later panels were not always there.

Longitudinal Members

Shortly after the first steel Porsche was built, the first pair of longitudinal members started to rust. While Porsche tended to refer to all parts running along the perimeter of the cockpit as longitudinal members, the part commonly called by this name is the curved lower panel to which the jack spur was welded (number 27, illustration 5/2, page 12).

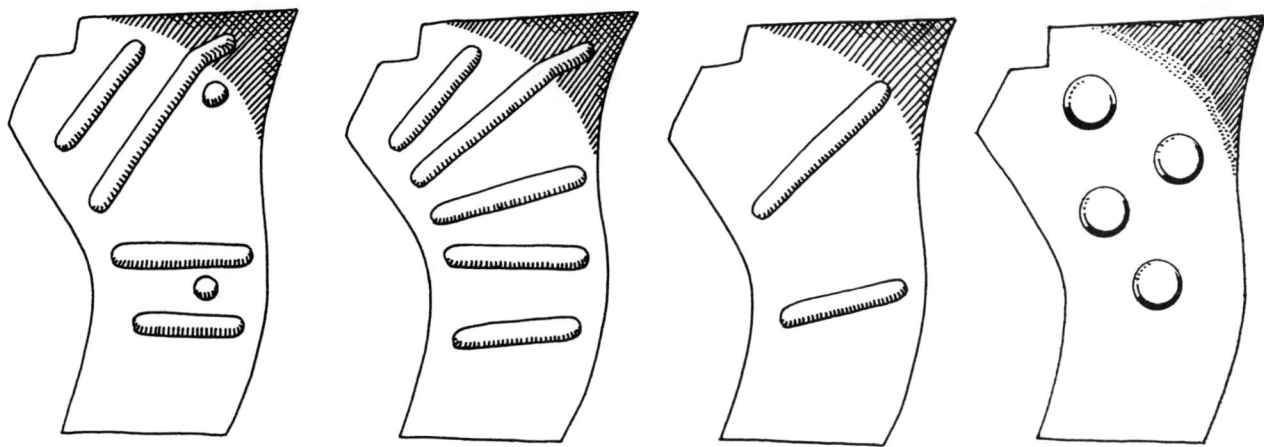

Front closing panel varieties, new to old (left to right)

Illustration 26 of the 1955 parts book (page 9) showed the entire box section, which included the front bulkhead, inner sill, heat conduit and jack spur. The forward part of this piece was described on page 14. Directly behind this was the panel which, on later models, housed the radio speakers.

The only change for the 356A was the addition of speakers in the front kick panels. The changes in the heating/defrosting system can be seen by comparing illustration 48 of the 356A book (page 11) with 5/2 of the B book (page 12) and 5/2C of the C book.

There were two changes between 1960 and 1965 in the speaker panel. The first was the T 6 356B change in the front bulkhead brought about by the fuel tank revision. The 356C had round, as opposed to the earlier oval, speaker holes. The parts book illustration does not reflect the actual part.

The internal tube which carried hot air to the passenger compartment was located between the inner sill and longitudinal. Both 356 and 356A had only a bare pipe with no insulation. The inner sill was changed slightly from the 356A to the T 5 356B models, with a modification of the brackets holding the now insulated internal heater tube. A similar alteration occurred with the introduction of the 356C.

The lower longitudinal, according to the parts book, was changed for the T 5 and 356C models. There was no perceptible difference with the T 5 but the change at 356C was the addition of drain holes. These had plastic plugs and their appearance was actually during T 6 356B production.

No mention was made of any changes in the jack spur, but two occurred. The transition from 356 to 356A brought about the first change. The earlier style of spur had a flat bottom, while the 356A steps up about half an inch (see illustration below). The modification was necessary due to the change in rocker panel.

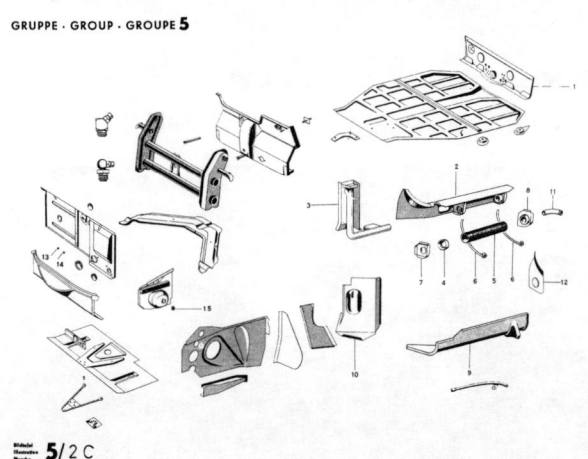

Illustration 5/2C, 356C Parts Book

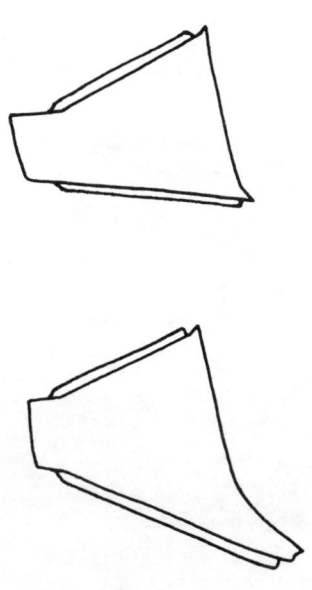

356 jack spur above, 356A/B jack spur below

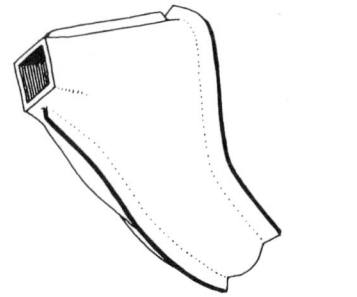 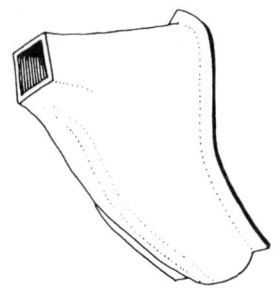

Early style jack spur with 90 degree welds, left. Late style with overlap welds, right

Sometime in 1963 the seam on the jack spur was changed from the more complex 90-degree angle to a simple overlap. Information supplied by 356 Registry members narrows the gap:

	Coupe Karmann	Coupe Reutter	Cabriolet
90-degree	213720	124562	159152
Overlap	215050	126711	159144

At the rear of the longitudinal member was a small flat panel shown in illustration 27 of the 1955 parts book (page 9). This was changed at the introduction of the 356A but was still basically flat. The T 5 356B and later cars had a round depression in this panel.

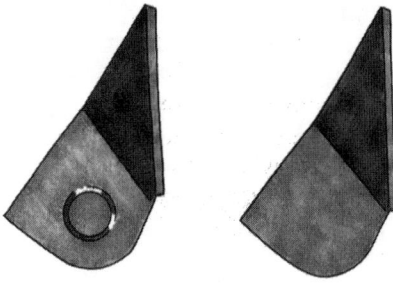

Rear closing panel for rear longitudinal, late and early

The 356B/C floor (above) differed from the earlier floor in the central rear area.

Floor

The floor, along with front and rear bulkheads, is often a critical corrosion repair area during restoration. The 356 and 356A floor were essentially the same; some changes in the tunnel area were the only significant differences. These were related to changes in shift, clutch cable and heater controls (see pages 114 -115). The front bulkhead was changed for the 356A model along with other front chassis changes previously discussed.

The rear bulkhead was not shown in the early parts books but undoubtedly changed. Since the transmission linkage access cover changed on the 356A, its different mode of attachment would at least necessitate different mounting hardware.

Seat mounts were modified from single stud to double slightly after the introduction of the 356A.

The 356B changed everywhere. The main floor pan lost the two round impressions at the front of the front half and developed a sag in the rear center due to revised transmission linkage. This required a different bulkhead. The front bulkhead was changed, for one reason because the dimmer switch moved from the floor to the steering column. Seat mounts were unchanged from the 356A.

The T 6 front bulkhead was modified for the new fuel tank. Seat mounts, too, were modified, replacing the dual stud with a single captive nut arrangement. The sole change for the 356C was a modification of the rear bulkhead to accommodate new brake cable mounting.

Dual stud seat mount on 356A and T 5 356B

Revised seat rail and mount of the T 6

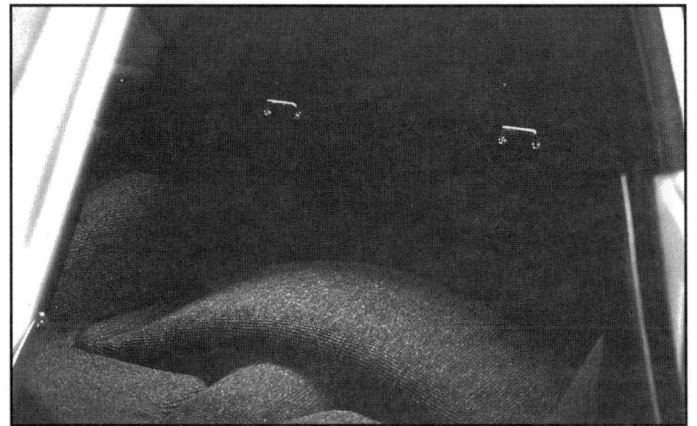
Rear interior area 1951 coupe, prior to parcel shelf

Early GT Speedster with parcel shelf

Naked late GT Speedster with no parcel shelf

Naked standard Speedster with parcel shelf

Rear Interior Compartment

Illustration 26 of the 1955 parts book (page 9) first showed the structural pieces that made up the majority of the rear interior chassis. These were the same for all pre-A models. Item number 19, which made up the flat area behind the rear seat or parcel shelf, was not present until the Model 52. Any changes made in this area between 1950 and 1952 were not officially documented.

The 356A brought a total change in this area with every piece altered. Carrera Speedsters had a special side panel available with roll bar supports. To save weight the T 2 aluminum-paneled GT cars did not use the parcel shelf behind the rear seat. Earlier steel-paneled GTs (up through at least #84461) retained the parcel shelf. The rear cross member (number 6) was different on Carreras with B-3 (gasoline) heating, but all others were the same.

With the introduction of the 356B and its altered rear seat area, everything changed again, but no further changes occurred until the introduction of the 356C. The rear seats were altered by shortening the backs. The platform, which held the seats, was changed.

Lower Rear Chassis

The lower rear chassis consisted of the torsion bar area and the structural area surrounding the engine and gearbox.

On the earliest cars, this section was relatively simple with flat side panels. The only changes in this area prior to 1955 were the rear bumper mounting plates, which changed with the three styles of bumpers. A modification occurred when lever shocks were replaced by telescopic ones in March of 1951, a change incidentally not acknowledged by the parts books.

With the 356A, everything changed. Side panels were more complex, and the rear torsion bar tube was modified to accept the 644 double-mount transmission. The shelf surrounding the engine was now a two level affair. The top level bolted in place and came in halves; the lower level was welded. The top level was not present when the larger Carrera engine was installed. The left side wall had holes for the oil sump plumbing. For pre-T 2 cars this wall was used for all models, while later 356s had non-perforated walls on pushrod powered cars.

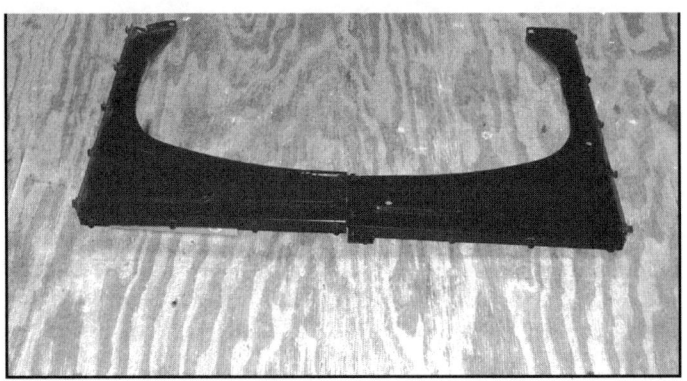
Removable 356A engine shelf

Early and late style fender braces

Gas heater on 356A engine shelf

Mesh screen protected Carrera oil tank

The rear fender brace was changed only once prior to 1959, at coupe 11779 and cabriolet 15051. This corresponded to when A-style bumpers were first installed on the 1953 models. Carreras had no left rear brace because the oil tank acted as a brace.

In 1960 everything changed due to the new gearbox. The engine shelf again became one piece and welded in (except Carreras which did not have this panel). The fender brace was changed for the final time and was used to support the bumper as well as the fender.

No additional alterations were made in the rear chassis until the introduction of the 356C. The torsion bar tube and the side panels were changed due to alterations in the bump stops. The engine shelf was modified for wiring access and the center was welded together.

Fitted standard in Carrera GS models and optional in other models was the Eberspächer gasoline heater, located in the engine compartment in the 356A and T 5 356B. The tail panel was altered for the heater's exhaust pipe and additional ducting was built into the chassis bulkheads. The switch in 356A models was above the lighter and on T 6 models was combined with the control for fresh air at the top center of the dash. The heater in the T 6 was in the left side of the front luggage compartment (additional information see page 79).

Chapter 3
Exterior Body Panels

Bumpers, Front and Rear

Five different types of bumpers were used on the 356 series Porsche. Chassis 5000, the first steel coupe, had wrap-around bumpers which covered the entire bottom portion of the nose and tail, similar to the aluminum cars built at Gmünd. These bumpers were attached via steel brackets to the chassis of the car. They appeared to be integrated into the body, but were removable. This type of bumper is generally referred to as "attached" or "body" style. According to the Porsche parts books, this type bumper was used through coupe 11300 and cabriolet 10250. The first points of confusion arise from a pair of alternate part numbers given in the 1953 parts book, 356.58.010 and 356.58.011 (front and rear), for these early bumpers shown in illustration 18. These were indicated as being fitted to coupes through 11778 and cabriolet 15050. This corresponds to the beginning of the 1953 model year cars. In the 1955 parts book these bumpers were described as fitting coupes through 11300 and cabriolets through 10250 just prior to the introduction of the Model 52.

The second variety of bumper was used on coupe 11301-11778 and cabriolet 10251-15050 (late Model 51 and Model 52), according to the 1955 parts book. These had the same part number as the earlier ones but may have been the "home market" bumpers which protruded slightly more than the original style, but were basically the same. These are described in Conradt's *Porsche 356, Driving in its Purest Form*. The chassis numbers are probably a bit off as these were supposedly first used in June of 1952, where the numbers quoted correspond January/February 1952.

A third type of bumper is not officially mentioned. They were "detached" bumpers, not the bottom-most

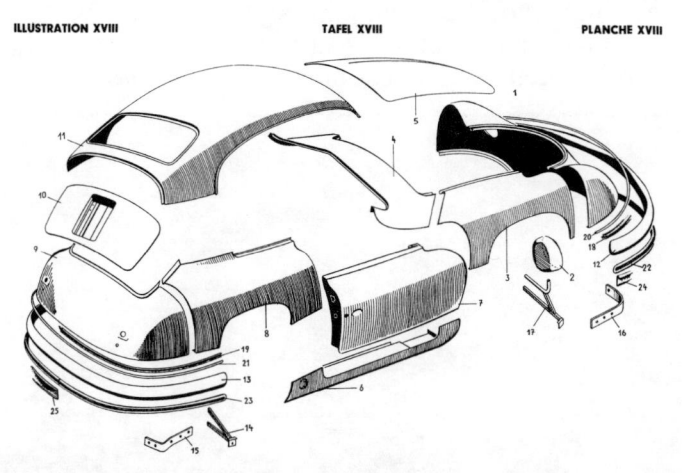

Illustration 18, 1953 Parts Book

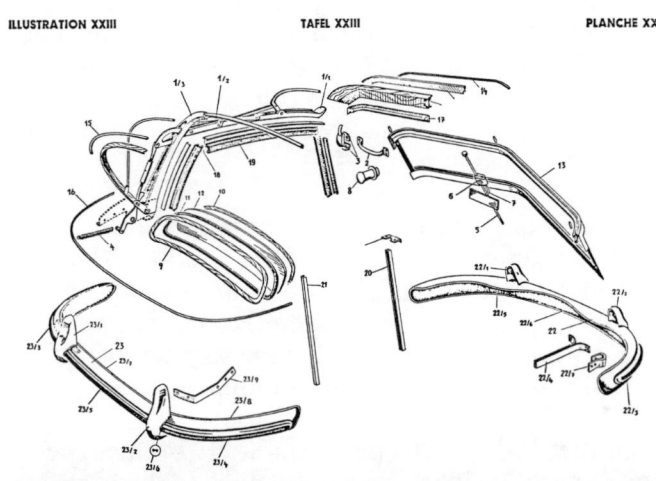

Illustration 23, 1953 Parts Book

19

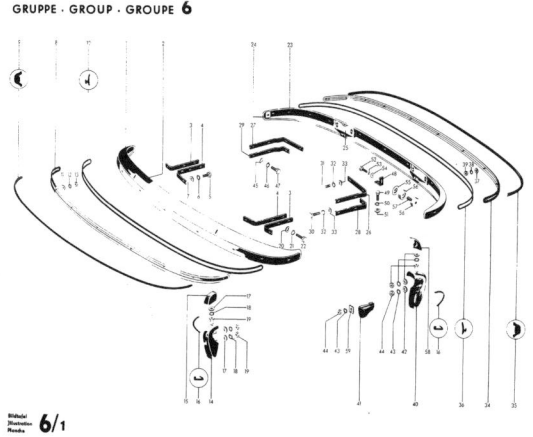

Illustration 44, 356A Parts Book

Attached bumper, front

Attached bumper, rear

Illustration 6/1, 356B Parts Book

exterior body panel. They fit quite close to the body, and nose and tail extension valances were added beneath the bumpers. The rear bumper wrapped around the fender to a lesser degree than the early type but wrapped considerably further than the type that followed. They were also slightly wider than the later style. It is interesting to note that these bumpers were illustrated in the 1953 parts book, but the version described in the corresponding text was the later style. These bumpers mounted via spring plates, which in theory could absorb some shock without damage. Each side had only a single spring plate; later bumpers had two.

These bumpers were so-called "export bumpers" destined for cars delivered to the U.S. Importer Max Hoffman felt the original type bumpers were not sufficiently high or strong to fend off American vehicles. These were likely first fitted in the summer of 1951 and were definitely in use by autumn.

Cabriolet 10075 had a peculiar variety of this type bumper, with a lower valance welded to the bumper. This may have been an early "prototype."

A fourth type bumper was used on the remainder of the 356 (from the 1953 model year) and all 356As. These are commonly referred to as "A" bumpers. These bumpers were separate from the body and mounted via dual spring plates, front and rear. They wrapped around the fenders to a lesser degree than the earlier export bumpers.

The single modification to this style bumper was the addition of cut-outs for exhaust pipes exiting through the bumperettes. This rear bumper was used on pushr-

Export bumper on Model 52 car

Rear lower valance, as used with export bumpers. Note leaded seam at wheel arch

The 356A type bumper did not wrap around as much as the earlier export bumper.

Early 356A rear bumper with exhaust below the valance

T 2 rear bumper with exhaust cut-outs

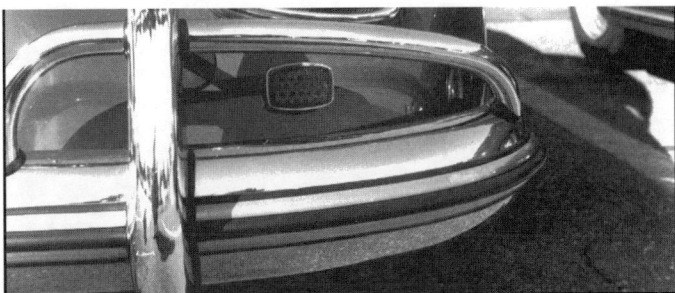

Chrome bumpers were optional starting with the 356A, although rarely fitted.

Police bumper featured a flattened area between the guards where a loud speaker was generally mounted.

Standard rear bumper for 356B and 356C

rod 1600 and 1600S cars built after 9/20/57 (T 2 body change). The earlier bumper without cutouts was used on all 356A Carreras along with lighter gauge spring plates. Chrome-plated bumpers were optional, although rarely fitted, as early as 1956.

The final bumper variety was found on 356B and 356C cars. These were much more complex stampings than earlier styles and were fabricated from thinner gauge steel than earlier bumpers. They attached via dual spring plates. A "police version" of the rear bumper featured a flattened top area between the bumper guards for mounting a loud speaker. Chrome bumpers were again optional.

Standard front bumper, 356B and 356C

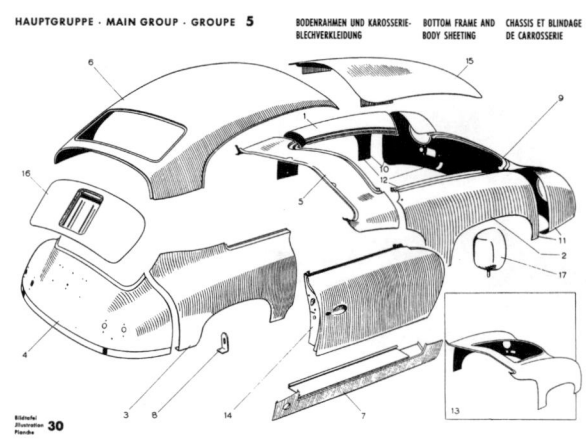

Illustration 30, 1955 Parts Book

Aluminum bumpers fitted by the Porsche factory have not been authenticated. Even GT cars, America Roadsters and Gmünd cars had steel bumpers. Obviously, bumpers were designed for protection of the car; racers were supposed to take them off at the track negating any advantage of aluminum. Separate part numbers were listed for 1960-on Carrera GTs, which corresponded to a lack of holes for bumper guards, not lighter weight bumper face bars.

Front Body Panels

Behind the front bumper one finds the nose. It seems reasonable to discuss the nose, front fenders, and front hood (commonly referred to as the "dog house" in the junkyard trade) at one time, since these panels were shared by all body styles.

The nose and front fenders in the 1953 parts manual, were those used with the early attached bumpers. The area where the turn signals mount was inconsistent. Most cars had slightly raised areas under the light unit. On these cars, the signal units were inboard of and below the headlights. Others had signal units in the same place, but mounted flush with the body. Later cars had flush-mounted signals directly below the headlight. Most cars seen in period photos show the inboard type; although, it is frequently not possible to determine if they are flush mounted. It appears that the first cars had no raised area and by mid-1950 the raised area was added and remained that way until the light units were relocated directly below the headlights. This was also the time that "A-style" bumpers first appeared on the 1953 models.

Most cars with export bumpers (1951-1952) had a slightly modified nose. The bolted *and* welded-on front valance panel with leaded end seams under the nose was mentioned in the parts books as well as a valance below the tail, but it does not have a part number assigned. Fenders were the same ones used with attached bumpers.

Raised area around front turn signal on a Model 51

The 1955 parts manual showed a nose with holes for horn grilles, described as fitting coupes from 52030 and cabriolets from 60550. This is an April 1954 change and coincided with the beginning of the 1954 model year. Chassis numbers authenticate this as reasonable. Information supplied by 356 Registry members indicates that coupe 51604 had no horn grilles

Revised location of turn signal on 1953 356

while 51605 did. This is "close enough" to the parts manual numbers considering assembly was not necessarily in chassis number order.

Noses on cars from October 1952 to April 1954 are thus officially unaccounted for. When the change was made to A bumpers, the nose was extended to go behind and below the bumper. From this time the turn signals were always located directly below the headlight units, mounted flush with the body and pointed slightly skyward. Grilles were not present.

It is interesting that the front fenders were not noted as being changed between 1950 and 1955. Obviously the fenders were lengthened at the leading edge of the wheel arch when the nose was extended in late 1952. The change was not reflected by a new part number because the part itself was hand finished in this area. In order to manufacture the newer, longer fender, it was only necessary to trim a little less steel off the pressing and roll a longer piece of wire into the wheel arch.

Front wheel arch profile, 356

The 356A, with its wider and smaller 15"-diameter wheels, had a subtly different wheel arch profile. The nose was unchanged from the late 356. In mid-1956 the position of the horn grilles was lowered about 3/4 inch. This corresponded to the introduction of American specification bumpers with chrome overrider protection tubes.

Front wheel arch profile, 356A

The front lid changed between 1953 and 1955. The only noticeable difference was that on the earlier cars the latch mount holes were closer together (42mm compared to 47mm on later cars) and there was no depression for the latch mechanism. The contour may have also been slightly different, suggested by the curvature on the base of early hood handles. There were no changes made for the 356A model.

Carrera front fenders were standard, but the nose and front hood were not. The Carrera lid was not

In mid-1956 the space between the headlight and horn grille was increased.

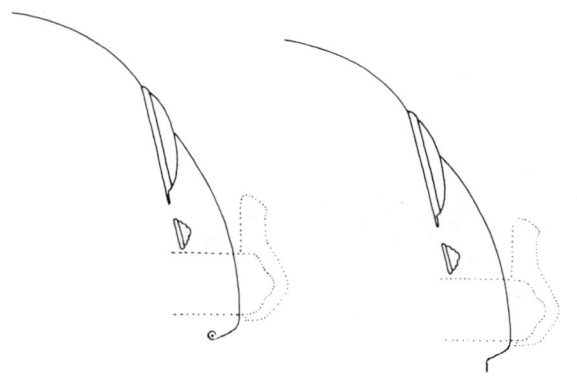

Illustration of the differences between standard nose panel and the wire rolled nose panel used on 356A Carreras

described as aluminum, although they were on late GTs. The difference in the nose was a wire rolled edge at the bottom, similar to the wire rolled edge on the fender wheel openings, where wire was used to form the edge. The standard nose panel (late 1952 - 1959) on non-Carrera models had a 90-degree flange at the bottom that was about a quarter inch wide and ran the width of the car.

23

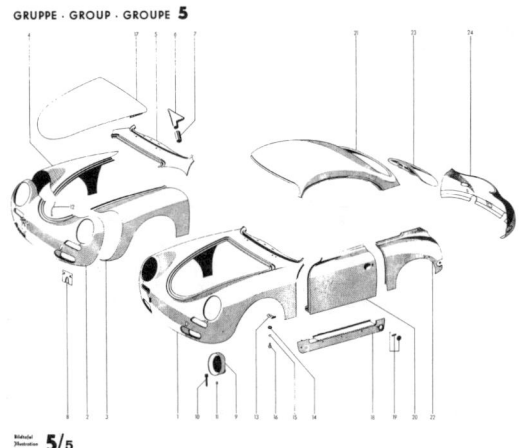

Illustration 5/5, 356B Parts Book

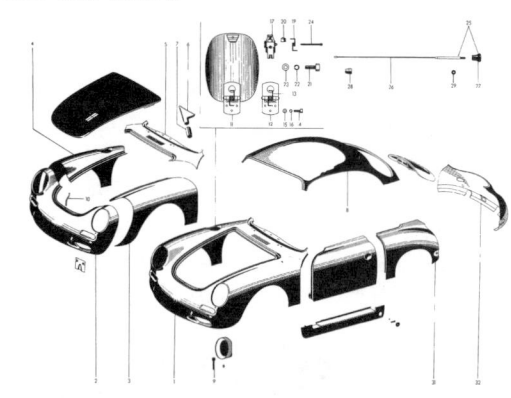

Illustration 5/5A, T 6 Parts Book

Lower latch area, T 6 356B

Modified lower latch area of the 356C

Nose, T 5

Nose, T 6

The 356B had an all new nose, fenders and hood. The T 5 hood was the same basic shape as its predecessor, and while they match fairly well around the perimeter, the contour was much different. The T 5 hood was flatter than the earlier hood, which created problems with fitting the appropriate hood handle if one attempted to fit the incorrect lid.

In 1962, the T 6 was introduced, with another complete revamping of front end sheet metal. The most easily identifiable change was the external gas filler lid on the right front fender on left-hand-drive cars. The hood was also enlarged and squared off in the front.

The 356C update was made without exterior changes, although the front hood was changed to accommodate the new "trigger" latch release mechanism.

Regrettably, manuals from 1960-on didn't mention Carrera models, although they indicated that standard panels were not used. The Carrera's front-mounted oil coolers required mounting brackets; there was also a wire-bead edge on the lower nose panel (not present on standard cars). Pushrod-powered GT models had the wire-bead edge, but not the oil coolers.

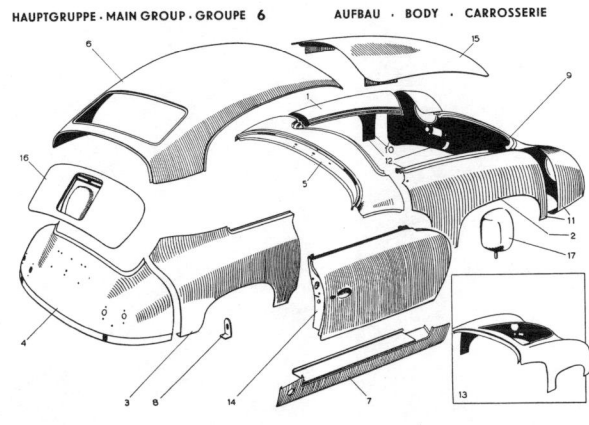

Illustration 51, 356A Parts Book

Cowl

The cowl is the section of the body between the windshield and the front hood. This panel, denoted as number 4 in illustration 18 of the 1953 parts book, remained unchanged through 1955. Coupes and cabriolets used the same cowl panel.

The Speedster, introduced in 1954, was significantly different in the cowl area to accommodate the removable windshield frame. The cowl was changed with the advent of the 356A Speedster because of the different gauge arrangement and addition of defroster vents above the dashboard. The subsequent Convertible D was not modified except that the windshield post mounting tubes were substantially longer.

The 356A coupe/cabriolet's cowl differed from the 356 model in two ways. Due to the curved windshield replacing the "bent" variety of the 356, the contour was changed. Another change was the incorporation of the padded dash top as shown in illustration 51 from the 356A parts book. This piece was used on all coupes and cabriolets, including Carrera models.

Cowl panels for the T 5 356B were unchanged from the 356A. It was again common to coupe, cabriolet and the new Karmann Hardtop. Roadsters shared the cowl with the Convertible D predecessor. They came with a different cowl section depending on whether the car had left or right-hand steering.

T 6 bodies had vents in the cowl panel, to provide fresh-air ventilation to the interior. This part was again common to all models except the Roadster. The T 6 Roadster cowl was available only for vehicles with left-hand steering, which suggested that right-hand drive T 6 Roadsters were not built. Unlike other T 6 models, the Roadster cowl had no vents.

The 356C featured a different part number, although the difference was not apparent; perhaps it was due to the change in the wiper/washer holes.

Cowl, T 5

Cowl, T 6

Doors

Illustration 18 of the 1953 parts book showed left and right doors with part numbers 356.51.325 and 356.51.326. One set of part numbers implied that early coupes and cabriolets shared the same doors. These early doors had an aluminum structural panel that held the inner door handle and window crank mechanisms. The window winder was in front and above the door handle. The entire inner door was covered by a flat aluminum panel.

By 1955, coupe and cabriolet doors had become separate entities. Different numbers implied some change between early and late doors. According to the 356A parts manual, the later doors fit coupes 11361-101692

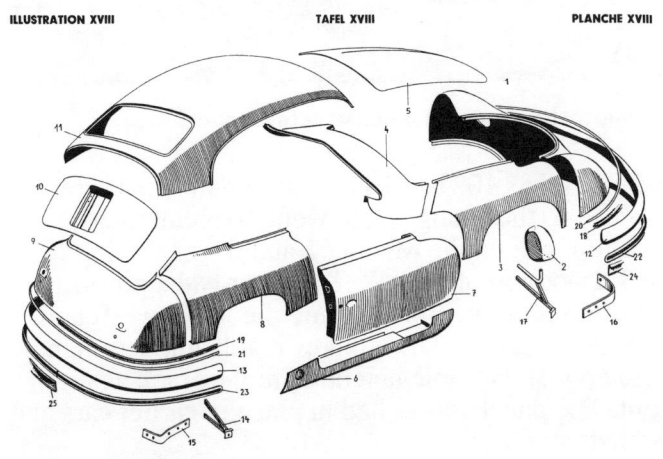

Illustration 18, 1953 Parts Book

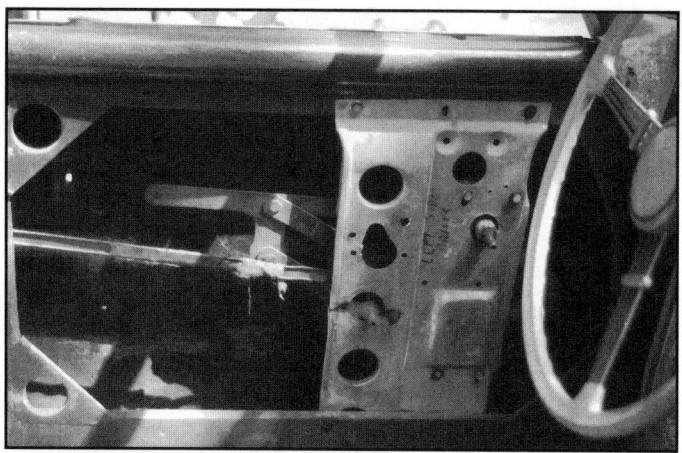

Early door with aluminum structural panel

Later door with steel structural panel

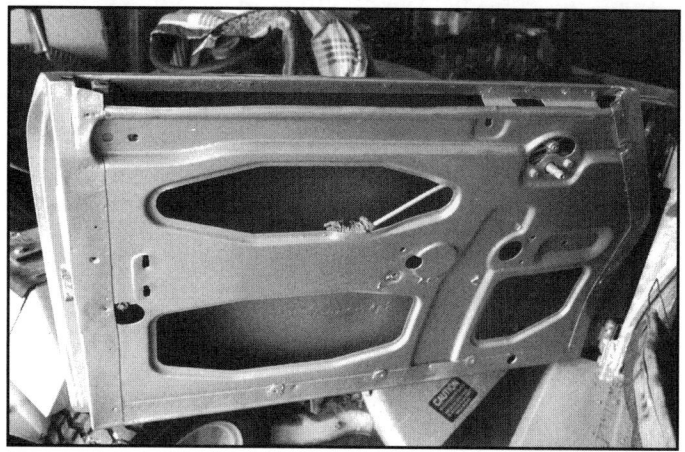

T 2 door with modified inner structural panel

Above left, early cabriolet with "coupe" doors, note the bolts to hold the window frame above and below the latch. This door also has the large early latch. Above right, T 2 cabriolet door shows no window frame bolts and lower latch position of the T 2.

Above left, 1955 coupe with bolts securing the window frame above and below the latch; notice also the smaller latch mechanism on a door stamped for the larger early latch. Above right, the Speedster door is markedly shorter when compared with the coupe door.

and cabriolets 10271-61892. These numbers corresponded to the change from wood to metal interior door-top trim on the Model 52 and the beginning of the T 2 body in mid-1957. This door had a pressed steel structural member holding the window lift and inner door handle. The window crank and door handle were now at the same height, with the crank again in front. The panel was bolted in place in earlier cars and welded later.

The coupe door had two formed depressions with screws which secured the door glass frame, absent on cabriolets (see photos). There were no other major differences, making it likely that doors were interchanged in the case of repair, when the need arose.

In mid-1955 the latch mechanism was changed to a slightly smaller version which had an accompanying change in striker plate (see photos). This change took place at coupe 53289 and cabriolet 60780 (and after Speedster 80324, actual chassis number unknown).

The Speedster door was substantially different, being lower at the rear than on coupes and cabriolets. These doors, which had no window channels, did not interchange with other models. This first door type was used on Speedsters 80001-83791.

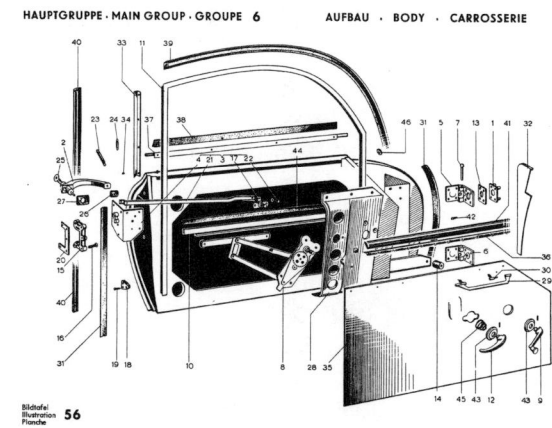

Illustration 56, 356A Parts Book

Illustration 6/3A, T 6 Parts Book

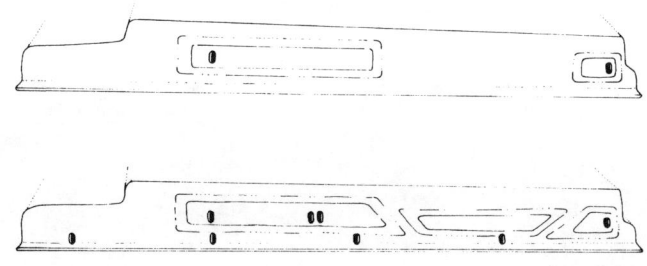

Door bottom stamping, pre-356C above, 356C below. Note drain holes on the latter.

In May or June 1957 an access hole was provided in the left door so a side mirror could be installed. It had a silver painted plastic cover.

The T 2 body involved many changes in the door, including substantial modification of the inner structure along with placement of window cranks and inner door handles. Another obvious change was the lowering of the latch mechanism to roughly mid-door height. In addition, the cabriolet door had an opening vent window; the coupe did not.

Carrera GT models of the T 2 series featured alumi-

The "straight-across" look door of the coupe and cabriolet

The downward sloping door of the Speedster. The slope continued in the rear fender.

The Convertible D door was basically a Speedster door with roll-up windows.

num doors, while the GS had the standard specification steel. No aluminum cabriolet door or earlier aluminum doors were listed (although, earlier aluminum panels have been alluded to).

The Convertible D had a new door. Effectively a Speedster door with roll-up windows, it was also used on all 356B Roadsters.

With the introduction of the 356B came a change in the coupe but not the cabriolet door shell. A structural change was made to accommodate the vent window in the coupe, already present in the cabriolet. Mirror access holes were now on both doors.

356C coupes and cabriolets had different doors from their predecessors. The indents in the bottom of the doors were changed, and brackets were added to support the arm rests, standard on the 356C.

Rocker Panels

There was only one major change in the rocker panel area, at the 1956 model year with the introduction of the 356A. The 356 models from 1950 through 1955 used a rounded, rolled under rocker panel. These were on all coupes through 55000, cabriolets through 61000 and Speedsters through 81900. The lower margin had the wire-rolled edge incorporated on leading and trailing edges of the wheel arches.

Later cars (356A, B, and C) used a flat rocker panel that did not roll under. While they had the rolled wire edge front and rear, the bottom edge was fairly flat with several depressions in the bottom margin for better drainage.

Carrera GTs used modified panels without holes for deco strips. The rear brace was filled in to provide a bulkhead for the oil lines. These lines went above the jack receiver on their way to the front mounted coolers. The jack receiver had a bracket welded to the top that held the lines.

The round recess toward the rear of the rocker panel was used for torsion bar access. When not in use it was filled by a flat round steel cover, held in place by a rectangular steel plate secured by a nut on the centrally located stud welded to the cover. This stud was prone to breakage during removal. The same torsion bar access cover was used on all years and models. It had no rubber seal, only a cloth spacer (usually a piece of interior vinyl) on the back.

Top, Coupe (without Sunroof)

The coupe roof panel, shown in illustration 18 in the 1953 parts book and illustration 30 in the 1955 book, was used through the 356 series ending at coupe 55000. There was no modification when the "bent" one-piece windshield replaced the earlier "split" two-piece glass.

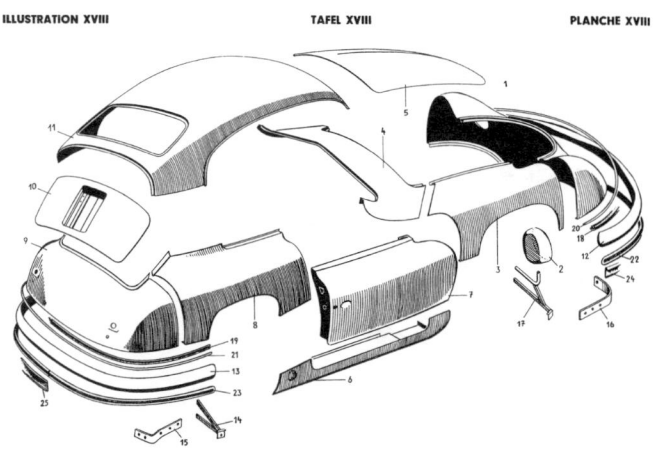

Illustration 18, 1953 Parts Book

Rocker panel, 1950 - 1955

Rocker panel, 1956 - 1965

Bent front top style was used through the 1955 model year.

Top, windshield area 1956 - 1961

Top, windshield area 1962 - on

Top, rear window area 1952 - 1961

Top, rear window area 1962 - on

The 356A coupe's top differed only in the curvature of the leading edge to accommodate the 356A windshield. Alternate part numbers are given in the 356A parts book: 644.503.501.00 and 644.503.051.00; the two numbers denote only a change in numbering systems.

A significant change was caused by enlarged front and rear glass of the T 6 coupe. The overall contours though, were similar. This top was used for the duration of 356 production.

There was no difference between Karmann and Reutter built coupe tops. There has been some confusion based on two different windshield seals available, one attributed to each coachbuilder. The original windshield seal 644.541.901.00 actually fits all models, while the 644.541.901.07 seal with a slightly longer outer flange was an "improved" replacement part.

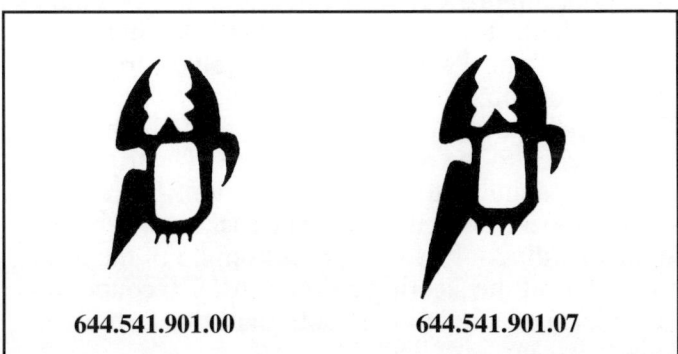

Top, Coupe (with Sunroof)

Sunroofs were offered as a factory-installed option from June 1954. Components for these sliding steel sunroofs were made by the German company Golde. They were not acknowledged by the parts books until April 1961, although accessories literature lists them as early as 1955. There are examples of earlier and some later cars with Golde fabric sunroofs, which may or may not be factory installations.

Early sunroofs had a rectangular shape with rounded corners. The leading edge had a slight V-shape matching the lines of the windshield. Water drain tubes ran down both front and rear roof pillars. The fronts emptied into the area in front of the doors. The rears could be seen running through the engine compartment just inside the lid. They emptied between the inner and outer tail panels. Drain tubes themselves were simply rubber tubing. Rails and interior trim were the same, as shown in illustration 6/6 of the T 5 356B parts book. Despite the fact that the 356A no longer had the "bent" windshield, all 1956 356As had the V-shaped sunroofs; the latest known chassis number with this type sunroof is a 1957 coupe, 58355. This was likely attributable to Golde, the company who built the sunroof, using up spare parts. The dimensions of this type of sunroof were 35 $1/2$" x 19" with the length measured at the center.

V-shaped sunroof on 356A

Non-V-shaped sunroof on 356A

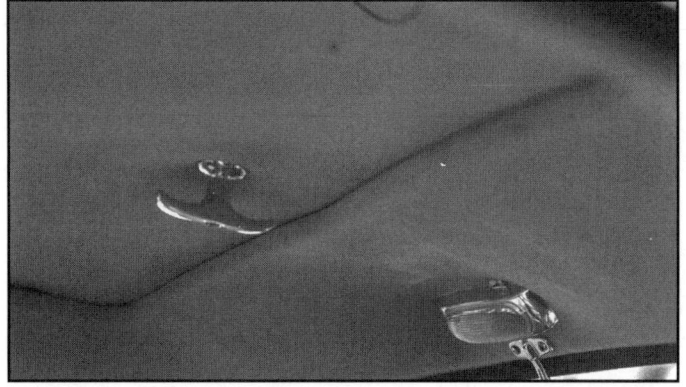
V-shaped sunroof with early T handle

Electric sunroof

356As from mid-1957 and 356Bs had the mechanical sunroof shown in the T 5 parts book. The "V" was no longer present, leaving the shape purely rectangular and somewhat shorter at 35 3/4" x 14".

A new sunroof operating handle appeared in 1957 when the "V" went away. Of the two handles, the shorter, later version fit inside a plastic cup, unlike the earlier version.

A complete inner subframe supported the sliding panel. Rubber seals flanked the sunroof front and rear only. No velvet strips surrounded the sliding panel, so water leaks were likely an occasional problem.

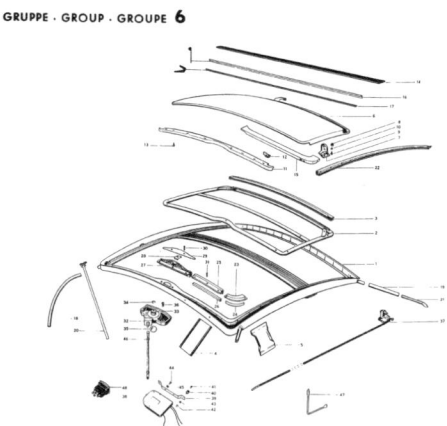
Illustration 6/6A, T 6 Parts Book

The electrically operated sunroof was illustrated in the T 6 356B parts book for the first time. It also noted that they were not fitted to Carrera GTs. The T 6 book was also the first manual to list a roof section especially for cars with sunroofs. Mechanical sunroofs were generally replaced by electrically operated ones with the advent of the T 6 body. There were a few examples of electric roofs in T 5s and mechanical roofs in T 6s. Both electric and mechanical roofs were offered as alternatives as early as the November 1959 accessory catalog. By the introduction of the 356C, only the electric roof was offered.

The outer panel of the electric sunroof had a different part number from the mechanical roof. The shape was slightly altered, being approximately 1/4" narrower and having more rounded rear corners than the mechanical type. Front drains again emptied into the front door hinge area; however, rear drains on coupes fitted with electric sunroofs had small slits in the exterior roof pillars. Two black or grey velvet strips surrounded the top insert to help prevent water leaks. The strip that sealed the leading edge and both sides was attached to the main roof section; the strip on the back was mounted to the sliding section. There was a single rubber seal at the rear. The rocker switch used to operate the roof was on the bottom lip of the dashboard, left of the steering column. All T 6 coupes and cabriolets had a hole in the bottom of the dash if the switch was not installed.

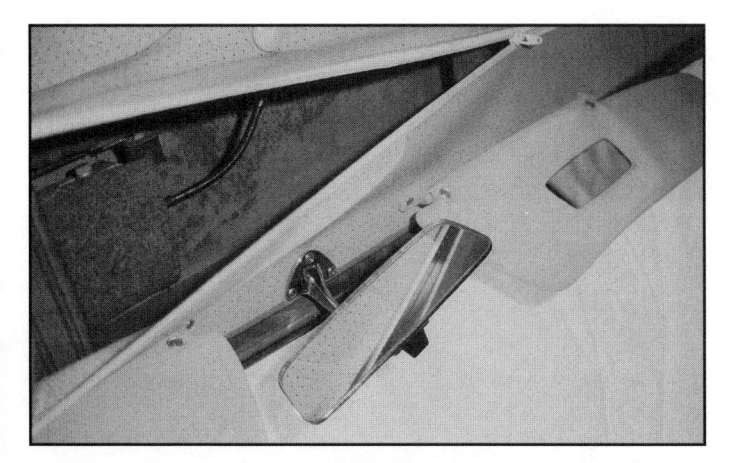

Zipper in electric sunroof headliner allowed access to the motor without removing the headliner.

Rubber tubes flanking the engine compartment allowed rear drains to empty between inner and outer tail.

Switch for electric sunroof was below the ignition switch.

Rear drain, electric sunroof

Top, Cabriolet

The cabriolet was introduced simultaneously with the coupe in 1950. Indeed, the first car, number 5001, was a cabriolet. A folding steel and cast aluminum frame carried two wooden bows, and the top was secured in the back via wood inset into the rear cowl. Aluminum tack strips fastened the fabric top to these wooden parts.

Early Reutter cabriolets were fitted with a glass rear window in a wooden frame, illustrated in the 1953 parts book. This style of top was altered in October, 1953 when a larger plastic rear window was introduced.

Tops for Gläser cabriolets had a rear window with external aluminum trim around it. Top bows were significantly different, the Gläser rear bow less rounded on the sides. Unlike later cars, the top was nearly flush with the rear body cowl when folded.

The early top frame was followed by one only slightly different in appearance, which had a soft top with a plastic rear window. This frame was shown in illustration 31 of the 1955 parts book; the soft top was shown in illustration 32. Cabriolet tops of cars built by Reutter before the 356A had a steel piece, mounted to the front top bow. This extended beyond the front of the fabric part of the top and was painted the

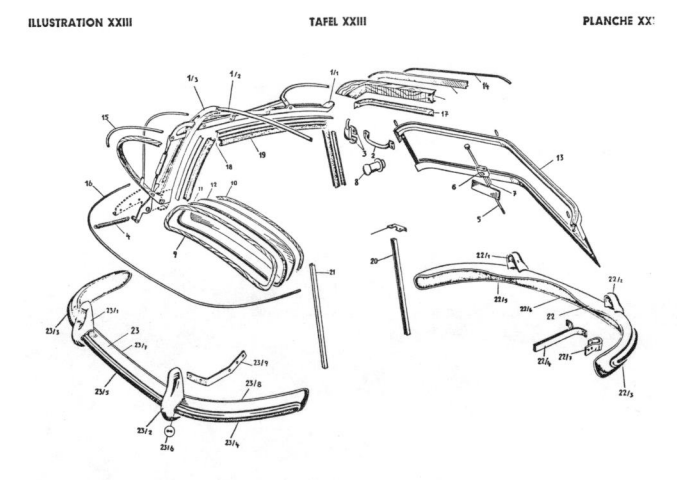

Illustration 23, 1953 Parts Book

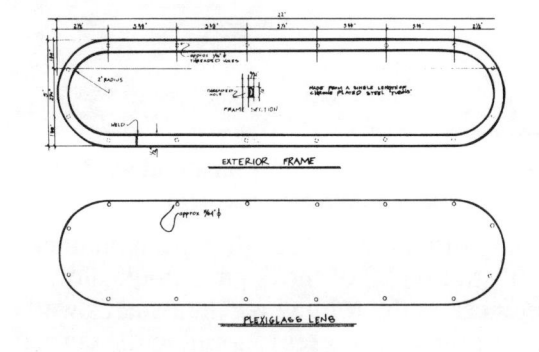

Aluminum frame for Gläser back window

31

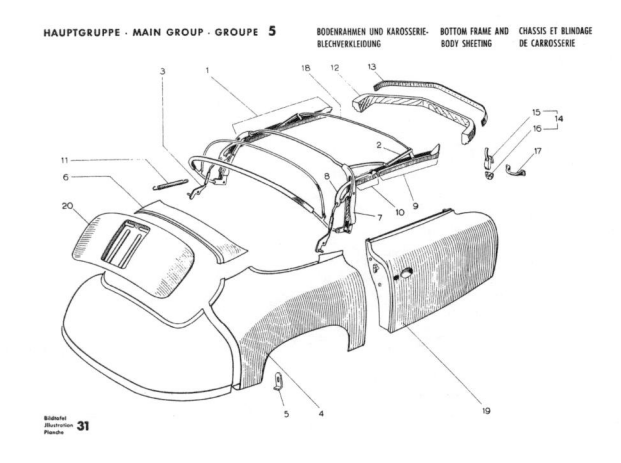

Illustration 31, 1955 Parts Book

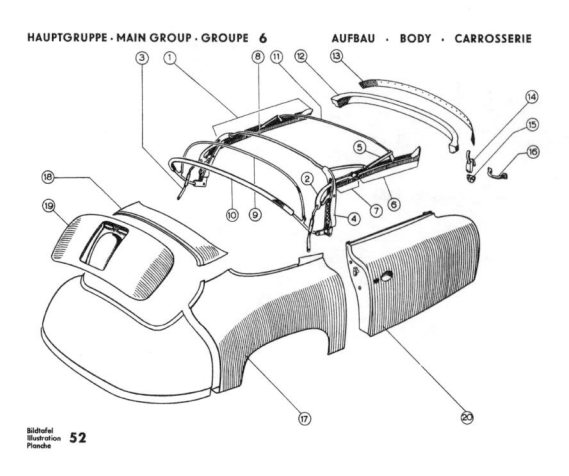

Illustration 52, 356A Parts Book

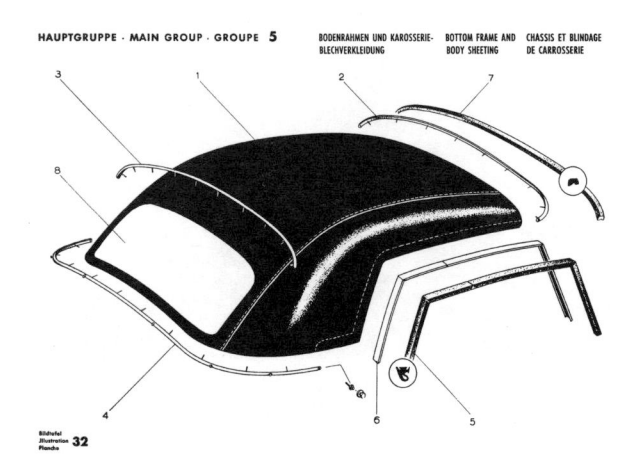

Illustration 32, 1955 Parts Book

Illustration 8/1, 356B Parts Book

color of the car. On later cars the leading edge of the top was covered by fabric and the front tack strip was deleted, as had been the case on all Gläser cabriolets.

Painted steel piece on leading edge on a split window Reutter cabriolet; note, aluminum front tack strip.

The coming of the 356A brought with it another top frame. Illustration 52 of the A parts book showed subtle differences in the folding mechanism, as well as the curved front bow corresponding to the curved 356A windshield. This frame was used from chassis 61001 - 150000 (T 2 change). Illustration 54 showed the top (this illustration is the same as #32 in the 1955 book). The part number for the top (fabric part) was different from that for the earlier car. The aluminum tack strips, however, were the same indicating only a minor change.

In 1958, beginning with chassis number 150001, the rear of the interior compartment was changed. A removable soft top was introduced that could be interchanged with the new removable hardtop. The new-style frame was first illustrated in figure 8/1 of the 356B parts book and remained unchanged from 1958 through 1965.

The T 2 top was much different from the earlier version. Its rear window was much larger, improving visibility. The rear aluminum tack strip was removed due to the elimination of the wood inset in the rear cowling (the new top was secured at the rear by turnbuckles). In March 1959 the middle aluminum tack strip was changed.

The 356B T 6 cabriolet top had a zippered rear window. This was a standard feature from 1962, and no additional changes were made until the last cabriolet was produced in March 1966.

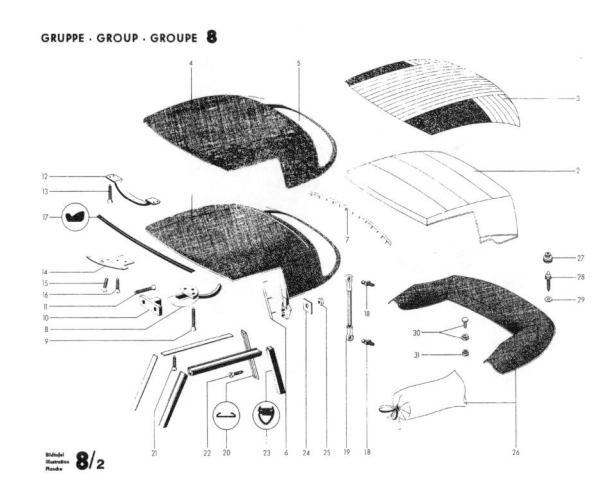

Illustration 8/2, 356B Parts Book

Removable Hardtop

The removable hardtop was offered for cabriolets starting with the 1958 model year (T 2). This steel top had fixed rear quarter windows. It was secured in the front with the same chrome clips used on soft tops, with turnbuckles in the rear (slightly shorter than those on soft tops) and by a bolt plate behind the doors. Removal was relatively simple. This top was first shown in the 356B parts book, illustration 8/5. The part number, 644.563.005.00, indicates no change from 356A to 356B. A rubber seal with aluminum insert was attached to the hardtop, where it mounted to the rear cowl.

The only changes to the hardtop were pop-out quarter windows and a sunroof option. The quarter windows don't appear in the 356B book but do in the T 6 book. Actual introduction of this feature coincided with the introduction in June 1961 of the Karmann Hardtop (notchback) or, as the Porsche factory appears to have called it, the Hardtop 61. This model, built in relatively small numbers in 1961 and 1962, was essentially a cabriolet with the hardtop welded in place. Some other features unique to this model are covered in the interior section (pages 117 & 133). As far as exterior sheet metal was concerned, it was a cabriolet.

356A with optional hardtop; note the fixed rear quarter windows.

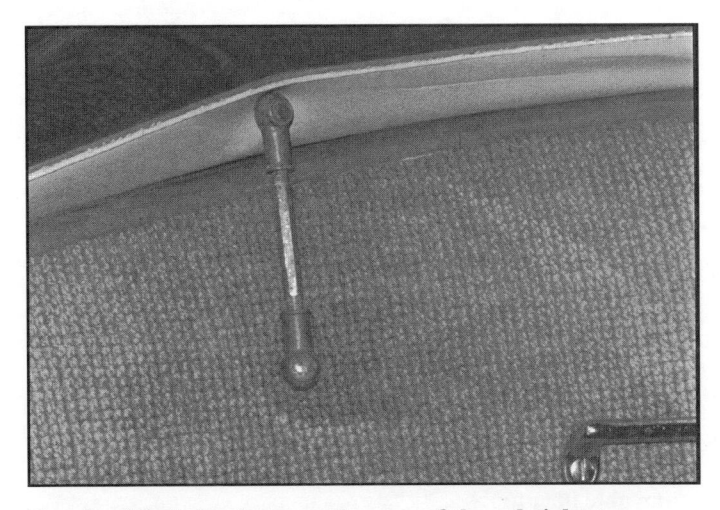

Turnbuckles helped secure the rear of the cabriolet top.

No additional changes were made on T 6 or 356C hardtops, although they had wider rear window trim. The lower seal trim was unaltered. It was possible to interchange any removable hardtop on cars from 1958 through 1965.

At least one 1959 356A cabriolet/hardtop was built with a mechanical sliding steel sunroof. This option was not officially listed in the accessories brochures, although this sunroof was definitely a Golde installation. A 1961-issued accessories brochure described the electric sunroof as an option for the cabriolet (hardtop) and "Hardtop 61" (Karmann Hardtop). This top mechanism was not identical to that of the coupe, in keeping with the slightly different contours of the top, but most mechanical components interchanged. Front and rear drains were visible on the top exterior.

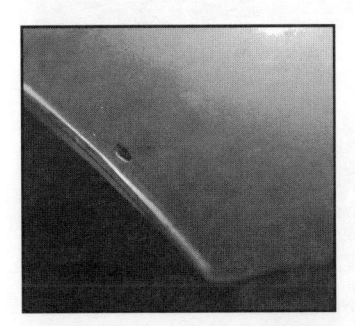

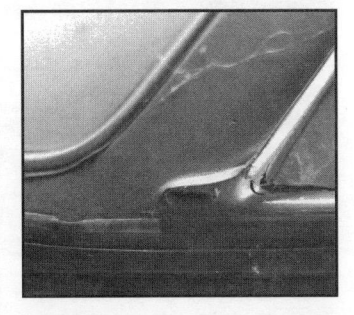

Drain locations, front and rear, T 6 hard top

356A removable hardtop with mechanical sunroof

From the side the Karmann Hardtop closely resembled a cabriolet with removable hardtop in place. Note that the rear window and rear quarter windows were larger than the removable hardtop's.

Karmann Hardtop

In the previous section the Karmann Hardtop model was described as being essentially a cabriolet with a hard top welded in place. This is not exactly true since the rear window and the rear quarter windows were larger. There was a distinct ridge above the windshield. When the T 6 body style was introduced the Karmann Hardtop received the larger windshield of the coupe, but retained the same rear window arrangement. The ridge above the windshield was not present on the T 6.

Sunroofs were optional on all Karmann Hardtops. They are described in the previous section.

The distictive ridge above the windshield on the T 5 Karmann Hardtop

Frameless, hinging quarter windows of the "Notchback"

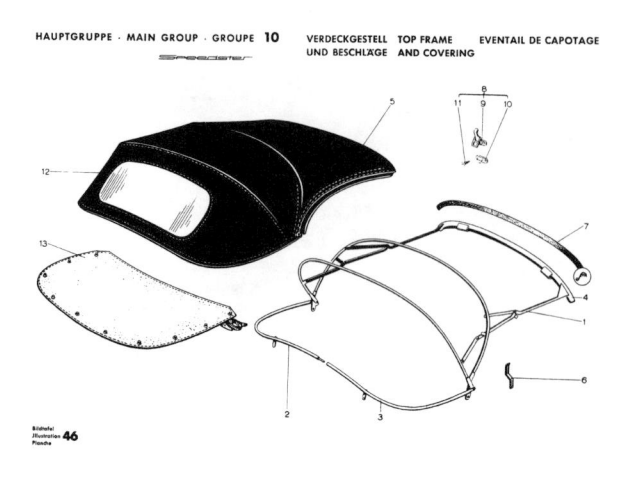

Illustration 46, 1955 Parts Book

Top, Speedster

When the Speedster was introduced, it featured a tubular steel removable top frame. This, along with the top and half-tonneau were shown in illustration 46 of the 1955 parts book.

This top, referred to as the low-bow top, was standard on all Speedsters through 1956. The high-bow top, allowing the driver slightly more head room and increased visibility via a larger rear window, followed the low-bow top.

Top frame, low bow top

Top frame, high bow top

Low bow top with small back window

High bow top with larger back window

Exactly when it was introduced is a problem. The parts books were seemingly unaware of such a change. The May 1957 book shows that no change had been made to that point. It may have been a T 2 or 1958 model year change, or it could have occurred as a running change in mid-1957. On low bow tops the second and third bows were lower by 1 to 2 inches, shorter in length and the side bolt boss was different. Oldest recorded high-bow top is 83025. Since all top frames were interchangeable, and since many cars and their original tops became separated, this change may never be properly documented.

Fiberglass hardtops were manufactured in the U.S. by Glaspar of boating fame. A factory version of this hardtop was made for late Speedsters. Tops were also made by Dynamic Plastics, Plasticon, Wilga and doubtlessly others.

Glaspar tops were by far the best designed, best finished and arguably the best looking. They had a single curved rear window with a rear seal (for the window) which had a white rubber lock-strip insert. Opening rear vents had chrome castings and fittings, original-style cloth headliner and factory latches at the windshield. A pair of aluminum castings screwed to the windshield posts to hold the front of the side curtains.

The good looking Glaspar hardtop

The Dynamic Plastics top had a compound curved rear window with a seal similar to the one on the Glaspar top. The similarity stopped there, however. This top had a foam rubber headliner, possibly sprayed on, crude wire latches and a moulded fake scoop above the rear window (8" - 10" long, 5" - 6" wide). Round I.D. decals on both sides read, "Dynamic Plastics, Compton, Calif."

Dynamic Plastics top

The Plasticon top was virtually identical to Dynamic Plastics top without the rear scoop. It had a single curve rear window with lock-strip insert, crude front latches and possibly a carpet headliner. The decals said only "Plasticon."

By the time the T 2 modifications occurred, Porsche made their own removable hardtop. It was similar to the Glaspar top, but had more elaborate hinging plastic quarter windows. The latch mechanisms for these windows were the same ones used on coupes. The rear window had a black rubber seal with black lock strip. Plexiglas side curtains were offered with this top.

Plasticon top

35

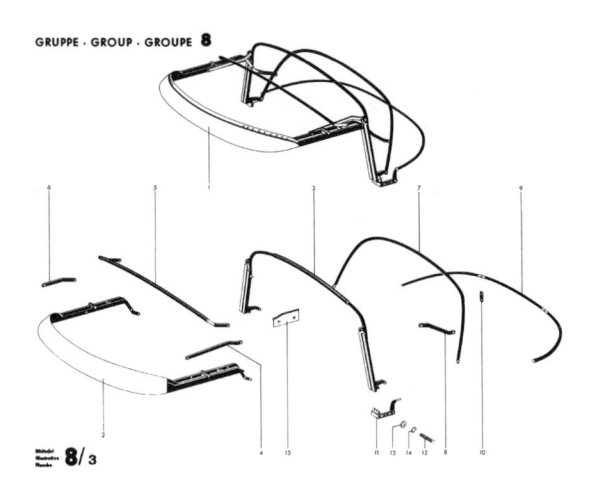

Illustration 8/3, 356B Parts Book

Illustration 8/4, 356B Parts Book

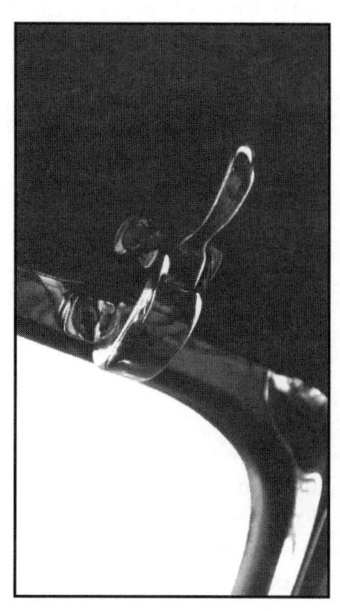

Top, Convertible D and Roadster

The tan folding steel top frame of the Convertible D evolved from the Speedster top to accept the higher windshield frame and roll-up windows. It had tubular steel construction with a steel front bow unlike the wooden bow of the cabriolet. The rear window was enlarged even more than the high-bow Speedster.

The Roadster top was unmodified from the Convertible D, however, latches and guide pins were changed in early 1960 at chassis 87825 (see photos). A zippered rear window was not offered.

Convertible D top with larger window and gutters

Top frame, Convertible D

The top latches on the Convertible D (left) were identical to those used on Speedsters. They were modified in early 1960 to cabriolet style hinges (right).

Convertible Top Material

All soft tops were cloth. The material, known as "Allwetter," was 100 percent cotton. Early cars had a coarser weave with a larger diameter fiber, and cars later than 1955 (or 1956) had a slightly finer weave than the similar Mercedes-Benz fabric both made by Happich. Regardless of exterior color, all had a tan inner surface with herringbone pattern. Information provided by Porsche factory publications and 356 Registry members yields the following colors:

356 - 1950 - 1955	Beige, Beige-Rosé, Grey-Blue, Black, Dark Blue, Grey, Brown, Blue-Grey, Grey-Green (Speedsters: Black and Beige only)
356A - 1956 - 1959	Black, Beige
356B - 1960 - 1963	Black, Beige, Grey
356C - 1964 - 1965	Black, Beige, Grey

Boot on 1951 cabriolet

Cloth boot on 1956 cabriolet

Tonneaus and Boots

Cabriolets had top boots made from the same material as the top. They came in a vinyl bag with a drawstring and were first illustrated in the B parts book, although they were certainly available before this. All factory photos of cabriolets from 1951 showing cars with tops folded have boots. It seems reasonable that a change was made at chassis 150001 (T 2 body change), but there is no information to confirm this.

Tonneau covers for early cabriolets were vinyl. Colors matched interior color, and some of these colors used were rather interesting (see color chart, pages 135 - 137). From 1958 on cabriolets could have cloth tonneaus as a factory option in two forms: one accommodated the soft top frame, the other did not.

Speedsters came standard with a vinyl half-tonneau. Reference to this was made in both 1955 and 1957 parts books. A full tonneau, as shown in the accessories book, was available, although it was not in the parts manuals. There is no indication of when it was introduced, but the car in the accessories book is a 1955 356, indicating it was probably available shortly after the Speedster's introduction. Colors available included black, tan and red; material was upholstery-type vinyl.

Optional Speedster full tonneau

Roadster boot

No boot or tonneau was shown in the parts book for Convertible D or Roadster; however, they were present in the accessories brochure. Accessory numbers 9630 and 9632 were described as "tonneau cover and cover for Roadster," respectively. Both were vinyl and the latter was a boot.

Lock Posts

Changes in lock posts corresponded basically to changes in doors, although there were some additional differences. The rear of the lock post was shown in the 1953 parts book (number 14, illustration 17). The same number was given for coupe and cabriolet, but in reality the two were not exactly the same. One difference was the post forming the leading edge of the

The Speedster half tonneau

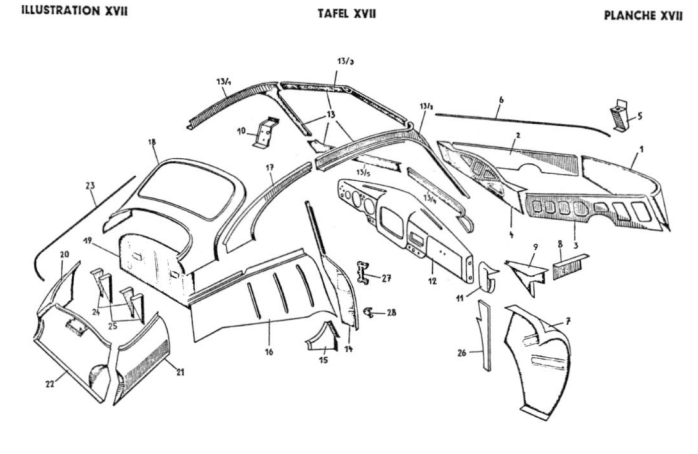

Illustration 17, 1953 Parts Book

rear quarter window, found only on coupes. Obviously this was not present on cabriolets. Cabriolet lock posts were also slightly wider at the top.

A change in lock post was made at coupe 11361 and cabriolet 10270, corresponding to the change from wood to metal door tops on the Model 52. The lock post was narrower at the top, matching the cross section of the door. Separate coupe and cabriolet lock posts were first officially available at this change, cabriolet posts being slightly wider at the top. This newer lock post was used until the introduction of the T 2 body in mid-1957.

Moving the striker mechanism to mid-door for the T 2 necessitated a redesign of the lock post. Mid-1959 the lock post was modified when the aluminum door wedge guide was deleted.

356Bs used the lock post from the T 2 356A body. T 6 bodied cars, though, had a small circular indentation

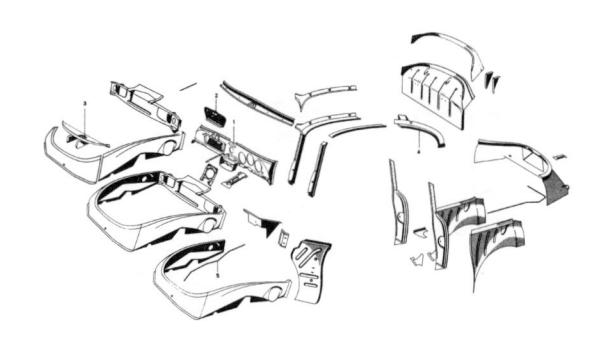

Illustration 5/3C, 356C Parts Book

at the bottom edge of the lock post. This change was not executed on the soon-to-be-discontinued Roadster. The actual chassis number when this occurred is unknown, but this information was provided by 356 Registry members.

	Cabriolet	Coupe-Reutter
No Impression	159144	113035
Impression	159276	116884

	Coupe-Karmann	Hardtop
No Impression		201965
Impression	210045	

No additional changes were made through the remainder of production. The Speedster used a shorter lock post corresponding to the sloping door. Changes in Speedster, Convertible D and Roadster lock posts mirrored the changes listed for coupe and cabriolet.

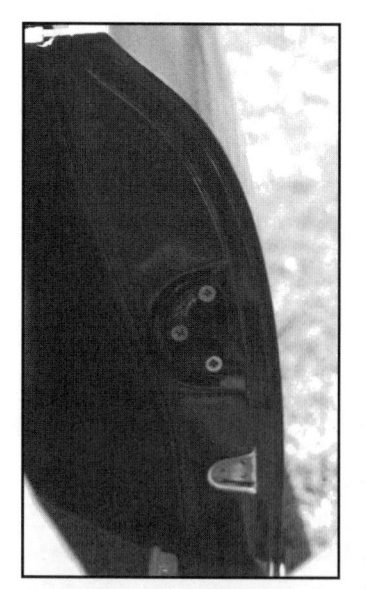

Left, coupe door jamb with high striker. Right, Speedster with high striker. Note the relative position of the striker plates. Mounting screws should be black.

Left, T 2 cabriolet door jamb with wedge. Right coupe door jamb with round impression. Note that cabriolet jamb is wider at the top.

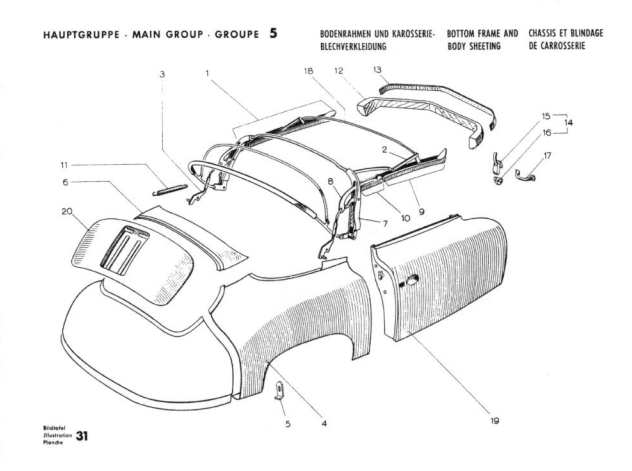

Illustration 31, 1955 Parts Book

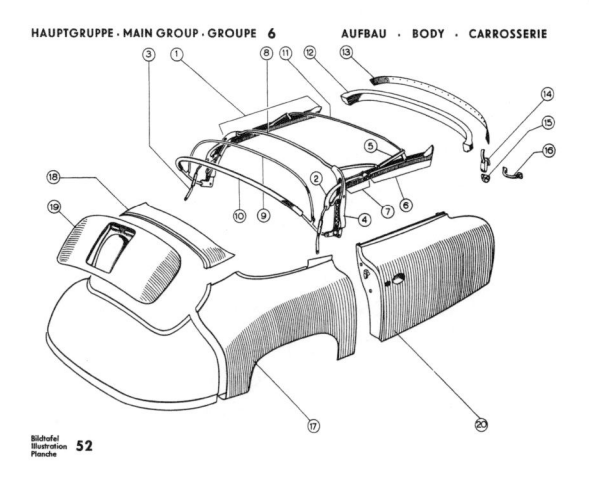

Illustration 52, 356A Parts Book

Rear Cowl

On coupes the piece below the rear window and above the deck lid was manufactured as part of the top. As mentioned earlier, the only change occurred between the T 5 and T 6 356B when the rear window was enlarged.

On open cars the rear cowl was a separate panel above the rear lid which connected the rear fenders. The first place this cabriolet piece appeared in the parts books was illustration 31 in the 1955 parts book. It appeared again in illustration 52 in the 356A book. As there was no mention of this in the 1953 book, one can only assume that this piece remained unchanged from 1950 through 1957 for Reutter cabriolets. Gläser cabriolets had larger rear lids and a different wood tack strip area.

The change at cabriolet chassis 150001 (T 2) corresponded to the change in top and the associated removal of the rear wooden tack strip. No further changes were made through the final 356C.

The rear cowl of the Speedster was considerably different than that of the cabriolet, being longer and having no recess for the tack strip. It was shown in illustration 45 in the 1955 parts book. In the 356A parts book, two alternate part numbers were given, which indicated a change in numbering systems rather than an actual change in the part's configuration.

A new part number was noted with the introduction of the Convertible D, due to the shape of the rear cockpit and modified top mounting. The 356B Roadster's rear cowl was unchanged from the Convertible D.

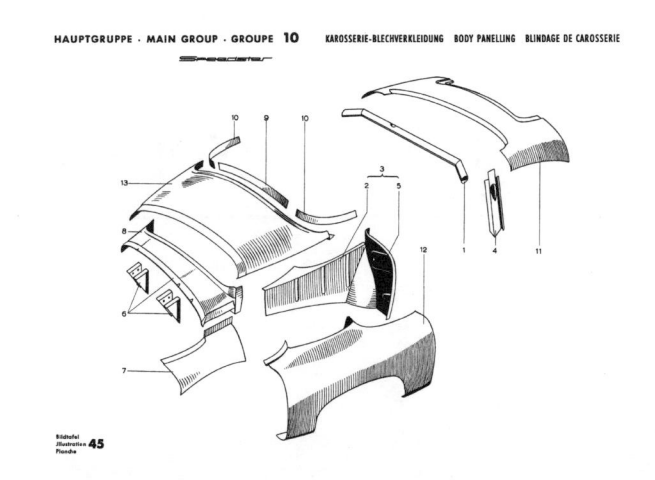

Illustration 45, 1955 Parts Book

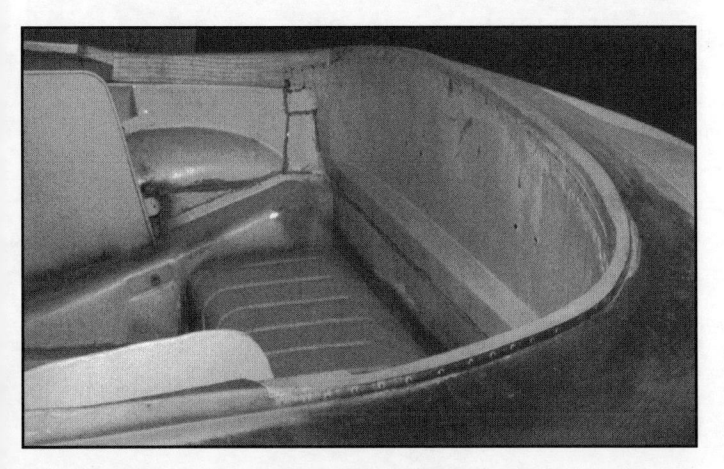

The wood tack strip of the early cabriolet

The revised rear cowl area of the T 2 cabriolet

39

Rear Fender

While the basic shape of various body styles of 356 Porsches was essentially the same, the contours of the rear fenders differed subtly as can be seen in side view pictures. The fastback roofline of the coupe blended into the rear fenders more steeply than the open cars. This prevented rear fenders from being substituted between models.

Illustration 18 of the 1953 parts manual showed the rear fender of a coupe, but nowhere in this parts manual was a cabriolet fender described. Since the top edge and contours were radically different, one can assume this was an omission.

Illustration 30 from the 1955 book showed the coupe fender, which had the same part number as the one in the 1953 book. Illustration 31 (previous page) showed the cabriolet fender. Note the tremendous difference. Illustration 45 (previous page) showed the Speedster fender, which was lower due to the sloping door and very different along the top edge. Its contours were somewhat similar to the cabriolet. As with the front fender, no change was noted when attached bumpers were replaced by A-style bumpers.

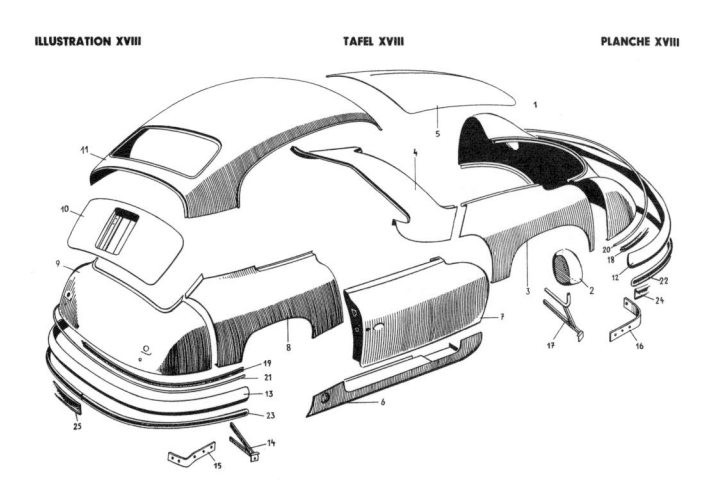

Illustration 18, 1953 Parts Book

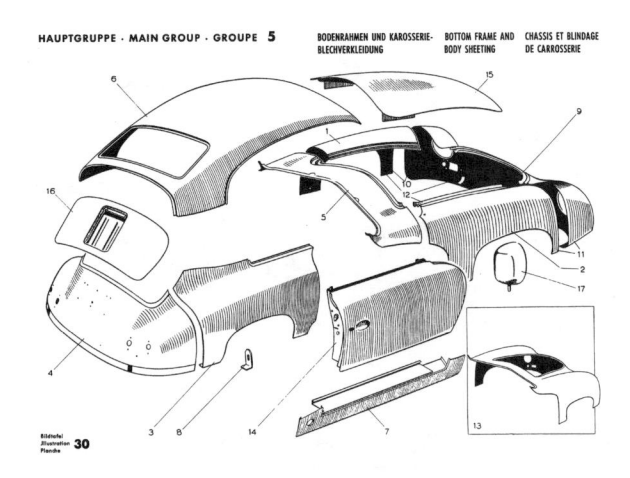

Illustration 30, 1955 Parts Book

Rear fender line, coupe

Rear fender line, cabriolet

Rear fender line, Roadster

The 356A, with its wider and smaller 15 inch diameter wheels, had considerably altered wheel arch profiles in the rear (see photos). The Carrera Speedster rear fenders were listed separately and described as having "wire reinforcement," meaning that the bottom rear edge of the of the fender had the same rolled wire edge as used on the wheel arch.

Rear arch profile, 356

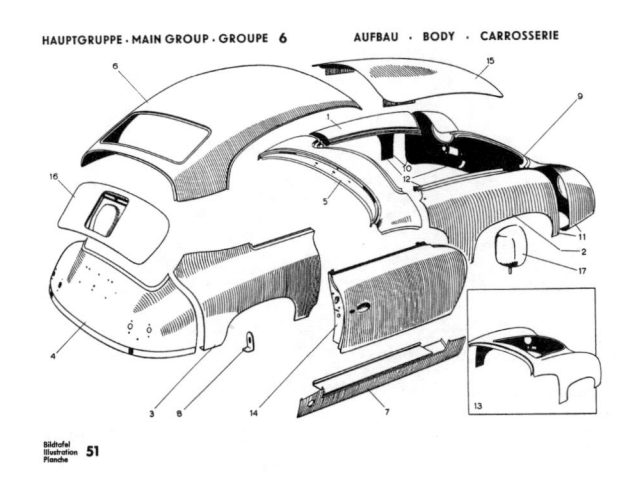

Illustration 51, 356A Parts Book

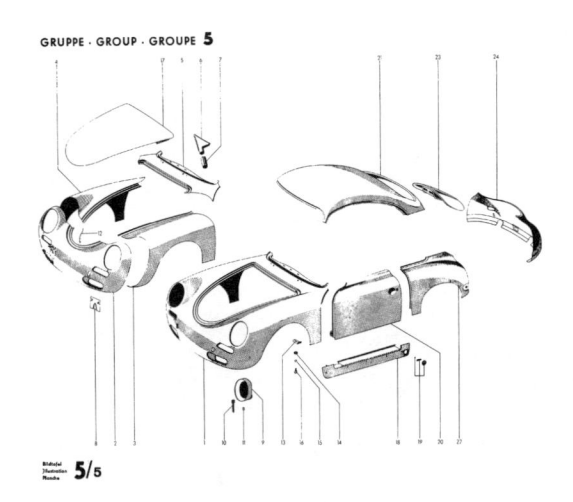

Illustration 5/5, 356B Parts Book

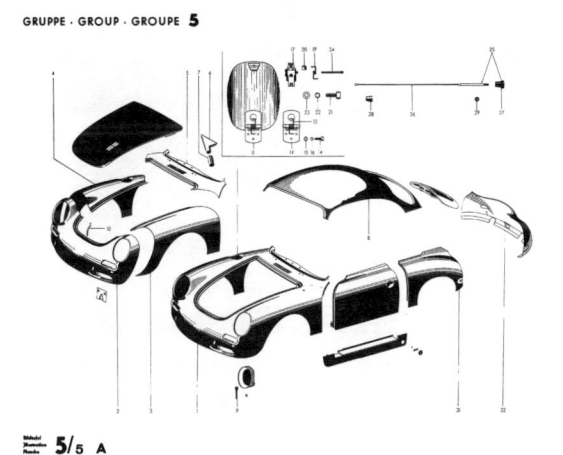

Illustration 5/5A, T 6 Parts Book

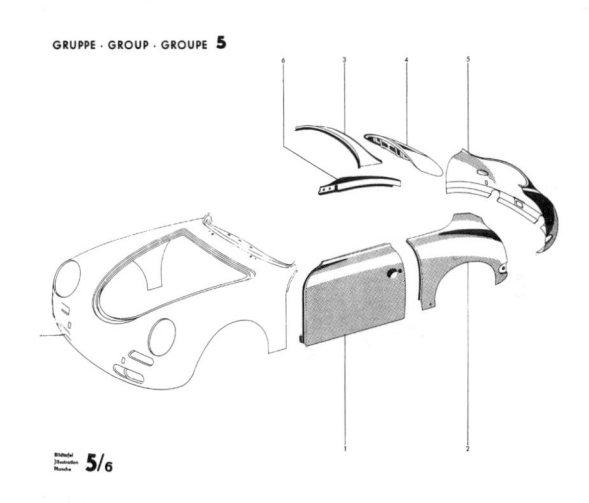

Illustration 5/6, 356B Parts Book

356A coupe fenders were unchanged from 1956 through 1959 with no alternate number listed for Carreras. Illustration 51 of the 356A parts book was nearly identical to illustration 30 in the 1955 book. Aside from the wheel arch, there appeared to be no significant difference. Illustration 52 from the 356A parts book showed the early cabriolet rear fender. A change occurred at chassis 150001 to accommodate the new soft top mechanism and the removable hardtop. The difference was at the top leading edge of the fender. No change in contours were apparent.

The Convertible D rear fender differed from that of the Speedster around the rear cowl where the top mounted; its other contours were identical.

Illustration 5/5 of the 356B parts book showed the difference from the 356A, the indentation and hole for the rear bumper. Illustration 5/6 showed the different fender for the open car. The cabriolet part was different from Roadster, again along the cowl edge.

The T 6 coupe illustration (5/5A) showed a different fender, due to the altered rear lid and cowl area, but the basic shape was essentially unaltered. T 6 cabriolets and Roadsters were unchanged from their T 5 counterparts in this area. 356C models were identical to T 6 356Bs.

Rear Deck Lid

Rear engine compartment lids of coupes and open cars were similar in appearance, giving the false impression that they were interchangeable. While T 6 cars were obviously different, the lids on earlier cars can be confusing. The easy way to differentiate between them is to look at the inside of the lid. On coupe lids prior to the T 6 model, the hinges mounted on the engine protector under the grille. Hinges were less than one foot apart. Open car lids had braces that served as hinge mounts, nearly two feet apart.

On T 6 double-vent cars, there was a tremendous difference in sizes of the lids. The coupe's was much larger. The cabriolet/Roadster lid had two vents but was identical to the earlier lids in external dimensions. The hinge location was altered; both coupe and open car hinges were separated by more than one foot.

The rear lid listed in the 1953 parts book and the

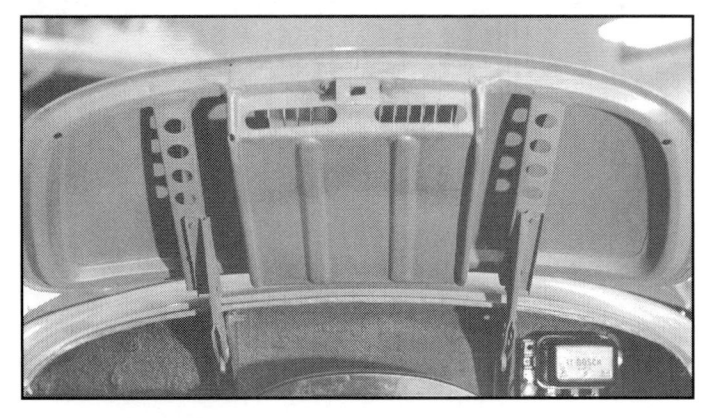

Wide spaced hinges and flat engine protector identify open cars built prior to the 356A. Open cars had additional sheet metal brackets where the hinges bolted.

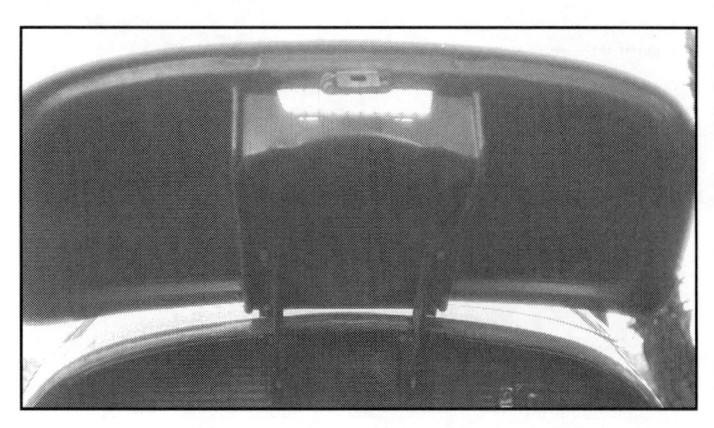

Hinges on coupes prior to the T 6 model were close together. 356As and T 5 356Bs had a bump in the engine protector.

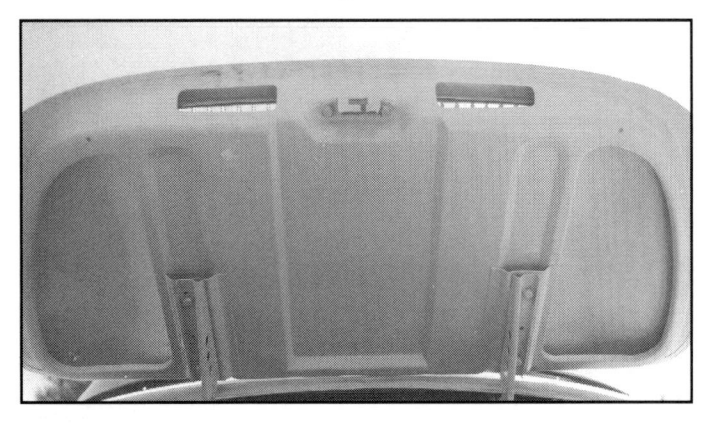

Early T 6 lids did not have the central row of louvers.

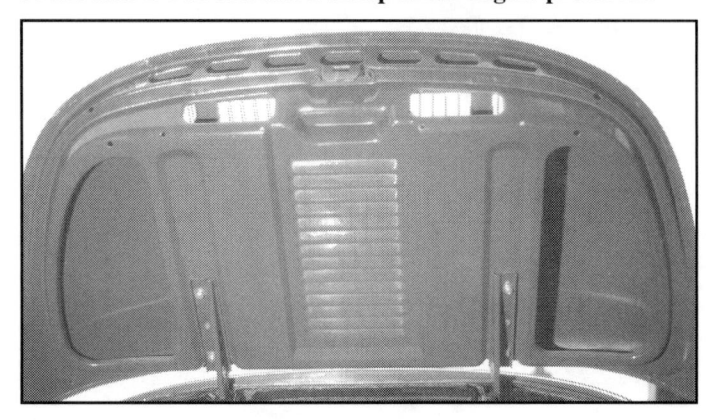

T 6 coupe lid with central louvers. Note oval vent holes and the way the hinges mount directly to the lid.

one listed in the 1955 book had different part numbers. The early lids, 1950 and 1951, were slightly wider. When they were changed is not noted. As with fenders, cabriolet lids were not mentioned until the 1955 parts book. From the illustrations and accompanying photos the early lid was identified by the flat engine protector with two longitudinal ribs. Cabriolets and Speedsters used the same lid. In fact, on all open cars, as well as Karmann hardtops, rear lids could be freely interchanged, 1953 through 1965, requiring adaptation of only the latch mechanism. Early cabriolets built by Gläser had considerably larger lids.

The 356A lids were easily differentiated from 356 lids by the bump in the middle of the engine protector and four corner threaded receptacles for luggage rack mounts, which had to be modified to accommodate the fan housing on the Carrera engine. Aside from that, coupe and cabriolet lids were essentially identical to those of earlier models.

Three coupe lids were listed in the 356A parts book. The first was the standard lid shown in illustration 51. The two others were for Carreras. One was steel, one aluminum; both were single-grilled, louvered lids.

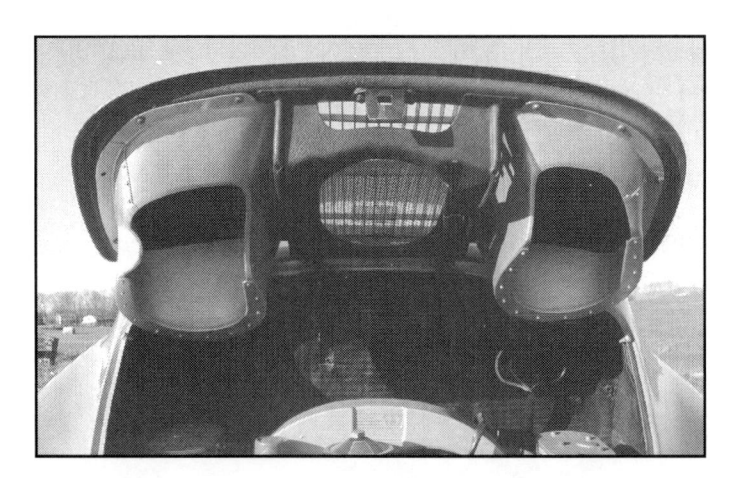

Carburetor ductwork and mesh center on Super 90 GT

Lack of inner structure on Carrera 2 cabriolet

42

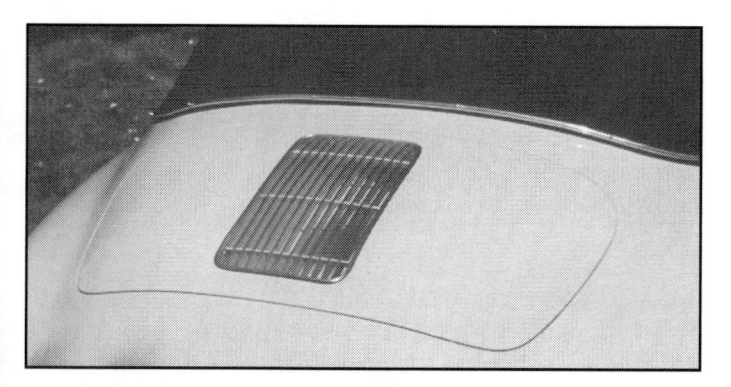

Reutter cabriolet

The T 6 lid was the same size as previous open car lids.

Wider rear lid on Gläser cabriolet

The small coupe lid used through the T 5 356B

Moving along to the 356A cabriolet/Speedster, there were again three rear lids. The first, again, was the standard lid. The second was for Carrera cabriolets (steel with louvers). The third was the aluminum variety used on Carrera GT Speedsters. The 1958 models had five louvers on each side of the vent. A sixth louver appeared on the pushrod and Carrera GT Speedsters built in 1959.

A final variation of the 356A lid was the dual vent permutation used on the 1959 Carrera Deluxe (GS). The part number for the open car's lid, 644.512.001.26, was the same number later used for the T 6 Roadster and cabriolet lid.

The standard rear lids on T 5 356B cars were unchanged from the 356A. The GTs had the six-louver lids found on the 1959 GTs. The coming of the T 6 saw the lid of the coupe grow in overall size, change shape slightly and sprout an additional air

The much larger T 6 coupe rear lid

vent. The open car version only sprouted the vent. The engine protector was much larger on these lids, and most had a row of louvers down the middle; early examples do not have the louvers. The survey indicated that louvers appeared in early 1963, between coupes 211114 and 212039. Rear lids remained unchanged for the 356C models.

Five louvers on 1958 GTs

Six louvers on 1959 GTs as well as T 5 GTs

Tail Panel

The only tail panel (the part of the outer body behind and below the rear lid) shown in the 1953 book had part number 356.51.315. This, according to the 1955 parts book, was appropriate for coupe 5001-11360 and cabriolet 35015-10270. A second tail, with the same part number, fit coupe 11361-11778 and cabriolet 10271-15050 corresponding to the Model 52 introduction. A third tail, 644.503.081.00 was listed for coupes from 11779 and cabriolets from 15051. This corresponds to the 1953 bumper changes discussed on pages 19 - 22. This final tail had a slightly raised section in the center where the tail pipes exited.

The early 356A, before the T 2 body change, used the same tail panel for both coupes and cabriolets. At coupe chassis 101693, cabriolet 150001, and Speedster 83792 (T 2 change), two cut-outs for the exhausts were added. At this point coupe and cabriolet/Speedster tail panels became non-interchangeable.

Four tail panels were listed for Carrera models, one with wire reinforcement without the tail pipe cut outs for GT coupes, one for Carrera GS coupe, one for Carrera GS cabriolet, and finally one with wire reinforcement for Carrera GT Speedster. The wire reinforcement was a rolled bottom edge, while the GS cars had a flanged bottom edge similar to non-Carreras, but without the exhaust cut-outs.

Toward the end of 1959 some 356As came with a small rectangular flat area where the back-up light was destined to appear on 356Bs. There was no light or hole, just the flattened area. This late-1959 change was not noted in the parts books, but survey results show that it occurred between coupes 106732 and 107664.

New bumpers, raised taillights, and other subtle modifications came with the 356B. There was one tail panel for coupe and one for open cars.

The new T 6 meant another change in the coupe tail due to the revised deck lid. The T 6 cabriolet piece also changed part number, although fenders, lid and bumper remained the same as the T 5. The only difference was holes for the model designation scripts and the weld nuts for the muffler skirt described below. 356Cs were unchanged from the T 6 356B.

Below the tail panel on the T 6 bodied Carrera 2, a louvered steel skirt covered the exhaust system. The bottom edge of this skirt was rolled wire like the wheel arches, and the last two digits of the chassis number were stamped on the back. It mounted to the body with slotted oval screws into weld nuts on the tail. A vinyl seal separated the two steel panels. Skirts were not used on earlier cars.

Raised center area on Pre-A tail panel

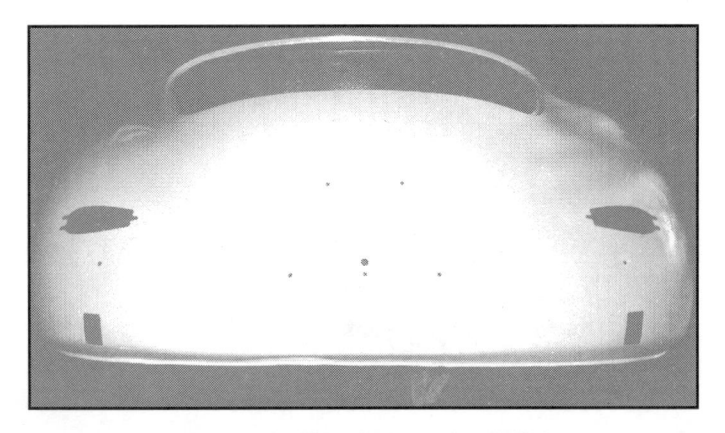

T 2 tail with exhaust cut-outs

Straight across bottom of the 356A, prior to T 2

Muffler skirt on the Carrera 2

Chapter 4

Exterior Trim

Bumper Trim, Front and Rear

The early bumpers used from 1950 through the Model 52 came with one of four types of trim strip. These were 1) flat-style aluminum, 2) small grooved aluminum, 3) 356A-style rubber and aluminum and 4) wide VW bus-type rubber and aluminum.

The gospel according to the Parts Books went something like this: The 1953 book gave three choices: 1) plain smooth 356.58.305 and 356.58.306, 2) strip with slot 356.58.306 (Hmmm), 3) Model 52 with rubber insert 356.58.307 and 356.58.308.

The 1955 book confused matters further. It stated that 356.58.305, "decorative strip with channel" fit front and rear of all coupes 5001 - 11130 and all cabriolets 5015 - 10200. Next it assigned a "decorative strip alu polished without rubber" to coupes 11131 - 11300 (!) and cabriolets 10201 - 10250 a different deco, 356.58.306 front and rear. For coupes 11301 - 11778 and cabriolets 10251 - 15050 there was a "decorative strip with rubber profile." These had different part numbers front (356.58.037) and rear (356.58.038). The final variety was 356.58.328 (644.505.041.00) front and 356.58.329 (644.505.043.00) rear. This 356A-style was said to fit coupes 11779 on and cabriolets 15051 on (1953 model year).

Skimming the given information for something re-

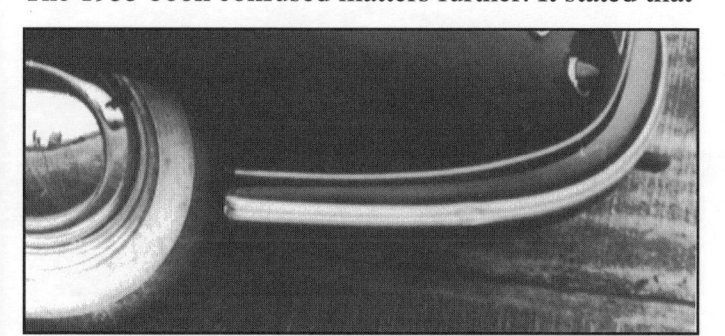

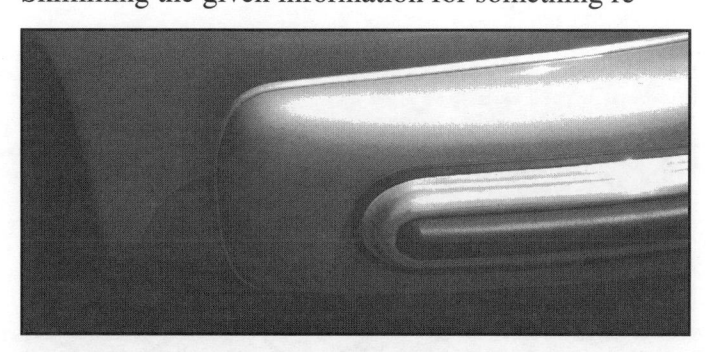

Grooved-type bumper trim

Bus-type bumper trim on export bumper

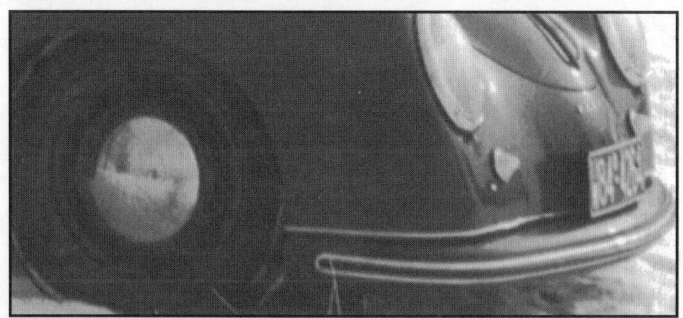

Flat-type bumper trim

A-type bumper trim on Model 52 home market bumper

Chassis #11321 (or is it actually #11421?)

Chassis #11332

Chassis #11340

Chassis #11415

Of course, this bears little resemblance to fact. The earliest car information is a factory photo of a 1950 coupe; no chassis number was supplied, but due to a number of details it was obviously one of the first few; it had the grooved bumper trim. Cabriolet 5135 had grooved trim. Coupe 5430 had A-style trim, however it shows signs of being updated by the factory circa 1953. Coupe 5599 had flat trim.

Of the five-digit chassis numbers, cabriolets 10158 and 10405 had flat trim, and from the four pictures showing a 1952 Swedish rally start, coupes 11332, 11340 and 11415 had flat trim while 11321 had 356A-style. Coupe 11111 and cabriolet 12355 also had A-style trim.

There were also many examples of bumpers with the wide VW bus trim, which had a thick rubber insert and some had removable pointed ends. Most export bumper type cars seem to have had this trim; although some had A-style trim. Yet another variation, on cab-

The narrow B/C bumper trim

Flat trim on 356A GT

sembling a chronological history, it appears that from 5001 through coupe 11130 and cabriolet 10200, all cars came with grooved bumper trim. At this point and until coupe 11300 and cabriolet 10250, they came with flat trim. Then the bumpers and trim changed, the trim being the very wide VW bus-style trim shown. At coupe 11779 and cabriolet 15051 for the 1953 model year the A-style bumpers appeared and through 1959 there were no additional changes.

356B GTs had flat trim with finished ends.

riolet 10075 with the unusual export bumpers, was bus trim split into left and right pieces. On this car there was a 12 inch gap in the center between the left and right sides. Inside ends were rounded, and no bumper guards were fitted. Later cars with export bumpers also had unique aluminum perimeter trim not used on other bumper styles.

One final piece of bumper trim unique to early cars with attached bumpers was a half-round aluminum molding above the front and rear bumpers. There were two different versions: early cars have a molding which rolled under the nose, while the later-style bumper molding butted up to the bumper without rolling under.

The A-style bumpers which started at chassis 11779 and 15051 all featured the familiar rubber and aluminum trim up through the 1959 models. There were exceptions. On Carrera GTs flat aluminum trim, similar to the trim used on early attached-bumper cars, was used. As on the early cars, this trim wrapped around the bumper ends.

The 356B and 356C shared a trim strip similar to the 356A but slightly narrower. 356B GTs had the flat aluminum molding, but on this model the ends were rounded, approximating the shape of the original deco strips. The T 6 Carrera 2 had standard trim strips.

Bumper Guards, 356

Bumper guards are the next area of controversy. Most attached-bumper cars have no bumper guards. This was true for most European cars. They were also not listed in the parts books. The test car in the July 1952 *Mechanix Illustrated,* however, showed that some cars had them, most likely U.S. models, even before the introduction of export bumpers. It is possible that some of these guards were a concave shape, as with the 1949 Gmünd cars.

Bumper guards for export bumpers were shown in illustration 23 of the 1953 parts book. They were aluminum castings, although pressed steel, chrome-plated guards exist.

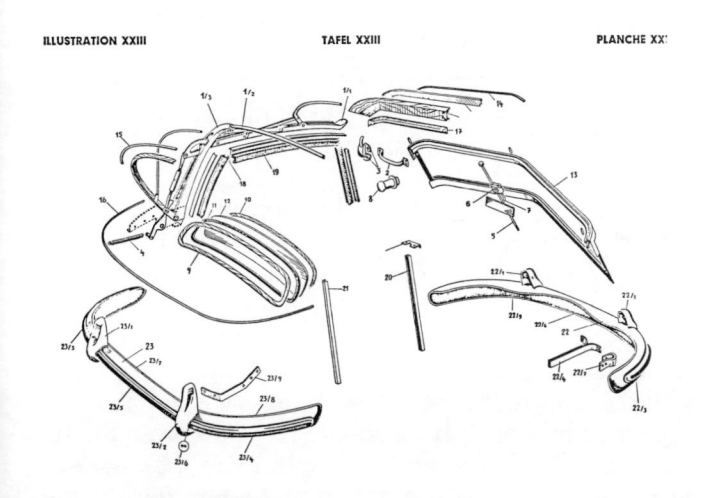

Aluminum guard on export bumper

Two types of guards were listed in the 1955 book for cars with A-style bumpers. The low, bright-anodized aluminum guards, 644.505.031.00 and 644.505.032-.00 (left and right) were interchangeable front to rear (that is right front to left rear and left front to right rear). They were first used, according to the parts book, at coupe 52030 and cabriolet 60550 for the 1954 model year. Earlier cars had chrome-plated steel versions. The steel guards were attached by two bolts to mounting plates in the guard.

Low, wide anodized aluminum guards used on the 356

Bumper Guards, European 356A

European 356As used bright-anodized aluminum bumper guards with the same part numbers used on late pre-As. The parts book noted "maximum width 64 mm from 356A." This dimension, in reality, represented a change, as earlier guards were distinctly wider.

Two other types of guards became available on the 1958 model: 644.505.031.01 and 644.505.031.02. It was noted that they were made from different materials with the ".02" having the part number cast into the bumperette. The parts book stated that these were "interchangeable in pairs." The 01 was an anodized cast

Illustration 23, 1953 Parts Book

Low European-style guards, 356A

356A with low overrider tube

aluminum alloy, while the 02 was chrome-plated cast aluminum. These were both low style bumperettes, not used in conjunction with overrider tubes.

At coupe 101693, cabriolet 150001 and Speedster 83792 (T 2 change), rear guards became different from fronts due to the exhaust running through the bumperette. There was only one part number for these, the heavier, chrome-plated, cast aluminum version. Carreras continued to use front bumperettes in the rear, since their exhaust system still exited below the bumper.

A cast aluminum bell-shaped funnel, 644.505.305.-00, was press-fitted into the rear guards to direct the exhaust through the opening.

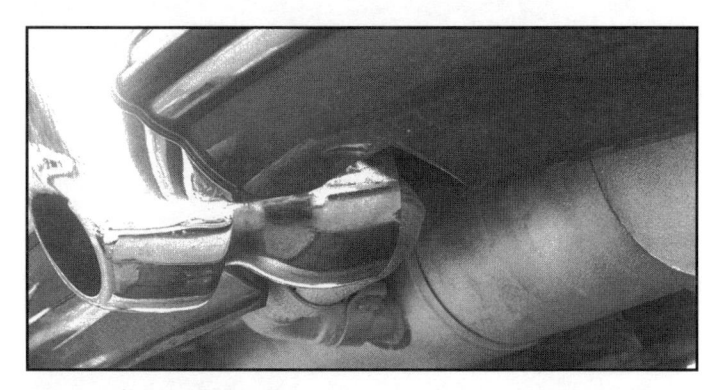

Aluminum exhaust funnel on T 2 356A, note originals were rough cast, not polished.

356A with high overrider tube

Bumper Guards and Trim, U.S. 356A

U.S. bumpers were easily distinguished from others by their chrome-plated steel overrider tubes. The bumper guards used were taller versions of the ones described on page 47. They had a notch for the overrider tube and were, like the European variety, interchangeable front to rear. These were on all non-Carreras from mid-1956 through the end of 1959, according to the parts book. They actually were not used on Carrera GTs but were standard on the Carrera GS. Illustration 44 of the 356A book showed the general arrangement. The oldest cars on file having U.S. bumpers were 1956 Speedster 82624 and coupe 57751; Speedster 82616 and coupe 57355 did not have them.

The height of the front overrider tube was increased in February 1959. Lowest chassis numbers on file with high tubes were coupe 108313 and cabriolet 151615. At this point, Carrera GS models were also fitted with this type of bumper.

By raising the notch and stud to accommodate the higher overrider tube, the front guard could no longer be used on the rear of Carrera models.

Initially, a single tube spanned the rear bumper. It was illustrated in the parts book, which stated to replace it with the split rear tubes. The change was apparently requested by police because the tube obscured the license plate. Exactly when the split rear tubes appeared is uncertain, although it was a bit after the tail and license light configuration was altered, which was

Painted steel support tube that penetrated the nose and tail on 356As with U.S.-style bumpers

The first rear overrider tubes mirrored the front.

Pre-T 2 and Carrera models had front guards installed in the rear.

T 2 cars had exhaust-through-the-guards styling.

coupe 100001, cabriolet 61700 and Speedster 83200 in March 1957. One 1957 GS Carrera, 100765, had the single tube overrider.

At the T 2's body introduction, a rear bumperette change occurred similar to the "exhaust through the bumper guard" described for the European configuration.

Peculiar to U.S. cars were the four holes in the body from which the bumper support tubes emerge. Added to help support the heavy, U.S.-trimmed bumper, the tubes were mild steel and always were painted silver. The front bumper support tubes were lengthened when the height of the overrider tube was changed in 1959. A rubber grommet protected the body where the tube passed through.

Bumper Guards, 356B and 356C

The bumper change for 1960 meant new bumper guards, two-piece units of chrome-plated zinc alloy die castings. As on late 356As, the exhaust exited through the lower half of the rear guard. The exhaust was guided by a sheet metal funnel which bolted in place on the lower guard. Due to the location of the funnel, carbonization and discoloration of the bumper guard often occurred, so aftermarket companies developed exhaust extensions. These were not available from Porsche.

356B and 356C Carreras used front guards in the rear because the exhaust once again exited under the bumper. Aluminum guards were apparently made for such cars but occasionally turn up randomly on other models. GT Carreras came with no guards at all. The rear bumpers of all 356Bs and 356Cs carried twin Hella license lights; these were never modified.

The massive 356B/C bumper guard, front and rear. The aftermarket exhaust extensions helped keep carbon residue off of the guard.

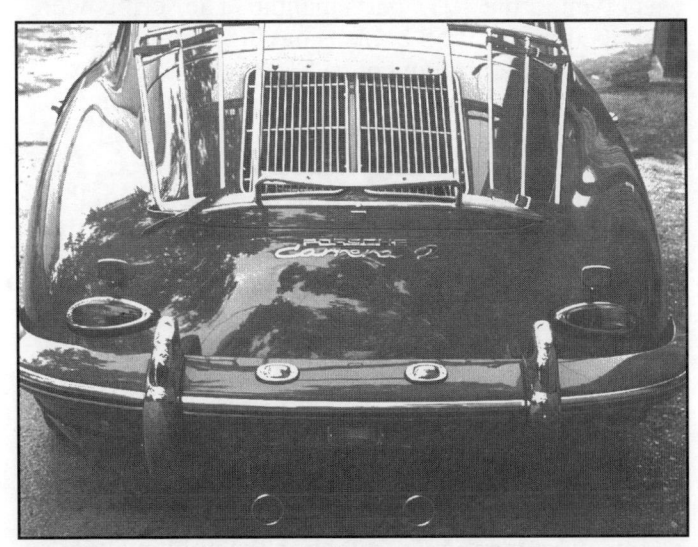

The Carrera 2 used front guards on the back.

The Porsche script for 356 and 356A

The rear Porsche script 356 and 356A

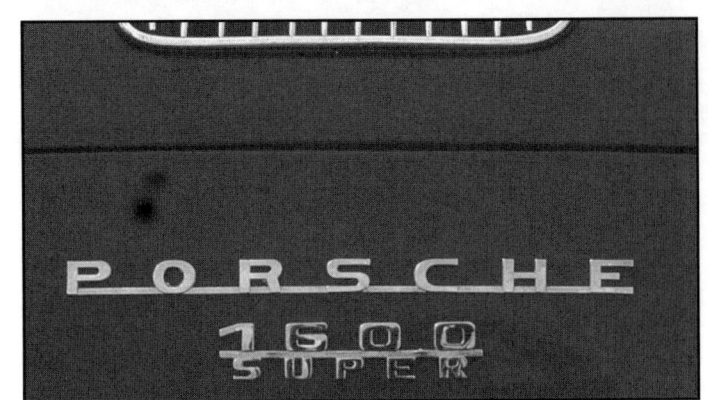

Only early 1960 356Bs had front scripts.

The T 5 script was longer than its predecessor.

Porsche Scripts

Since the first 356 rolled off the assembly line, each one had proudly carried the name of its creator. The cast metal scripts fore and aft on most 356s were what announced to the public at large the owner's good taste in automobiles.

Starting with chassis number 5001, the Porsche name appeared as a cast aluminum plate on the nose and tail, below the corresponding lids. The scripts were identical front and rear. The part number 356.58.036 was given in the 1953 parts manual. The scripts were described in the 1955 book as having "hollow rivets" and were used through coupe 51585 and cabriolet 60368. These scripts had seven rivets. From this point, full rivets, or solid pegs, were used on all scripts. This Porsche script had only five rivets. The aluminum script 644.559.301.01 was used from the chassis numbers listed above through the end of the 1955 model year on all cars except Speedsters, which used gold-plated brass scripts.

The part number given in the 1955 parts book for the gold-plated script for nose and tail was 540.58.303. The 540 prefix implied its use on Speedsters. It was possible that other models may have been fitted with gold scripts, although none were reported in the survey. In the 356A parts book the gold and aluminum scripts were mentioned, although the gold one was given the number 644.559.301.00. It seems reasonable that this was the same as 540.58.303.

The script changed with the introduction of the 356B in late 1959. It was similar in appearance but was about an inch longer. Like earlier scripts, it mounted with five studs. Early 356Bs had them on the front and back, but most had them on the back only. Which cars did and which did not is a troublesome question. If overall impressions mean anything, it appears that all very early 1960 cars had front scripts, and a great number of Roadsters had them. Since Roadsters were not built by Reutter, it is likely that they were discontinued at different times. Front scripts were not used on any models after 1960. (The T 6 rear script is described on page 71)

Headlights

It is safe to assume that early Porsche 356s came with whatever headlights were being used in Wolfsburg that year. The most obvious difference between VW and Porsche units was the absence of the VW logo on the Porsche lens. Most early cars came with removable bulb-type headlights. The 1953 parts book had a listing 356.62.014 for Hella lights and 356.62.013 for Bosch units. Both were non-sealed beam type. As no further description or chassis numbers are listed, the implication is that either unit could have been used.

The 1955 book listed Bosch and Hella units and the familiar Hella clear lens sealed-beam unit. This light

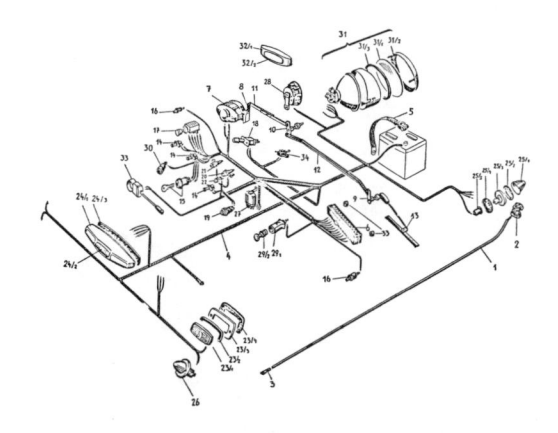

Illustration 22, 1953 Parts Book

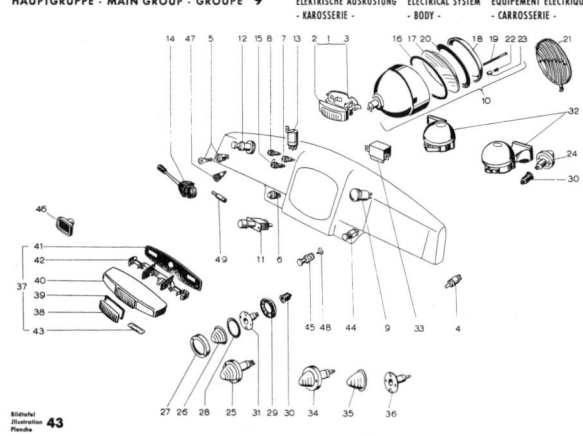

Illustration 43, 1955 Parts Book

unit was available as early as July 1950, when VWs were first officially imported to the U.S. where sealed beam lights were required in some states. The oldest car in the survey with this style light was 10158, a 1951 cabriolet. A vestigial oval on the lens was on early sealed beam units. Trying to authenticate this information is difficult because of the vulnerability of the lens and replacement ease.

The pre-A 356 had no parking lights in the headlight, using dual-filament turn signal units for both signal and running light functions. Adjusting screws were at the same height (lower third) on either side of the sealed beam headlight unit.

Headlight grilles were standard equipment on Speedsters and optional on other models in the 1955 model year. They were chrome-plated, pot-metal castings. This grille was inserted in place of the lens on the sealed beam headlight unit, requiring no modifications, but special mounting screws with knurled knobs were required.

The 356A parts book listed the Bosch and Hella symmetrical units described above as well as the Hella sealed-beam unit. In addition, Bosch and Hella asymmetrical headlights were listed.

The sealed-beam headlights remained unchanged un-

The Bosch symmetric headlight unit

The Bosch asymmetric headlight unit

The Hella symmetric headlight unit had both adjustment screws at the bottom of the light. Bosch adjusters were at 9 and 12 o'clock positions.

The Hella asymmetric headlight unit had diagonally placed adjustment screws, as did the Bosch asymmetric unit.

51

The early cast headlight grille

Late wire-mesh headlight grille

til the turn signal units changed from two-pole to one-pole at coupe 100001, cabriolet 61701 and Speedster 83201 (March 1957, the time when teardrop taillights were added). At this point the parking light bulb appeared in the headlight unit directly in front of the sealed beam unit. Both pot-metal and wire mesh headlight grilles were available on the 356A. The pot metal grille replaced the glass lens, while the mesh grilles were installed over the lenses allowing their use on non-sealed beam lights. Mesh grilles continued to be offered through the end of 356C production.

Headlight units on 356Bs were unaltered. The parts book listed both Hella-made sealed-beam units and Bosch standard and asymmetrical units. The standard units were for left-hand traffic. Both of the non-U.S. units had parking lights built into the headlight. The sealed-beam units no longer had the parking light within the headlight. Instead, the parking light bulb hole was covered by a piece of silver painted cardboard or metal.

According to the parts book, no additional changes were made. But this was not the way it was. A headlight unit with diagonally opposed adjustment screws appeared, with no parking light or cardboard covered hole. From owner's surveys it appears that T 5s and some early T 6s had the early-style light, while 356Cs had the later style. There seems to be a tremendous number of cars with variations on this theme, likely due to the ease of replacement and the abundant VW replacement units. From information provided, the change appeared in late 1963 with the earliest diagonal unit on cabriolet 159469.

Early Hella sealed beam headlight unit

Hella sealed beam headlight unit with parking light bulb

Hella sealed beam headlight unit with parking light cover

Hella sealed beam headlight unit with diagonal adjusters

It is worth mentioning that numerous factory photos exist showing rows and rows of 356s with sealed beam headlight units without the actual sealed beam in place, obviously finished cars waiting for export. This implies that sealed beam units were either importer or dealer-installed, as were the headlights on VWs of the time.

Turn Signals

The first 356s came with a round turn signal unit with a conical plastic lens. The front and rear signal units were identical except for color. The fronts were clear (or amber), and the rears red. These light units were single-filament and functioned only as indicator lights. There were at least two different light units. Both had indentations on each side where the rim was mounted. The first type was made by Hella and had a dome shaped lens with concentric rings. The later unit had a taller lens which was "pointy" and had ribs converging at the apex. This unit was unmarked, but was likely made by SWF. These appeared early in production, certainly by the Model 51 cars, but seem not to have been used on cars built by Gläser.

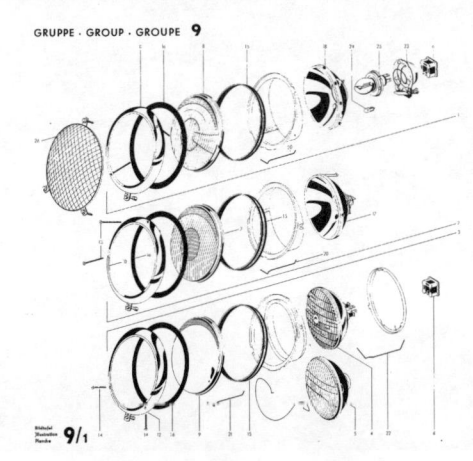

According to the 1955 parts book, the first SWF, two-poled (dual-filament which functioned as turn signal and running light) beehive light units were on coupe 11779 and cabriolet 15073 for the 1953 model year. The white lens on this front turn signal unit was pebble grained on the inside surface. The lenses were plastic, although some early cars had glass lenses. This unit was used until coupe 100001, cabriolet 61701 and Speedster 83201, when a taller clear beehive on a wedge shaped chrome-plated block appeared. This was a single pole unit.

Illustration 9/1, 356B Parts Book

Hella (left) and unmarked SWF (right) turn signal units

Early beehive turn signal unit

Late, tall beehive turn signal unit on wedge base

356A wedge turn signal unit with twist-on lens

The 356B/C turn signal unit

At coupe 104090, cabriolet 150640 and Convertible D 85503, a revised wedge unit with a twist-on lens was first used. Again, this was a single-pole unit manufactured by SWF. It was replaced on the 356B by the two-bulb unit, the final permutation of the front turn signal unit. European models had only a single bulb as the parking light was within the headlight. U.S. cars had clear lenses, while most other countries had amber lenses. These units were the first to be sided, left and right.

Fog Lights

Fog lights were optional equipment on 356s as early as 1951. Many early competition photos showed both round and rectangular lights on the bumpers of 1950 - 1954 cars. The official 1955 optional fog lights were small round units mounted on the bumper or recessed into the nose. Another rectangular bumper-mounted fog light was available on 356As. It was shown in an accessories catalog dated February 1959 and was for use on cars with U.S. bumpers. It mounted on top of the bumper, just outside the guard.

For the 356B the familiar Hella 128 unit became optional equipment; it had an oval shape and mounted below the bumper in the lower grille area. Rubber plugs were present in the three holes where the grille was normally mounted. Wiring for fog lights was present in all cars from 1954.

Nose mounted fog lights on a 356A

Hella 128 fog light unit

The early "no hole" hood handle

The handle with a hole was a Model 52 change

Early blunt crested hood handle

1956 356A with "pointy" crested hood handle and grey seals

Hood Handles

The first 356s were equipped with a small aluminum handle toward the front of the hood. These were not anodized and were mounted with three studs. Initially, they had no hole in the front. According to the 1955 parts book this handle was used from chassis 5001 until coupe 52844 and cabriolet 60693, but, another handle with a hole in it, existed. It was first installed on the Model 52.

The Speedster-inspired 356A-style handle with the enameled Porsche crest commenced at coupe 52845 and cabriolet 60694 (November 1954 for the 1955 model year). All but the first Speedster used this handle or a reasonable facsimile. The 356A-style handle, mounted with two nuts at the back and one at the front, was a bright anodized aluminum casting. It was used through the duration of the 356 and all of the 356A series. A couple of subtle variations were present with this handle. Very early ones had a rounded front, while the majority were "pointy." There was also a reinforcement ridge on the inside of some handles. When first installed in 1954 the seals consisted of flat pads that did not protrude from the handle edge. By the introduction of the 356A light grey seals that were clearly visible were installed front and rear. By 1957 these were black.

The 356B and 356C cars came with a chrome plated pot metal casting much larger than the 356A handle.

The 356B/C hood handle was larger than the earlier ones, but used the same crest.

It used the same enameled crest. The original crest had an opaque red-orange colored enamel, not the red translucent color that Porsche began supplying as a replacement in the early 1980s.

Horn Grille

Horn grilles were first installed on 356s starting with the 1954 model year at coupe 52030 and cabriolet 60550. They were chrome-plated pot metal mounted with three tiny studs (designed to break off when removal of horn grilles was attempted). These grilles were used through 1959.

With the introduction of the 356B, the grilles were

Horn grilles appeared mid-1954.

B/C upper horn grille

Lower B/C horn grille

Carrera 2s did not have upper grilles.

modified. These bright anodized aluminum pressings were found above and below the bumper. The mounting hardware for the lower grilles consisting of small strips of metal, a flat mounting plate and clips was interesting, if not terribly practical (perhaps Porsche's response to complaints about breaking studs on earlier grilles?). Grilles were used on all 356Bs and 356Cs. Cars with fog lights did not have lower grilles. Carrera 2s did not have upper grilles (due to oil coolers).

Wipers

Illustration 22 of the 1953 parts book showed a very VW-like windshield wiper blade. Interestingly, an asymmetry was noted by different part numbers for left and right. These were most likely the wiper arms, which, in cross section, were circular. This information did not agree with the survey results, which suggest that left and right were identical. As with headlights, the necessity and ease of replacement make the wiper arms and blades difficult to authenticate. Many cars were likely updated, based on superiority of new designs and lack of availability of original-style parts.

Wiper blades were attached via set screws. Coupling pieces, which held set screws, were different, early to late: early was smaller, more contoured, with a 3mm screw, while late were squared off and had cheese head screws.

To further complicate, the 1955 book stated:

Coupe 5001 - 11778 and cabriolets 5015 - 15072 used a Bosch wiper system. This had a small, round, black Bosch motor and linkage like early VWs.

Coupes 11779 - 52029 and cabriolets 15073 - 60549 used SWF 1953 wiper system: Bowden cable/tube operated switch, and linkage in motor; parallel arm motion.

Coupes 52630 - on and cabriolets 60550 - on used the SWF 54 wiper system.

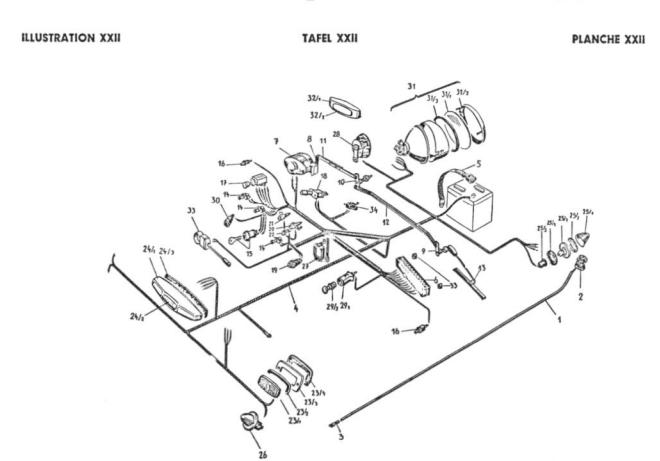

Illustration 22, 1953 Parts Book

All of these systems were single speed and ran off a

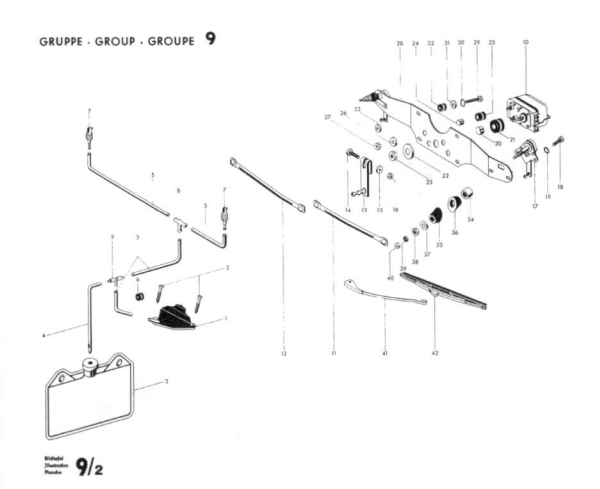

Illustration 9/2, 356B Parts Book

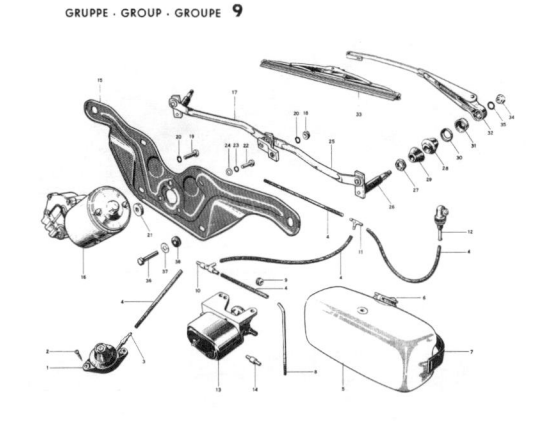

Illustration 9/2A, T 6 Parts Book

single wiper motor. The first two systems were sided with left and right wiper blades while the SWF 54 had only one type of blade. The SWF 54 was the familiar flattened arm with a set screw retaining the blade.

Another variation appeared in late 1954: the sided 225mm arms and 260mm SWF blades for the Speedster.

The SWF 54, which came with a bowden cable for operation of the switch and linkage in the motor, continued through coupe 10000, cabriolet 67700 and Speedster 83200 (mid-1957). Later 356As were apparently fitted with either the SWF 2400 or the Bosch WS 7/6 H system. Both were offered in a special order version which did not interfere with VHF reception. The two types were apparently used interchangeably, as available.

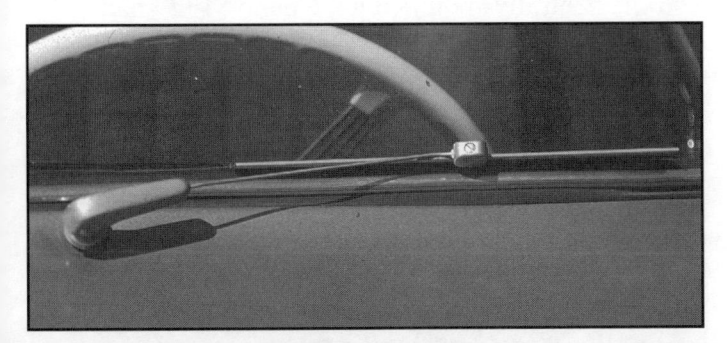

Asymmetry occurred again on the SWF 2400 arms, similar in appearance to the earlier SWF 54. A different arm was used for right-hand drive cars. The Bosch arm was not sided, but the end was hooked like 911 arms. Speedster arms were again sided and shorter than coupe and cabriolet counterparts. The wiper blades were the same for all models. No special mention of what was used on Convertible Ds was made, but it seems reasonable that the wipers used on the later Roadster would have been identical.

The T 5 retained Porsche's choice of electricals being Bosch or SWF, although motors were apparently interchangeable. The Roadster had the SWF 2400 arms and blades as fitted to some 356A coupes and cabriolets, while T 5 coupes and cabriolets used the Bosch arms and blades used on the other 356A coupes and cabriolets.

Early wiper arm with circular cross section

Shorter arms were used on Speedsters.

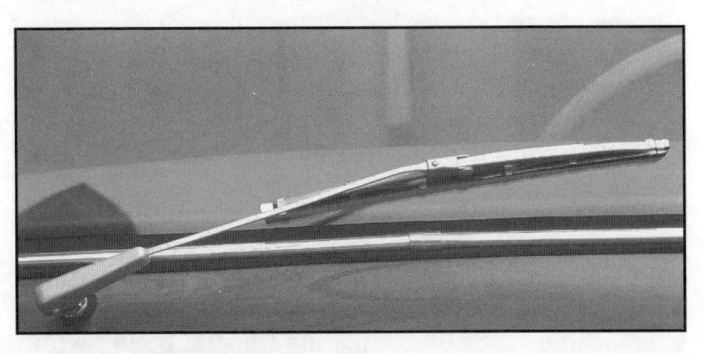

Flattened SWF arm with set screw blade

Unusual arm with external hooks

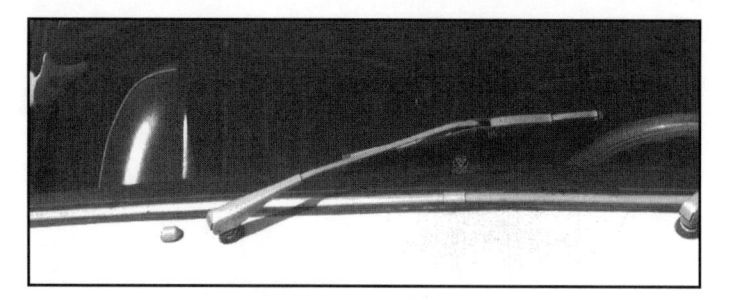

Bosch wiper arm with internal hook

These wiper arms were used on Convertible D and Roadster.

T 6 wiper arm with cap nut

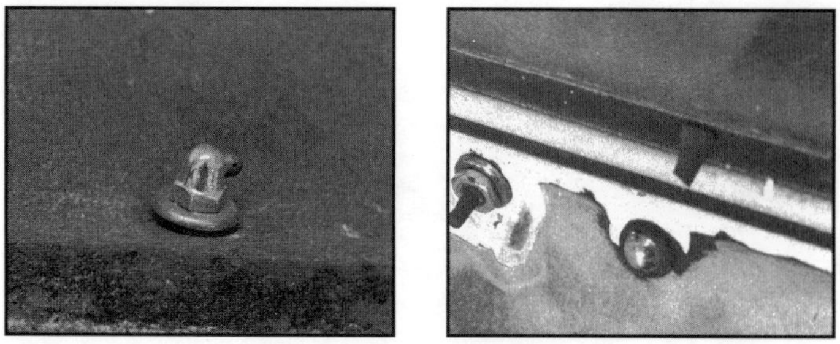

Cabriolet #5142 (left), low dome (right)

Higher dome (left), hexagonal jet (right)

Windshield Washer System

Windshield washers were fitted to nearly all 356s. The earliest cars had rather diverse jet nozzles and placement, which demonstrates either indecision or, in many cases, dealer (or owner) installation. A good example of this is on page 46, where four cars are illustrated within 150 chassis numbers. Two of the cars had jets inside the wipers, two had them outside.

The types of jets also varied. The oldest car illustrated, 5142, showed a unique form. Cabriolet 10200 had a single centrally-mounted jet. Coupe 51329 had a low domed model; the next, a 1954 coupe, was similar but not identical to the 1953.

The first 356s with windshield washers had a large rectangular glass bottle made by SWF. Location varied, but generally it was up by the fuel tank or down

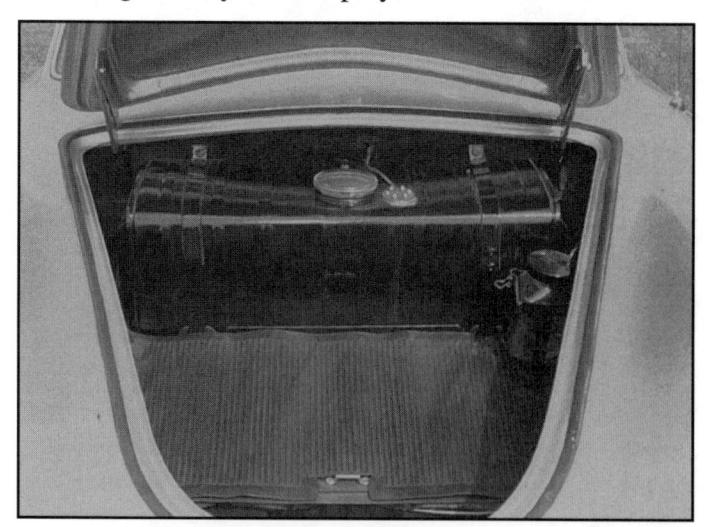

The T 6 ended the long history of wipers which mounted by a hex nut perpendicular to the wiper shaft. These cars came equipped with a new mounting which used a splined, tapered wiper shaft; it was threaded on the end so the wiper arm could be held in place by an aluminum cap nut. Wiper arms and blades were symmetrical and interchangeable for all models, 1962 through 1965. There was a difference between the wiper motors of right and left-hand drive models. Both were Bosch and there were six and twelve volt versions (to match the electrical system of the particular car).

The mounting hardware that protruded through the body is another point of interest. Pre-1956 cars had a chrome nut and spacer but not the rubber bases seen on later cars. A number of different wiper gearboxes (the part mounted under the cowl from which the wiper shaft protruded) were used up to 1955 - 1956, with differing shaft diameters and shaft housing lengths.

The 356A parts book was the first to mention the rubber spacers at the base of the wiper arm. The ones listed in the 356A book were the same as those listed for T 5 Bs. The T 6 hardware was significantly different, which can be seen by comparing illustration 9/2 with illustration 9/2A.

Glass washer bottle location 1954 356

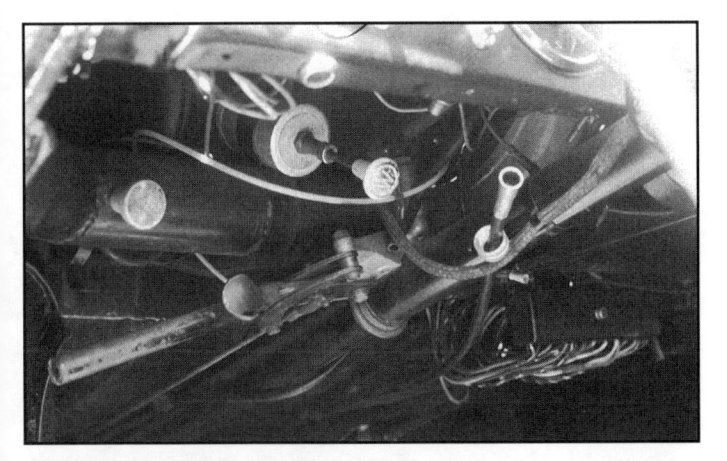

Hand pump mounted on the defroster tube.

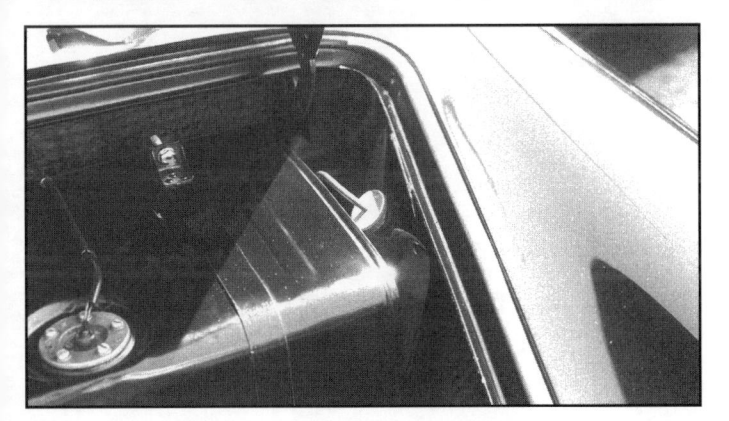

Washer bag located alongside the fuel tank

by the battery, both on the driver's side. During this period SWF offered aftermarket washer kits to upgrade cars not so equipped. These were similar to factory systems, utilizing identical nozzles, glass reservoirs, and hand-operated or electrical pumps.

For the 1955 model year, the glass reservoir was replaced by a flat nylon bag. The first official mention of the change was in the 1955 parts book, which also showed the 1955 - 1959 hexagonal jet, often associated with the 356A, starting at coupe 52908 and cabriolet 60707 (early 1955 model year). The washer solution was propelled by a hand-operated pump which mounted under the dashboard.

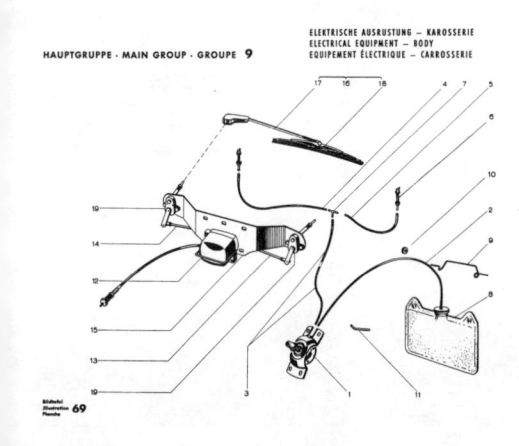

Illustration 69, 356A Parts Book

Left, the washer nozzle first used on the Convertible D; Right, the 356C washer nozzle

Rubber foot pump found on 356B/Cs

The 356A had a foot-pumped windshield washer as shown in illustration 69 of the 356A book. The washer system was altered in the Convertible D including the washer nozzles.

The T 5 featured a rubber SWF foot pump and the external nozzles first seen on the Convertible D. The washer bag was unaltered from the 356A. Washer bags came in a variety of colors. Grey, blue and black were colors most often described, although a yellow one was submitted on the owner survey. There was no chronological sequence in regard to color; however, blue was the most prevalent color.

The jet and pump were basically unaltered for the T 6. The washer reservoir was different, being a hard plastic reservoir as illustrated in 9/2A (page 57). The extra capacity was necessary for the optional electric washer. 356Cs were about the same, the only change being a flat dual jet nozzle. These had a bright anodized cover and were later used on 911s and 914s.

The T 6 washer bottle

Aerials

Sharing the cowl with the wipers and washers was the aerial, which with the exception of the 1953 book, didn't appear in the parts books at all. In many cases they were dealer-installed. Nearly all were installed close to the windshield on the left front fender. The hinge pillar had a hollowed out section for the antenna. Hirschmann and Bosch aerials were most frequently used, although theoretically any brand in any location could be "original" if dealer-installed. The two brands described in the 1953 book were Kathrein and Hirschmann.

One early factory photo showed an aerial in the center of the cowl directly in front of the windshield on a 1950 coupe. Another popular location on coupes of the time was on the roof just above the center of the windshield.

For 356As the accessory books listed a hand-cranked, retractable aerial. An electric aerial, which functioned via the on-off switch on the radio, could be ordered. Interestingly, the 356B seems to have come only with a manually-operated antenna. No mention was made of the manufacturer, but most 356Bs had Hirschmann aerials.

The 356C accessory book showed an illustration of a T 6 with a manual Hirschmann unit. Other options were a lockable aerial for either 6 or 12-volt system. The lockable version seems to be Hirschmann again; the electric model was definitely a Hirschmann.

Early aerial with red plastic tip

Lockable Bosch aerial was a common replacement.

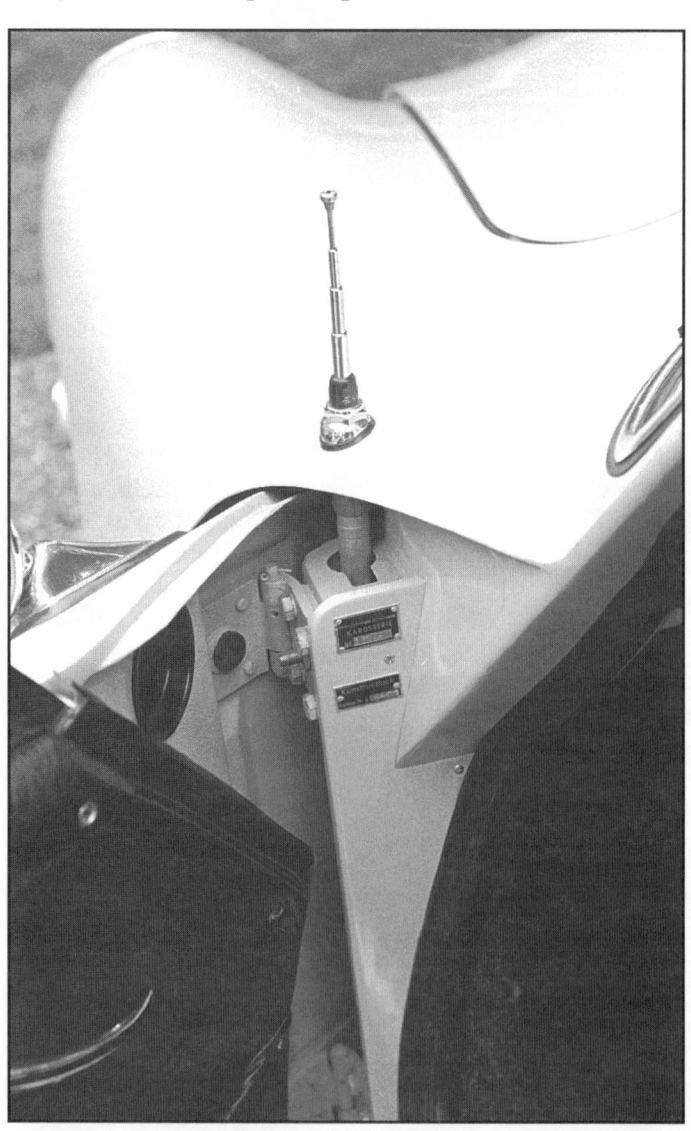

Lockable Hirschmann aerial showing hingepost mounting

The split windshield lacked any bright trim.

The Speedster windshield frame

Windshields and Trim

Divided two-piece windshields were installed, per the 1955 parts book, to coupe 11360 and cabriolet 10270, the last Model 51 cars. The same windshield was used for coupes and cabriolets. The rubber molding around the glass had no aluminum trim, and a rubber seal went between the window halves.

All this seems to go well with the photos of the four early cars (page 46), with the exception of 11321, which had a one-piece windshield. The bent windshield fit the same hole as the split windshield, which made re-tooling the top forming dies unnecessary. The rubber profile around the glass was different in that a groove was present to hold the aluminum trim. This trim was not bright-anodized, only polished. A small clip was present at the top and bottom to cover the ends of the left and right side trim pieces. Despite the bend in the windshield, these clips were not bent. Again, the same windshield was used for coupe and cabriolet models.

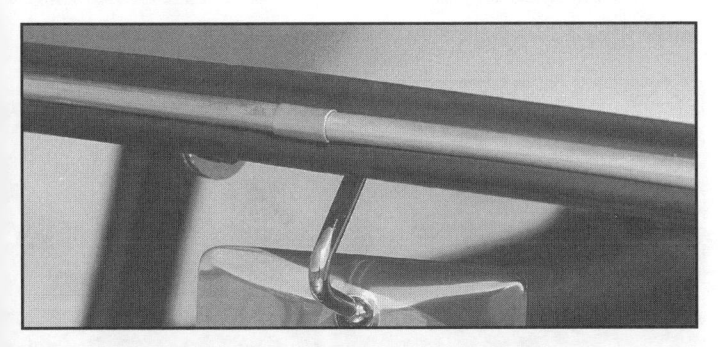

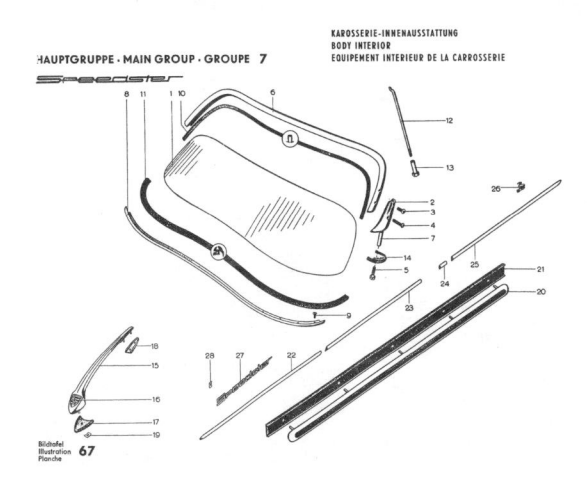

Illustration 67, 356A Parts Book

The Speedster, of course, had a unique low curved glass windshield. The windshield frame and two low posts were chrome plated brass. A single rubber seal went around the sides and top of the glass, with a second seal below the glass and two small rubber pads below the windshield posts.

356A coupes and cabriolets used the same seal as the 356 coupes and cabriolets. The aluminum trim was also identical in cross section although it was contoured to the new shape of the glass. The center clip was unchanged for the 356A, but longer on T 5 cars. Coupe and cabriolet trim was the same.

The Convertible D was also unique in the windshield department. Its taller brass posts required a different windshield than the Speedster. The Roadster was ba-

Small clip on "bent" windshield

Longer late windshield clip

Convertible D/Roadster windshield frame

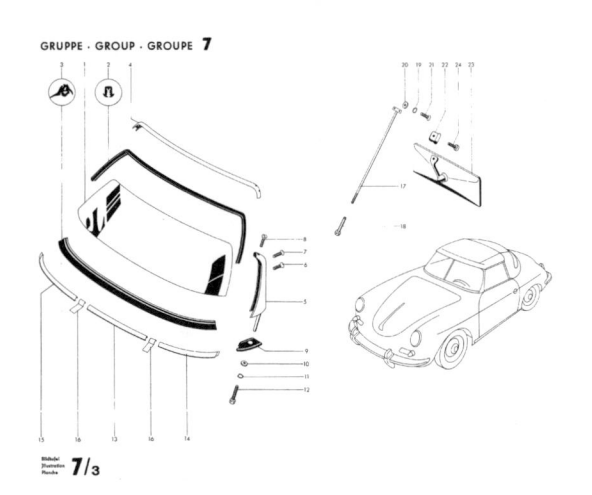

Illustration 7/3, 356B Parts Book

Early Roadster windshield post (left), and late post (right)

sically the same as the Convertible D but differed in several areas. First, the posts went from brass to pot metal in late 1960 at 87316, likely a cost savings measure. Also, according to the parts book the windshield actually changed in early 1961 at 87516. The later windshield was approximately 7/8 inch taller. Top latches were also modified at Roadster 87825, making top frame swaps with Convertible Ds and earlier Roadsters difficult (they can be adapted with careful drilling and threading).

The T 5 356B coupe and cabriolet windshield assembly was identical to the 356A. T 6 coupes and Karmann Hardtops were different from cabriolets. This windshield was taller and somewhat narrower than earlier cars; although the same seal was used for

The T 6 coupe windshield was taller and had wider trim.

coupes and cabriolets. Cabriolets used the same windshield as previous coupes and cabriolets. Karmann and Reutter coupe windshields were the taller one previously mentioned. The T 6 windshield trim was broader and bright anodized. No change was made for 356C models.

Fender Scripts

Very early Speedsters varied from later Speedsters by having a different side script. This script was located on the upper third toward the back of the front fender on both sides. Earlier cars had rounded letters much like the Spyder name plate; while later cars had the more familiar squared off letters. The change occurred around 80029, quite early in production. GT Speedsters had no scripts at all. Other Speedsters occasionally lacked scripts, if so ordered. There were also factory photos showing Speedsters with both Carrera and Speedster fender scripts and early Convertible Ds with Speedster scripts and fender scripts reading "Speedster D." The Speedster script was the later style with the D being separate. This was not acknowledged by the parts book, nor have any such vehicles apparently survived.

Early Speedster script

Late Speedster script

Some Carreras had their names on both front fenders. The large 644.559.325.00 script was found only on fenders of 356A GS cars. GTs, T 5 356B GT cars and Carrera 2s had no fender scripts. Carrera Speedster, 81072, had the small Carrera script followed by the Speedster script.

Two additional side scripts existed for production cars, the gold-plated "Continental" script used in 1955 and "European" script used on 1956 models.

356A Carrera script

The short lived Continental script

The shorter lived European script

Coachbuilder Badges

Nearly all early 356s came with the name "Reutter" proudly displayed on the right front fender. The Gläser-built cars had Gläser badges on both fenders until apparently badges became scarce, at which time they appeared only on the right side, then not at all. Chassis 10165 had no badge.

Reutter badges on the earliest cars were of painted aluminum (5135 owner's survey), followed by a cloisonne version on chrome-plated copper. Both versions were secured by slotted screws. Those with sharp eyes will notice that 11451 (page 46) had an angled Reutter badge (not currently available as a reproduction). The next type was similar to the enameled version but was painted on flat aluminum. This was used in 1953 and likely earlier. Use of this type badge continued until the familiar oval Reutter badge appeared with 1955 models.

This large oval Reutter anodized aluminum badge with black border was fitted from 1955 through 1960, when a smaller oval badge came into use. The exact point at which the smaller Reutter badge was fitted is uncertain as is the last use of such badges. The newest car on the owner's survey with a large badge fitted was coupe 117015, late 1961. The last recorded use of the small badge was coupe 123512, early 1963. Both were secured with round-headed aluminum rivets.

All U.S.-spec. 1955 coupes and cabriolets were Continentals. The owner's survey results indicate that all 1955 model year cars, except Speedsters, showed evidence that "Continental" scripts were originally installed. The "European" script used on both coupes and cabriolets in early 1956 was discontinued before the end of the model year, apparently not a successful marketing tool. The latest Europeans known are coupe 55154, cabriolet 61064.

Large Reutter badge

Early Reutter badge. The first ones were cloisonne, later versions, painted.

Small Reutter badge

Karmann badge came in cloisonne and painted aluminum. Drauz badge was fitted on Roadsters and Convertible Ds.

Other coachbuilders, such as Drauz, D'Ieteren, and Karmann, all labeled their product with appropriate badges, as illustrated. Karmann badges were either anodized aluminum on earlier cars or a fired ceramic version on later cars. Later cars rarely had badges. Owner's survey results: the latest aluminum badge 200949, earliest ceramic 210436, latest ceramic 213040.

One last point of interest is that in the parts book both Drauz and Reutter badges were listed as being available in English and German. Karmann badges were offered in English only. With the exception of the word "Belgium," D'Ieteren badges were in French, so it seems reasonable that only one badge was produced.

Side Moldings

Upper side moldings were first installed on Speedsters. There were four pieces on each side, aluminum extrusions, bolted to the body and door. They were not available before the production of the Speedster. They may or may not have been on everything built later. As a rule, most Speedsters, Convertible Ds and Roadsters seem to have them, and most coupes and cabriolets do not.

Aluminum side molding on Speedster

Lower side moldings, on the rocker panels, also appeared first on the Speedster. They resembled the bumper trim but had a wider rubber insert. Initially, they were located directly below the bottom of the door. They were moved down about a half inch midyear. Rocker moldings were simultaneously fitted to coupes and cabriolets late in the 1955 model year. The 356A models used the same molding and it was mounted below the door bottom with similar spacing as the late 356.

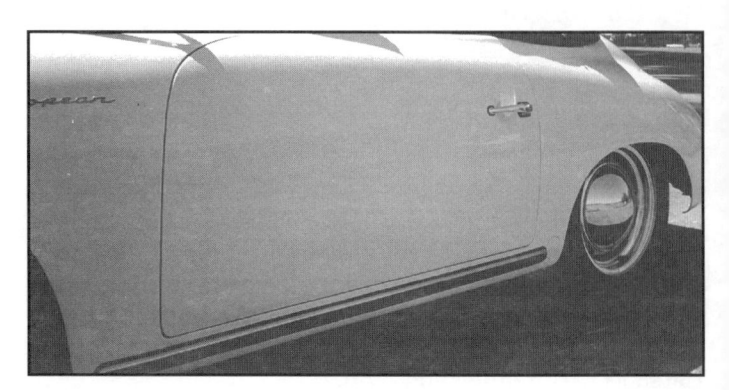

356/A rocker deco

The 356B had a thinner rocker molding with the insert narrower than on bumper trim. While there was no official change in them after 1960, early rocker moldings had finished ends with no visible split, while later cars (and all 911/912s) had a horizontal split at the end of the molding. This later style was bright anodized; earlier versions had no protective coating. Carrera GTs had no rocker moldings.

Late 356B/C deco ends were unfinished. Note also D'Ieteren badge, which should be mounted with solid rivets.

GTs did not have rocker moldings.

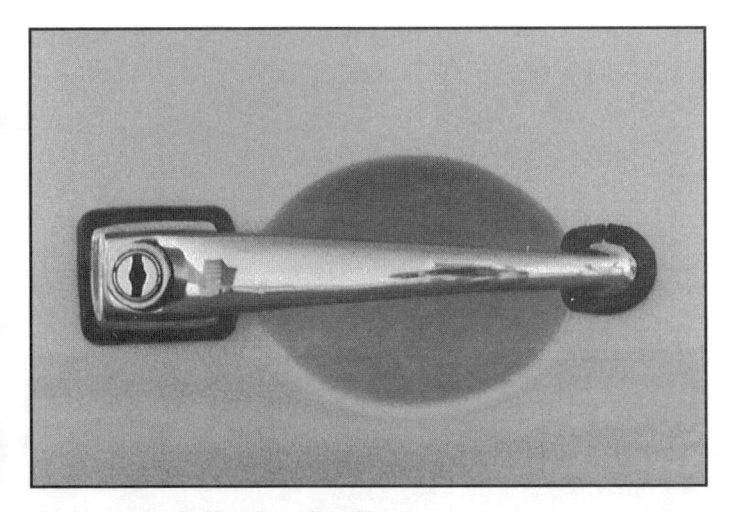

Early squared edge door handle

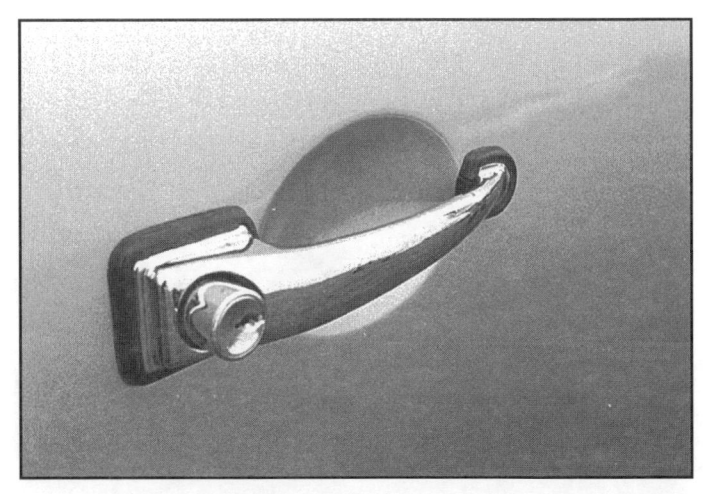

Later squared edge door handle with new style lock cylinder

Late rounded edge door handle

Original Aero mirrors had a spine on the base.

Door Handles

Only one change of consequence occurred on door handles, between 1957 and 1958. The visible difference was at the rear part of the door handle, which went from a squared edge to a rounded edge. The change occurred at (or about) the T 2 change: coupe 101693, cabriolet 150000 and Speedster 83791.

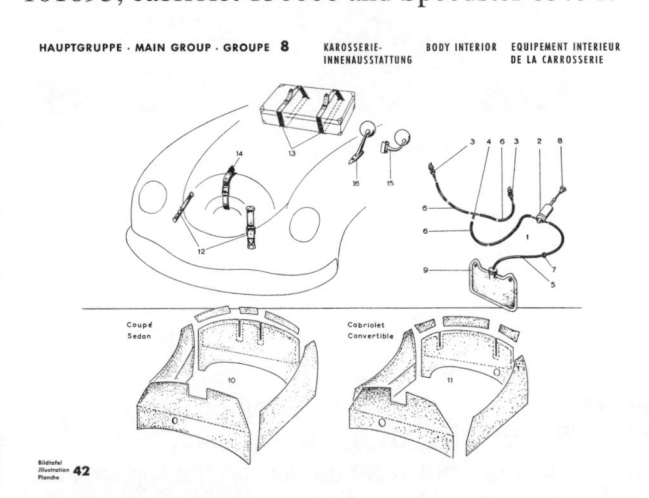

Illustration 42, 1955 Parts Book

Exterior Mirrors

Exterior mirrors were optional on all U.S.-spec. cars, but were standard in Germany from 1959. None of the 1951 coupes pictured on page 46 had exterior mirrors. The 356 parts book illustrated two mirror types, one for mounting on the fender edge (between the door and fender) and one for front fender top mounting. The latter were similar to the Lucas or Raydot mirrors fitted to contemporary British cars and were frequently dealer installed. Dealer and owner installed mirrors also accounted substantial additional variety.

The three commonly seen types of mirrors were the Aero, Ponto-Stabil and Durant styles. The first cars on the Registry survey to have Aero-style mirrors were of 1955 production. These were generally fitted through 1961. The T 6 Bs usually were fitted with the Ponto-Stabil varieties (the base seal on this mirror was grey rather than black). Several period photos showed Ponto-Stabil mirrors on 356As. Durant mirrors were fitted to 356C models as well as early 911s. Talbot mirrors were available as options as early as 1960. As with other mirrors, they could be fitted on both driver's and passenger's sides.

Original Ponto Stabil mirror had flattened outer ridge (repros don't). The base seal was grey.

A later Ponto Stabil-style mirror (made by Talbot) with subtle differences. Both types appear in factory photos.

Original Talbot mirror

Recent Talbot mirror with large green plastic spot

One final mirror was the aerodynamic Spyder-inspired one. These were generally seen on GTs, although they turned up on other models occasionally. The cover, painted body color, was made from either aluminum or steel.

Until the mirror access holes were placed in the left door (May/June 1957) and right door (T 5 356B), mirrors were located on the front fenders. After this they were nearly always mounted on the doors.

The aerodynamic GT fender mirror

Side Windows

Vent windows first appeared on T 2 cabriolets. The pivot was a pressed, flattened bracket. Inside was a chrome locking handle. The GT coupe of 1959 was the next to receive vent windows (all coupes got them at the 356B introduction). These were similar to the cabriolet windows but were angled on the top surface. The T 6 coupe and cabriolet had a modified conical cast pivot.

Durant mirror

Pre-T 2 cabriolets did not have vent windows.

Optional vent assembly on 356A coupe

The only change in coupe side windows was related to the addition of vent windows: cabriolets 1958, GT coupes 1959 (windows in GTs were generally Plexiglas), non-GT coupes 1960. Convertible Ds and Roadsters shared the same glass and did not have vent windows. Tinted glass was not mentioned in the option lists, but some 356Cs appear to have been so equipped. Karmann Hardtops had cabriolet windows. These non-laminated windows were made by Sekurit.

Rear quarter windows were originally non-opening.

The seal was identical in cross section to the windshield and rear window seals. The familiar hinged opening quarter windows appeared in late April 1951, shortly into the production of the Model 51. These were laminated and made by Sigla. The first cars with opening windows had knurled steel latch knobs. By mid-1951 an ivory plastic "crown" knob replaced the steel one. When this knob changed to the medium sized 1954 window crank style was not recorded. It seems reasonable that the change coincided with other knob changes for 1954. These knobs were matched in color with the other knobs in the interior. GT coupes had hinged frameless Plexiglas quarter windows.

Quarter windows for Karmann Hardtops and removable hardtops are discussed on pages 33 - 34.

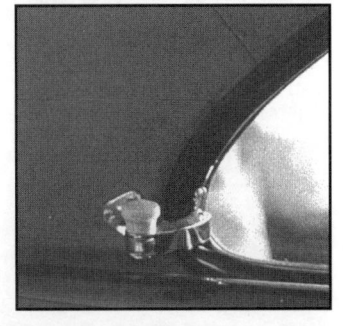

Early flattened pivot (left); Late conical pivot (right)

Early "crown" knob (left) and later medium knob (right)

GT coupes after 1960 had fixed Plexiglas vents (left). Locking chrome handle on vent window (right)

Fixed quarter windows were found on the first 356 coupes. The seal had the same cross section as the windshield seal.

Frameless Plexiglas quarter window on 356 SC GT

The back window of the Karmann Hardtop

Rear Window Trim

The rear window of coupes was first changed at the introduction of the 356A. It was not different in shape, but the retooling of the pressing allowed the cheaper non-laminated Sekurit window to be used in place of the laminated version by Sigla found on earlier cars. No additional changes were made through 1961. As with the windshield, the aluminum molding was not initially used. It was added at the Model 52. This unanodized aluminum molding was identical in cross section to the molding up front. The clips, top and bottom, were identical to those on the windshield trim between 1952 and 1961. The rubber seal was also identical in cross section to the windshield seal, only shorter.

The removable hardtop, introduced in 1958, had a glass rear window that was larger than the coupe's. Its seal and aluminum trim were similar to the coupe. The same clips were used. The Karmann Hardtop followed the same theme, but had a larger rear window.

Between the rear cowl and and the lower edge of the top was another seal with a larger aluminum insert and a center clip similar to the one used on the glass seals.

In 1962 the coupe rear glass was made larger, and the aluminum trim, as with the windshield trim, became broader and bright anodized. The T 6 removable hardtop, which had opening quarter windows, used the broader aluminum trim on the rear window. The seal and the glass were unchanged. The T 6 Karmann Hardtop had the wider aluminum trim but used the same glass and seal as the T 5. The removable hardtop cowl to top seal and trim was unaltered.

Early rear window seal without aluminum trim

Aluminum trimmed small rear window was used through the T 5 356B.

The larger rear window used on the T 6 also had wider anodized trim.

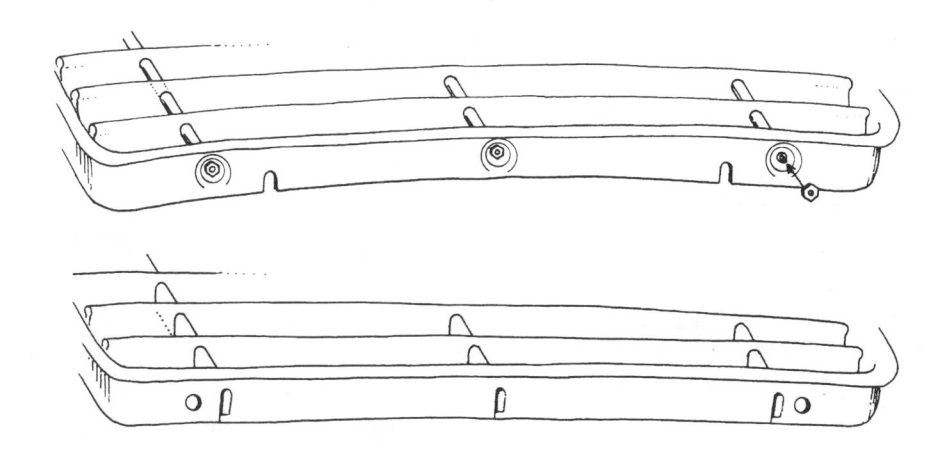

This illustration shows the three major differences in rear grilles. Above is a late style cabriolet which shows the slight curvature of the open car grille, the circular cross-pieces and the slots for mounting. Below is an early coupe which shows the flat profile, press-fit cross-pieces and round mounting holes.

Rear Grilles

From the first cars in 1950 through 1965, the rear grille was basically unchanged. Other than the fact that there were two instead of one from 1962 through 1965, the physical appearance of the grilles was altered very little. Even the first listing in the 1953 parts book showed different grilles for coupes and cabriolets. The difference may be seen from the side view, as the coupe grille was nearly flat and an obvious curve can be seen on the cabriolet. The part number changed in the 1955 book, but the grilles were not altered. The very first cars did not have seals between the grille and body, but they were standard by 1953. The seal was black vinyl and the split between the ends was at the bottom center.

Through mid-1960 the grilles were attached to the rear lid via screws through holes in the outer rim above the top horizontal bar and below the bottom bar. Later cars featured a slot through which the screws were inserted and these slots were located below the top horizontal bar and above the bottom bar.

The next change was shortly after the introduction of the T 6 356B, although no part number change accompanied it. These aluminum grilles were bright anodized and had vertical ribs bolted in place, with cylindrical cross-pieces rather than the earlier press fit variety. Information obtained by owner's survey was inconclusive regarding the anodized finish, but most, if not all, had it.

Early rear grille with press-fit cross-pieces

Late style rear grille with circular cross-pieces

The early Reutter rack on a Model 52 cabriolet

Chrome-plated Leitz rack with two sets of mounting holes could be installed on single or double grille lids.

This Reutter rack would fit single grille lids only.

The Leitz rack doing its thing.

Luggage Racks

Although not a parts manual item, luggage racks could be found in the accessory books from the 356A onward. Factory photos show them as early as 1952. Two manufacturers made fairly similar factory fitted devices. Leather straps could be added to both to hold skis.

Painted racks were manufactured by Reutter from 1952 through 1965. Some were painted the color of the car, although most later racks were painted silver-grey. The earliest racks were somewhat smaller (see photos above). Prior to the introduction of the 356A models it was necessary to drill holes in the rear lid engine protector for attaching. After that time all rear lids came with four threaded holes for the mounting hardware.

By 1960 optional chrome-plated racks were being manufactured by Leitz. Due to their utility and continued production they have become much more common today than during the era when the cars were produced.

Both Reutter and Leitz original single-grille racks have only one set of mounting holes (4), while dual-grille racks generally had two sets of holes (8) so that they could be mounted on either single or dual-grille cars.

Early aluminum script

T 6 Porsche and 60 scripts

The elusive 1300 script

Scripts with shine up light were slightly lower.

T 5 356B with larger Porsche script

T 6 356B with S script

Script placement on the Carrera 2

Small Carrera script on 356A GT

The unusual T 5 Super 90 script

Script placement on the 356C

Taillight placement on the earliest 356s

Rear Scripts

The rear Porsche scripts through the T 5 356B were identical to those used up front, as described on page 50. They were always centered on the tail panel approximately three inches below the rear lid.

The T 6 Porsche script was mounted only in the rear, never up front. It was modified again with only two mounting studs. Externally the difference was visible via the change in the bar connecting the letters. Up to this point a solid bar at the base of the letters was used, but on the T 6 script, the P-O line and H-E line are half way up the letters. This script was used on T 6 356Bs and 356Cs.

At or around the introduction of the Model 52 Porsche began affixing a script below the Porsche script on the tail which gave the engine type and size. The oldest car in the owner's survey which had a rear engine-type script was 11994. The newest without holes (implying no engine designation script) was number 10960. One earlier car, 10798, had holes in the body but no script remaining.

Apparently 1100-cc engined cars never had engine designation scripts. According to the 1955 parts book, 1300, 1300 SUPER, 1500, and 1500 SUPER badges were available in aluminum or gold. Part numbers for the aluminum badges all start with a 356 prefix, the gold with 540, *implying* once again that the gold badges were for Speedsters.

The 356A parts book listed the 1300 badge as chrome (earlier cars were definitely aluminum), which may explain the chrome-plated Porsche scripts that were available. The 1300 SUPER, 1600 and 1600 SUPER were gold; a small Carrera badge, 644.339. 326.00, was also on the back of appropriate cars.

356Bs came with the same badges: Carrera, 1600, 1600 SUPER plus the new SUPER 90. These were all gold-plated.

The T 6 356B brought a change in engine designations scripts: 60, S and 90. In addition, 2-liter Carreras featured the large Carrera badge 644.559.325.00, formerly on front fenders, and a gold "2" on the tail panel.

356Cs had C and SC engine scripts. Carrera 2s used the same script arrangement as on the T 6 B version.

Taillights

The rear indicator light on the first 356s was identical to the early front turn signal light, differing only in lens color. The taillight was the rectangular Hella-made light directly above the signal unit (page 71).

According to the 1955 parts book, at coupe 11779 and cabriolet 15073 (1953 model year) this arrangement was replaced by the two familiar beehive light units. The inside unit was the brake light, the outside unit was the taillight and turn signal.

The outside unit was a two-poled light with a red lens. The inside unit originally carried a 15-watt bulb and a dark orange lens. At coupe 53210 and cabriolet 60765 (early 1955) this unit was revised to accept a 20-watt bulb.

With the 356A, the miracle of rewiring transformed

U.S. spec. all red teardrop taillight

Red/amber teardrop taillight

the inside light of the pair to become the taillight. It had a red lens. The outside unit became the turn signal/brake light and was dark red-orange in color.

At coupe 100001, cabriolet 61701 and Speedster 83201 (March 1957), the teardrop unit appeared, combining tail light, turn signal and brake light. This configuration continued throughout the remainder of the production. The only variation was the difference in all red U.S., red-amber European and amber-red Italian lenses.

Original style beehive lights

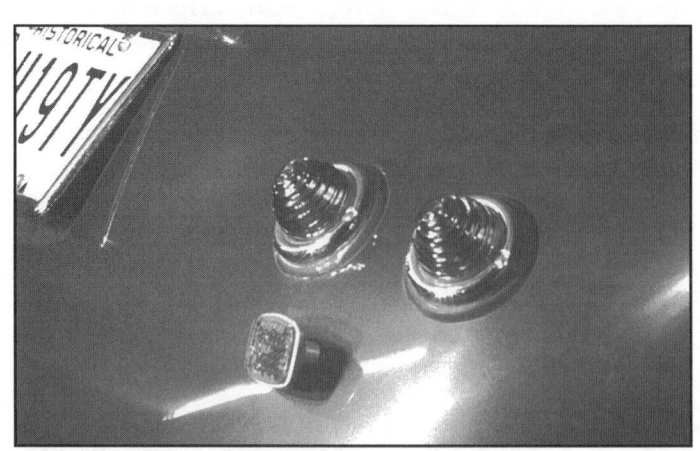

Taller replacement lenses on beehive lights

Early license light with central brake light

Location of Hella logo

License Light, Back-up Light

In the original taillight configuration, the brake light was in the center of the large chrome-plated Hella license light unit, located over the license plate. When the beehive lights were introduced, the center lens changed from red to clear and changed from brake light to back-up light function. Due to lower bumpers on earlier cars, their license lights were also lower.

At coupe 100001, cabriolet 61701 and Speedster 83201 (taillight change) the license light went from shine-down to shine-up, under the license plate. It is worth noting due to reproduction light units – that originals had the number 1431 and Hella logo on top center of the chrome-plated housing (some very early ones did not). The center lens also had a Hella logo. License light lenses were held in place by solid rivets.

The 356B brought paired Hella license light units on the bumper. These remained unchanged throughout the production of 356Bs and 356Cs.

Back-up lights on 356Bs and 356Cs were beneath the bumper. All but French-specification cars came with clear lenses; French cars had yellow.

Shine-down license light with central back-up light

Shine-up license light

The 356B/C license light

The 356B/C back-up light

The SWF reflector with aluminum base

ULO reflector on pod

Reflectors

Rear reflectors were first used when twin beehive lights replaced the earlier arrangement at the 1953 model year. They were below the lights, but above the bumper. Made by SWF, they had a steel back and glass lens. The diamond reflector pattern was larger than later ULO units. Aluminum spacers with small rubber pads were placed between the reflector and body to achieve the proper angle.

In 1960 the reflectors were changed. The new ones were manufactured by ULO and had plastic lenses with aluminum backs. There were two placements: on most European cars they were below the bumper; on most U.S. cars they came on little chrome pods above the tail light. Either configuration was correct, as it was a customer option. Having both on the same car, however, is wrong. When installed in the low position, plastic spacers were used. When on pods, early cars had a slotted chrome screw (which looked suspiciously like the rear seat pivot screw) filling the hole under the bumper. By late 1960, cars had vinyl plugs in the holes. Survey results placed the change between coupes 87973 and 88805.

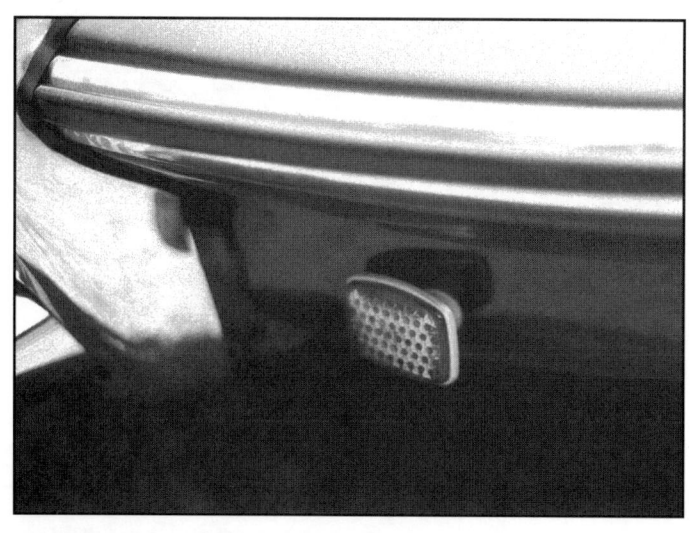

A slotted screw was in lower reflector hole in early 1960.

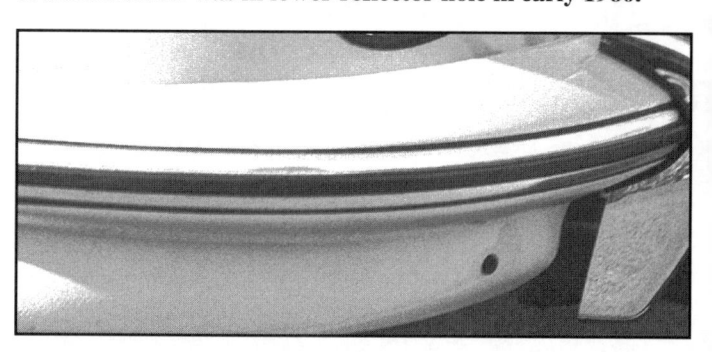

From late 1960-on the lower holes had small vinyl plugs (which often disappeared!).

Wheels and Hub Caps

The first steel cars produced used 16 inch diameter wheels also found on VWs of the same era. They had a 3 inch rim width and no cooling slots. The 1953 parts book stated that they were for use on 1.1 and 1.3-litre cars with 1.5 litre cars having slotted wheels. The actual appearance of slotted wheels took place in mid-1951. No chrome-plated wheel was listed, although it appeared in the 1955 parts book. Slotted wheels were $3 \frac{1}{4}$ inches wide. There were a number of subtle variations in the slots based on time (or perhaps place) of manufacture. Colors of wheels seem to be controversial. Body color was a definite possibility. Alternatives were white rims with body-colored centers and body color rims with white centers. Some solid wheels were pin-striped. Silver wheels were found on red and blue Speedsters.

356B/C reflector mounted below the bumper

Solid 16" wheel.

Slotted 16" wheels; note holes for attaching "turbo" rings.

The moon hubcap was used on both 15" and 16" wheels.

Vented aluminum "turbo" ring for slotted 16" wheels; note hollowed out lug bolts.

Only one type of hubcap was originally supplied for the 16 inch wheel, the familiar baby moon. Early moons differed by being flatter and "pointier." They were $3/16$ inch shorter and $5/16$ inch smaller in diameter. Factory photos of very early cars showed a moon-type hubcap with a ring in the center, where the "VW" logo would have been on a VW hubcap of that era.

There were two types of trim rings. The louvered "turbo ring" was aluminum, finished in dull silver. The description in the 356A accessory book – which was odd in the first place because they were not available for 356As – stated: "Qualitest wheel rings are bolted to the wheel, and cannot be lost or stolen. They are finned in the direction of rotation to aid brake cooling. Heads of the fastening bolts serve as sound interrupters." A chrome-plated beauty ring was also an option.

356A 15" wheel; note lug nuts.

The half aluminum Carrera wheel had a different offset than the standard wheel. Note crested hubcap.

The 356C disc brake wheel; note valve stem retaining wire.

The silver non-enameled crest on the flat stainless cap

Optional Rudge knock-off wheels

The 356A was equipped with 4 1/2 x 15 inch slotted wheels which could be supplied either primed, silver-painted or chrome plated. The fact that they were available primed implied that colors other than silver were offered on 356As, as on earlier cars. Body colored rims were common prior to the introduction of the T 2. Also listed was a light alloy wheel for the Carrera GT, with steel center and aluminum rim. Listed but not illustrated in the A parts book were the optional Rudge (standard wheels were made by Lemmerz and Kronprinz) knock-off wheels. These were available only in chrome finish and required replacement of brake drums for installation. A 2 kg copper hammer for removal was also listed. Wire wheels were also available as they appear in some factory photos, as did knock-off 16" wheels on earlier cars.

Three types of hub caps were listed for 15 inch wheels. The baby moon carried the same part number as the one for 16 inch wheels. A light alloy (which translates to aluminum) moon was listed for Carrera GTs. Crested caps, the ones with the lumps, were listed for use on 1600S and Carrera De Luxe. These were first used on T 2s. They were listed in the optional equipment booklet, meaning that they could have been fitted to any model. The crests used on these caps were always ceramic.

The T 5 and T 6 wheels were unchanged from the 356A except that Rudge wheels were not listed as an option, although they continued to be offered on drum brake cars. Crested hubcaps continued to be standard on Super, S-90 and Carrera models and remained optional on Normals. The 356B parts book was the first to list the little wires that secured the valve stem in an upright position during high speed touring. These cannot be installed on some aftermarket Brazilian-made chrome wheels due to the incorrect positioning of the valve stem hole in relation to the wheel slots.

The disc brakes on 356C models necessitated a considerable change in the wheels. Disc brake wheels came in the same three finishes (primed, silver and chrome-plated) and chrome was standard on Carrera 2 models. They remained the same size at 4 1/2 x 15 inch. Hub caps (the flat ones) were listed with and without crest. The caps without crests were found on 356Cs built in July and August of 1963. Only one type of crest, the silver non-ceramic type, was listed, and that had a "901" part number. A number of cars had the ceramic crest, as did some early 900-series cars. Valve stem retainers differed from the drum brake versions.

Lug nuts never changed, according to the parts manuals. The early cars with VW brakes had lug bolts different from the VW bolts of that era by having deeply recessed head centers for weight savings. These bolts were not shown in the parts books but were used through the introduction of the 1953 models.

Optional tire combinations were listed in the 356B and 356C accessory books. Standard tires were not listed. The 356B buyer had a choice of 165-15 Conti-Radial, 165-15 Dunlop SP, 165-15 Michellin X or 5.60-15 white walls (no manufacturer listed). All but the latter was standard on S-90s. For 356Cs, the following were listed as optional (standard on SCs except for the whitewalls): 165-15 Conti-Radial, 165-15 Dunlop SP, 165-15 Michelin X, 165-15 Phoenix and 5.60-15 Phoenix whitewalls.

Chapter 5

Luggage Compartment

The front compartment of the 356 Porsche was designed to contain the gas tank, spare tire, battery, a fair amount of electrical wiring, tool kit, jack, washer reservoirs and occasionally tiny pieces of luggage.

The Battery and Associated Hardware

Starting from the ground up, so to speak, the first piece of hardware to consider is the wooden battery platform. These were in all 356s and early 1956 356As, but were not in later cars. The first cars had two large slatted platforms that covered most of the battery compartment floor. From the Model 52, platforms were constructed from approximately 1/4 inch thick wood with blocks and strips to hold the battery level. The platforms were painted black. The illustration in the Speedster section of the 356 parts book showed a different, rectangular platform to accommodate the smaller battery fitted.

The braided copper ground strap of the earliest 356s remained basically unchanged until the T 6. The revised mounting for the strap allowed a shorter length to be used. No further changes were made.

The positive cable terminal on 356s and 356As had two screws to hold the cables in place. The part number was no different in the 356B book, but the illustration showed a terminal with three screws. The T 6

Ground straps, 356 - 356B (T 5) long, and 356B (T 6) - 356C short

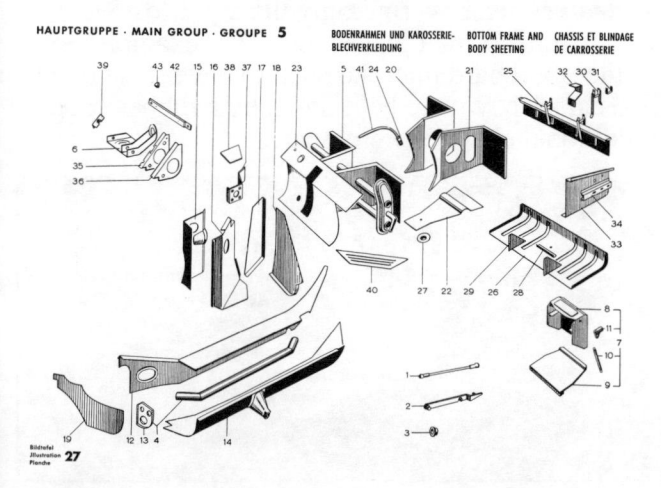

Illustration 27, 1955 Parts Book

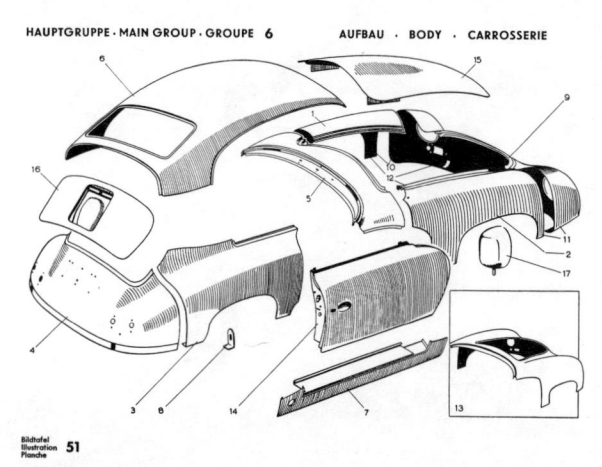

Illustration 51, 356A Parts Book

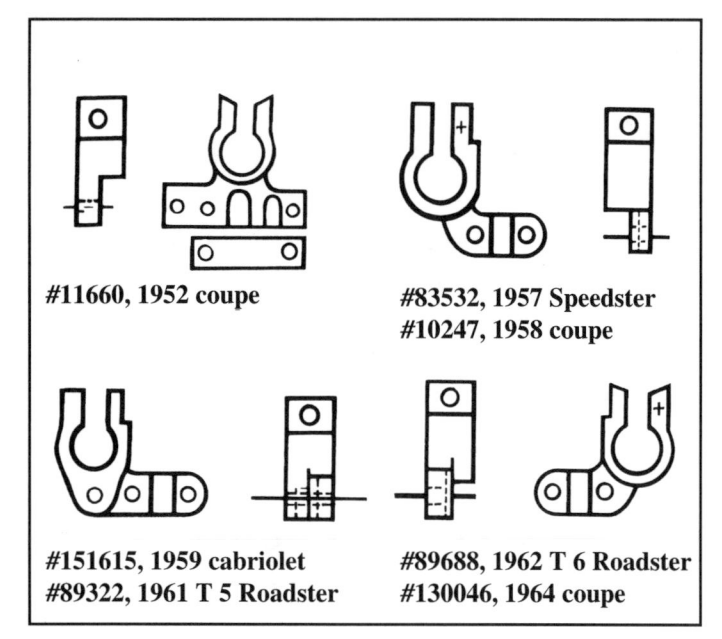

#11660, 1952 coupe

#83532, 1957 Speedster
#10247, 1958 coupe

#151615, 1959 cabriolet
#89322, 1961 T 5 Roadster

#89688, 1962 T 6 Roadster
#130046, 1964 coupe

Positive Battery Terminals

356 metal battery covers; the early style had wooden blocks, later style had metal tabs.

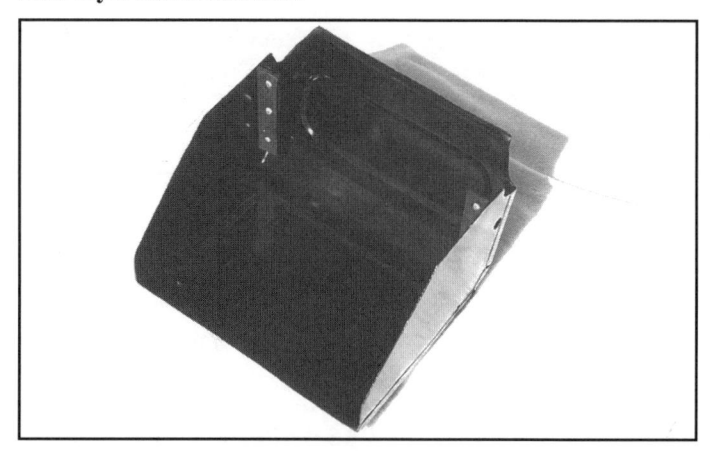

356 battery cover with metal tabs

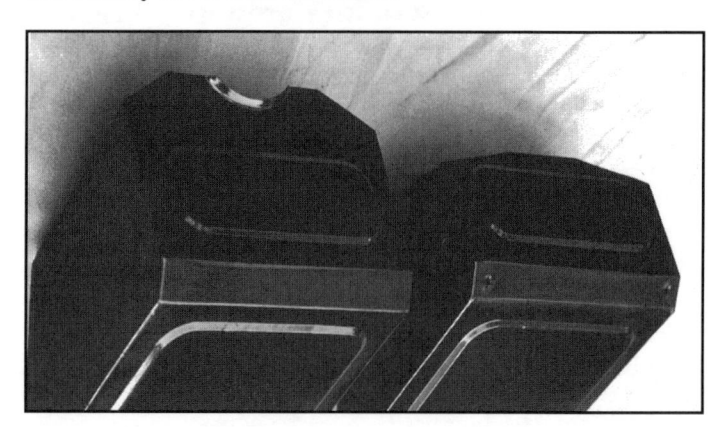

book used the same illustration but had a different part number. There was also a separate listing for a 12-volt terminal.

From 1950 through May 1952, the battery was mounted on the passenger's side of the front luggage compartment and was held down by a pivoting steel strap that was welded to the battery box side. The left side of this strap was secured by a spring clip. In June 1952 cars had a steel cover which secured the centrally-mounted battery. It was held in place on each side by spring clips. Early metal battery covers came in three varieties. The first version was separated from the battery by wood blocks; the later types had a rubber strip riveted to an angled metal piece on the battery cover. Due to a smaller battery, Speedsters retained the earlier wooden-block style.

Early 1956 356As had the third variety of metal cover, but it was soon replaced by a fiberboard version, which was unaltered on the T 5 356B. The T 6 had its

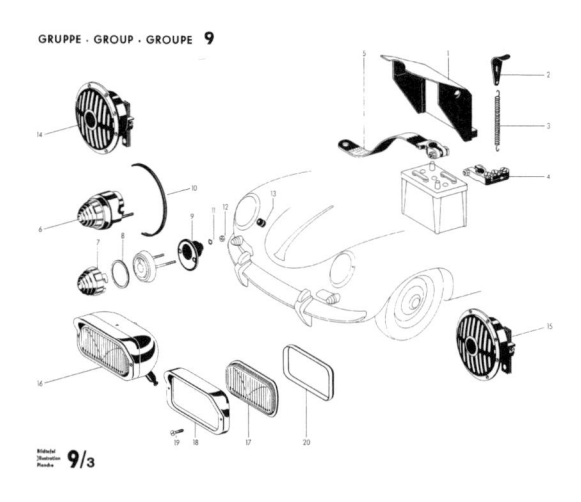

356A (left) vs. 356 (right) metal battery covers

battery relocated to the right of center, and with the new placement came a different battery cover, an abbreviated version covering only the top. Most were black vacuum-formed plastic, however examples exist in the fiberboard material used to cover fuse blocks on T 6 cars. They were held down by a rubber strap. No additional changes were made.

Illustration 9/3, T 5 Parts Book

Fiberboard 356A - T 5 356B battery cover

356C battery compartment showing plastic battery cover and optional blower

The Eberspächer T 6 gas heater

Other Battery Area Components

A fresh air blower was in the lower compartment with the battery. This was available as an option from 1960 through 1965.

The T 6 body had a hollowed-out area on the left side of the battery compartment to accommodate the optional Eberspächer gas heater.

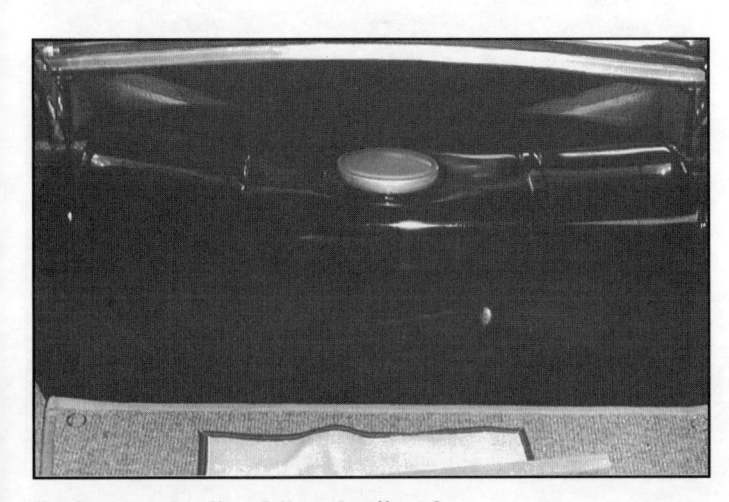

Early "strapless" and "ventless" tank

Fuel Tank

The first 356s off the line featured an under-hood fuel filler centered on the tank top. From 1950 through Model 52 cars, this tank was not secured by straps but was bolted in place at the bottom with brackets. This tank was replaced by a larger one held in place by steel straps. This type of mounting continued through the T 5 356B.

A vent cone behind the filler was added mid-1951. The cone sported a small rubber tube as an air vent and overflow tube. This tube disappeared behind the tank and eventually went down to the right of the tank and exited into the right front wheel well. Three different cones were noted. A very small and short variety was used through at least mid-1953. The second type was quite tall with the tube exiting straight out at the top. This was used during 1954 and probably until the tank with the depressed area for the fuel sender appeared mid-1955. The third and final type was slightly lower with the tube angled down and backward. This was used through the T 5 356B.

The three types of cones: Top, early low cone; middle, tall cone; bottom, lower cone with angled vent tube

79

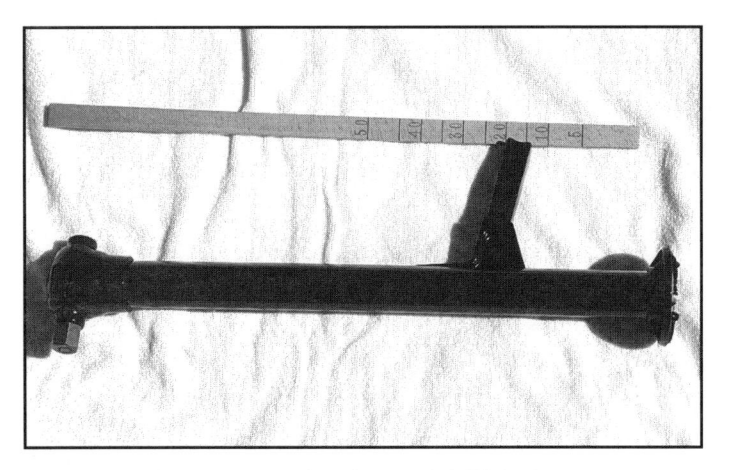

Early fuel dip stick and Bilstein "VIGOT" jack

The first tanks had no electrical float for a fuel gauge. A graduated wooden dipstick was supplied to determine fuel level. The first cars that had a fuel tank with sender, according to the factory parts book, were coupe 53527 and the cabriolet 60816, corresponding to mid-1955 at the introduction of the VDO fuel gauge. The Beck fuel gauge (described on page 93) had a different sender and tank. These were fitted from the introduction of the 1954 model, coupe 52030 and cabriolet 60350 until the introduction of the VDO gauge. No Speedsters had fuel gauges until the introduction of the 356A, so they used a tank without sender.

The standard 57-liter fuel tank on the 356A was unchanged from the late 356. An 80-liter tank was optional as early as 1956. The T 5 356B tank was largely unchanged.

The T 6 gave Porsche owners a new luxury, filling up without lifting the front lid. A gas filler door on the right front fender accessed the neck of the new, redesigned 52-liter tank. The original design featured a tank level sender in the bottom of the tank. The sender was moved to the top of the tank in mid-1962 at Reutter coupe 121224, Karmann coupe 211175 and cabriolet 157072.

Optional 80 liter tank; note replacement-type gas cap.

T 6 bottom sender tank

T 6 top sender tank

The black ABS liner that covered the T 6 fuel tank

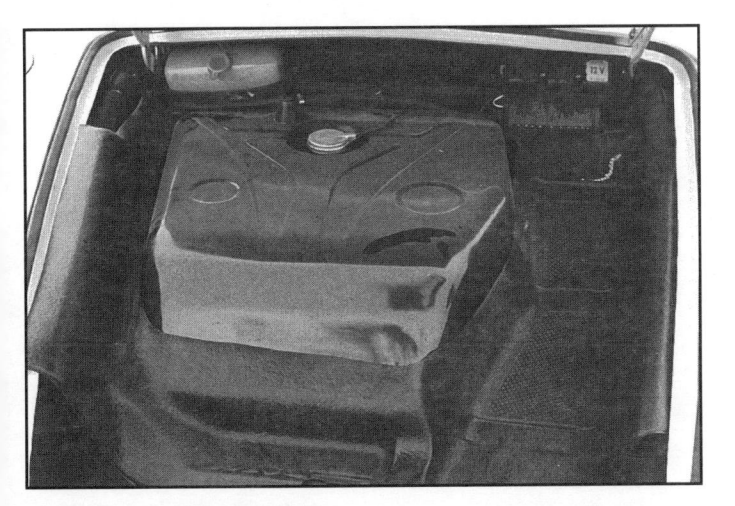

Optional 110 liter T 6 tank

Presumably the 70-liter tank was always an option on the T 6. It was standard for Carrera 2s and police cars. An even larger 110-liter tank was available, used in the 2-liter GTs.

The fuel tanks in right-hand drive T 6 cars differed from the left-hand drive cars. The first right-hand drive T 6 cars used the same tank as the T 5 and did not have the filler lid on the fender. A special tank developed for right-hand drive cars is described on a supplement to the T 6 356B parts book on a page dated 4/64. This tank was unlike the T 5 or left-hand drive T 6 tank, but it allowed use of the fender filler.

Gas caps went through a brief evolution. 356, 356A and T 5 356B gas caps had a very finely knurled rim and were manufactured by Blau. Some replacement caps supplied by Porsche were similar in general appearance, but the rim knurls were much wider. The smaller cap on the T 6 and later cars never changed.

Other Luggage Compartment Features

Through the T 5 model, 356s had the fuse containing block under the dashboard. Breaking with tradition, the T 6 356B had the fuse block on the left-side firewall in the luggage compartment. It had a fiberboard cover replaced in the 356C by a white vacuum-formed plastic piece. Cars with 12-volt systems had a decal on this cover denoting that. All had decals listing the fuse circuits and amperage.

The front luggage compartment seal was roughly V-shaped in cross section. The open part of the V faced away from the opening, toward the outside of the car. Two flat metal corner plates helped hold the rearmost portion of the seal; the remainder was held in place by glue and a vast number of screws. Information supplied stated that slotted screws were originally used, with Phillips-head screws appearing mid-year 1955. The first cars had two piece front seals joined midway down each side with flat steel plates. Prior to 1955 this arrangement was was replaced by a one piece seal

T 6 right-hand drive fuel tank

Fiberboard T 6 fuse cover

White plastic 356C fuse cover

with the ends joined under the right-side corner plate.

The front latch mechanism was alluded to previously on page 24. All cars, 1950 through the last T 6 356B, had the simple spring and pin with the safety catch to the right. A change in bolt spacing was made between 1953 and 1955. The upper part of the latch was always painted body color. The bottom part was generally body color, as well, but on some T 5 and T 6 356Bs they were black. The mechanism of the 356C had a "trigger" release.

Early style front hood latch

Front lid hinges were another occupant of the luggage compartment. Gläser cabriolets had solid hinges, while all Reutter cars were "drilled for lightness." The front part was painted exterior body color, with the rear portion painted gloss black (as were those in the engine compartment). The inner surface of the front lid and the lip surrounding it were painted body color.

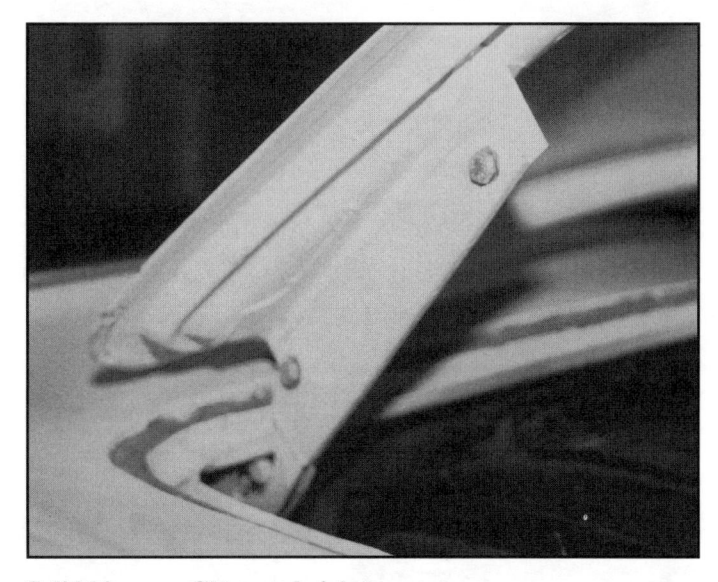

Solid hinge on Gläser cabriolet

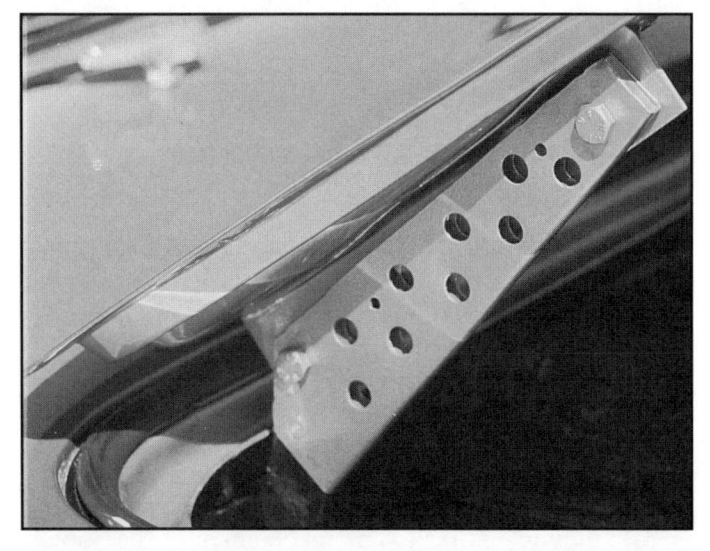

Drilled hinge on Reutter coupe

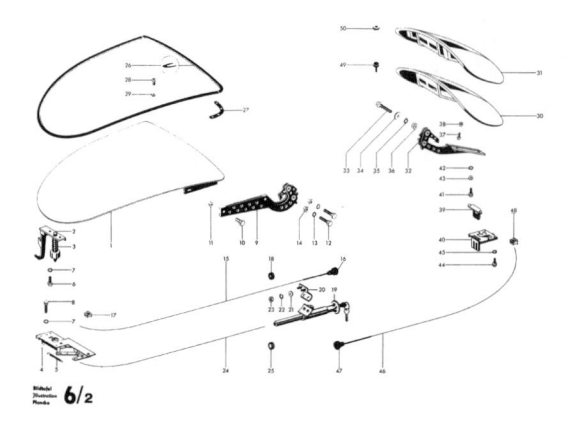

Illustration 6/2, 356B Parts Book

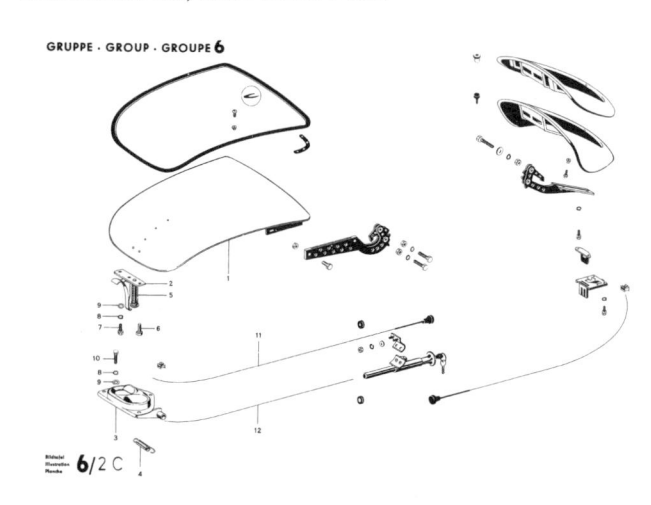

Illustration 6/2C, 356C Parts Book

The luggage compartment walls were covered with a textured black undercoat on 356B and later cars. Most early cars had tan cloth-bound carpet on the side walls of the luggage compartment. 1955 coupe 54205 had vinyl panels in dark grey-green color, as opposed to carpeting. Carpet and/or vinyl was not used after the introduction of the 356A. Instead a textured cardboard was found.

The first 356s had the spare tire laying flat under the front lid, with an aluminum false floor under the leading edge of the luggage compartment. The area under the tire was generally carpeted in these early cars. When the tire moved more closely to vertical for the 1953 model year, a ribbed rubber mat appeared. There does seem to be uncertainty over whether or not all Speedsters originally came with mats. Most restored "show-quality" cars seem to have them.

The T 6 356B and 356C had a large ABS vacuum-formed luggage compartment liner. A cut-out version was used on those fitted with the optional 70- liter fuel tank.

Leather spare tire straps appeared slightly after the

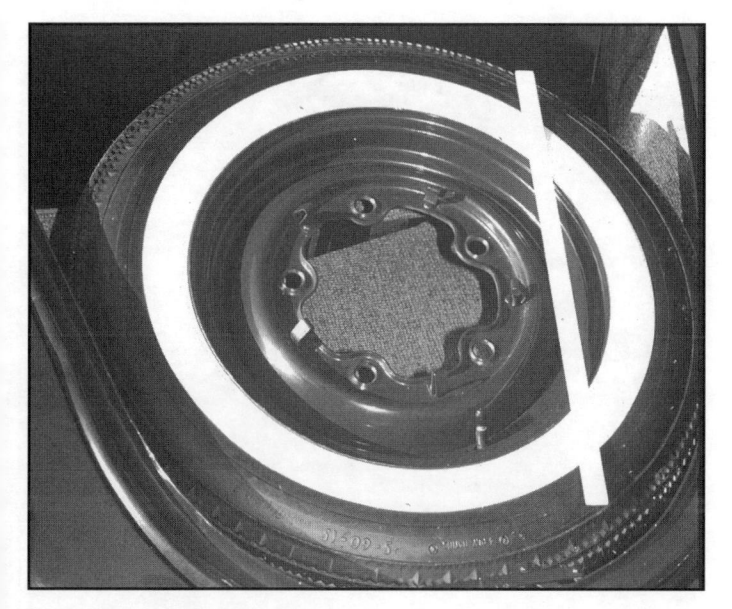

Early horizontal spare tire

1953 model year (see page 10). Many early Speedsters had a cloth strap 25mm wide and 876mm long, with a buckle 36mm x 60mm. This was used until at least 83501 (mid-1957).

Cloth Speedster tire strap

Leather tire strap

Tool Kits

The first detailed reference to tool kits came in the January 1955 parts book:

356.72.103	Tool bag
356.72.106	Jack without handle
356.72.108	Handle for jack
8x9 DIN 895	Wrench, 8x9 mm
10x14 DIN 895	Wrench, 10x14 mm
11x12 DIN 895	Wrench, 11x12 mm
17x19 DIN 895	Wrench, 17x19 mm
160 DIN 5244	Pliers, combination
356.72.101	Wrench, sparking plug
012.281 A	Socket wrench 36mm
DIN 5270	Screw driver, short
DIN 5270	Screw driver, long
L.709.02	Gauge, tire pressure
356.72.102	Speed handle, wheel
M14x1.5 DIN 74391	Bolt, wheel
547.09.305	V-belt, small

Note that the 36mm wrench was called a socket wrench, whereas a better translation from the German would have been "ring spanner," or, in French, hex key, which better described the flat generator nut wrench. Also, the wheel bolt, *kugelbund mutter,* was really a nut.

The presence of both jack handle and wheel fastener speed handle (typically a Hazet 772/2) indicates that this was a 356A-type kit or a late pre-A with the lever-operated jack. Cars with the early VIGOT jack would have had only the speed handle. It is interesting that a 13mm open wrench was not included, this being prior to standardizing on that size for 8mm bolts, when they had 14mm heads and nuts. The DIN 895 wrench was quite different from the usual chrome-plated Hazet #450s seen in most tool kits. The spark plug extended socket wrench (typically a Hazet 763) was turned by inserting a small tommy bar through holes in the end. The bar is not listed, because it was considered part of the wrench. The fan belt listed was for a small crank pulley, three-piece case motor, which also made this a late 356, early 356A kit.

Tool kit, 1954 356

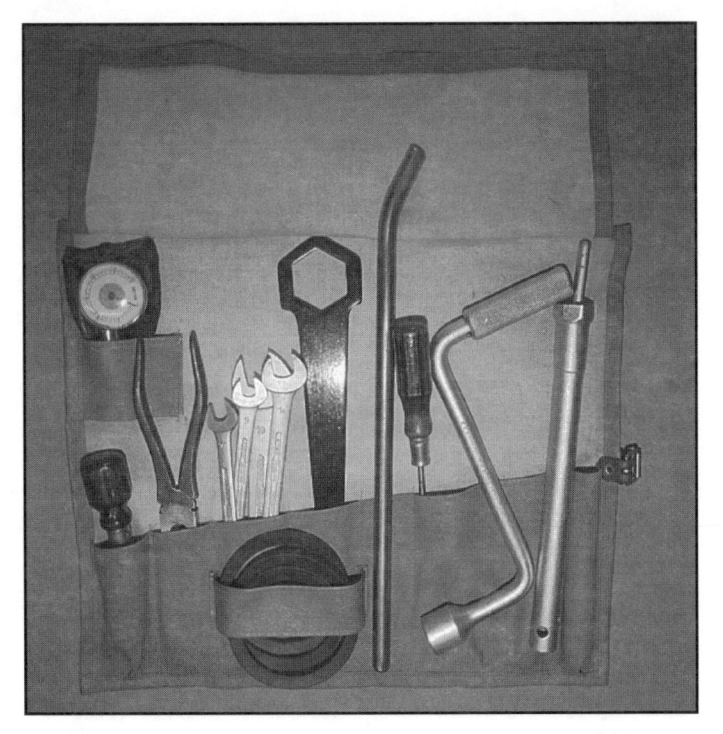

Tool kit, 356A

The difference between this early kit and a 356A kit, as illustrated in the 356A driver's manual, was the *kreutzschraubenzieher* or Phillips-head screwdriver, needed for the later cars.

One might reasonably ask if earlier cars had tool kits, and what did they look like? The wider jack clips in 356 cars held a larger VIGOT (Bilstein) jack (photo page 80), cranked up with the wheel nut speed handle. Phillips-head screws were not used, so there was no need for a cross-point driver. Wiring was attached to screw clamped terminals, so there was a need for a short, small tipped, flat-blade screwdriver. Otherwise, most service requirements were the same and similar tools would probably have been used.

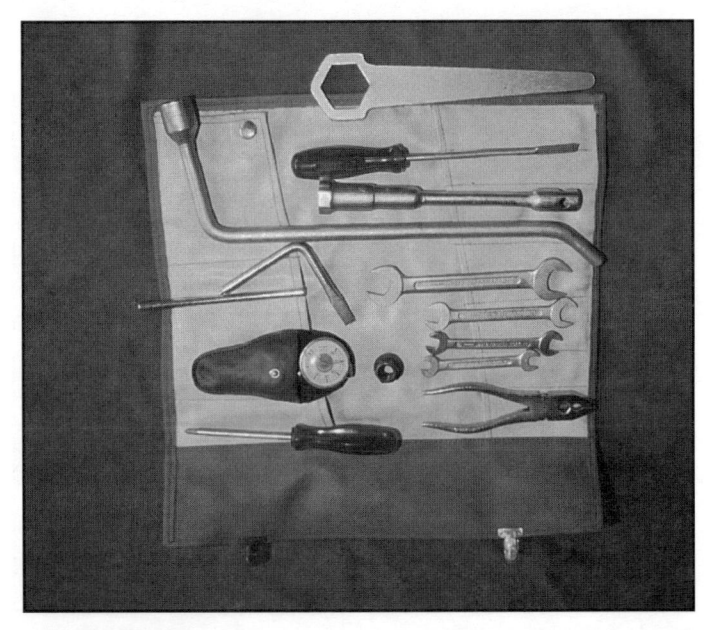

Tool kit, 356C

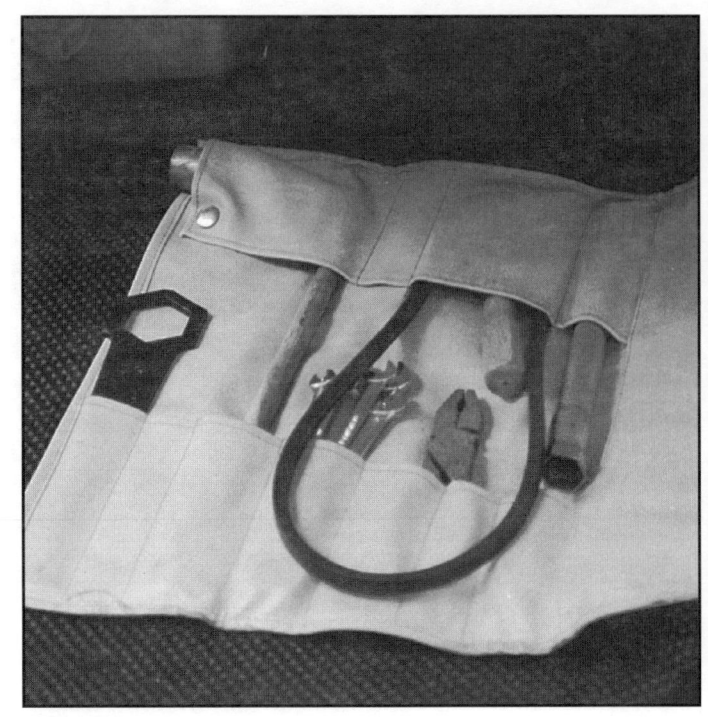

Tool kit, T 6 356B

One tool kit, which the owner claimed came from a 1954 Continental (sic.) coupe, was different from the kit above and caused skepticism among the authorities. One big difference was the 300-gm European machinists hammer in an eighth pocket (there were seven pockets in later kits). There were also three small screwdrivers, extra parts and a cloth pouch-covered tire gauge. The extra parts were a drain plug, wheel stud nut and rocker arm screw with a rubber plug for the pocket. The second small screwdriver had a small-tip blade; the large screwdriver (a Jorg) was flat-tipped. Other tools were as found in later tool kits. The kit bag was a bluish-green-grey vinyl cloth with a leather strap and buckle. The hammer was probably useful in cracking coconuts and was like the one in the picture showing hinge pin removal in the 1954 maintenance manual. There were at least two types of hammer, one with a logo in the outline of a gear, the other a Jorg.

Early 356B tool kits were identical to late 356A kits until sometime during the 1962 model production. An owner's manual dated January 1963 shows a number of changes: first, the jack was an updated design, the changes primarily were in the piece that fit into the jack mount on the car, which seemed to have been strengthened. A wood-handled hubcap puller was added, and the tire gauge included in earlier tool kits was deleted. The short screwdriver, also included in earlier tool kits was also deleted, leaving only two screwdrivers. There was also a slight change in design of the large regular screwdriver. Lastly, the four open-end wrenches were of slightly different design, being from a different supplier. The late 356B tool bag itself was smaller.

The June 1964 owner's manual for the 356C showed a fourth tool kit variation. In this one, the two wood-handled screwdrivers were replaced by two plastic-handled screwdrivers and the tire gauge with case was again included. The design of the open-end wrenches changed again to satin finish "no name" (as opposed to the previous Hazet) wrenches, and the generator pulley wrench was plated rather than painted black. The hubcap puller was different (though not shown in the photograph) due to the new flat-style C hubcaps. The major change, continued from the third tool kit configuration, was the combination wheel nut wrench/jack lever made by Klein.

All tool kits contained a fan belt, a spare wheel nut and a set of combination pliers which seemed unchanged through the period. Pliers in the 356C kit were chrome-plated; earlier varieties were black.

Carrera tool kits contained all tools in the pushrod tool kits except the plug wrench. Due to accessibility problems, their plug change device consisted of a wrench, ratchet, two extension pieces and a universal joint. There were four additional wrenches. 356B Carrera models had a special 36mm ring spanner; 356A Carreras had a 6 and 10mm wrench not in the standard kit.

Following is a list of the contents of four tool kits by date of owner's manual in which they are described. The X indicates the tools not included.

	Jan 1955	Oct 1956	Sept 1957	Jan 1963	June 1964
Short Screwdriver		(a)	(a)	X	X
Screwdriver		(a)	(a)	(a)	(b)
Phillips-head Screwdriver	X	X	(a)	(a)	(b)
Tire Gauge in Case				X	
1 Spare Wheel Nut					
Combination Pliers					
Open-end Wrench 8 x 9mm					
Open-end Wrench 11 x 12mm					
Open-end Wrench 10 x 14mm					
Open-end Wrench 19 x 17mm					
Generator Pulley Wrench					(c)
Spark Plug Wrench					
Spark Plug Wrench Pin					
Fan Belt					
Jack	X			(d)	(d)
Hubcap Puller	X	X	X	(a)	
Jack Lever	X			X	X
Wheel Nut Wrench	X			X	X
Wheel Nut Wrench/Jack Handle		X	X		

(a) Wood-handle
(b) Plastic-handled
(c) Plated rather than painted black
(d) Improved design

Early 356A bags were green and were closed with a tie string. Late 356A/early 356B (large) bags were light green with a coarse-grained leather strap. The late (small) 356B tool bags were mostly black, although some were blue; these tool bags fastened in the same way as the earlier bag, with a tie string closing. Late (356C) tool bags were generally black, white, red, blue or gray, with black and gray predominating. The 356C tool bag was of a different design, with metal fasteners provided for closing rather than ties.

Material for the green bags was a cloth-backed medium grain vinyl. Expanded vinyl was never used in any 356 A/B/C tool bags. The 356B series (small) bags were also of cloth-backed vinyl in the blue and black mentioned above.

Tool bags for the 356C series were made of one of three kinds of vinyl. One had a basket-weave texture; another was a very-coarse grained (alligator-like) vinyl. The third was a smooth upholstery-type textured vinyl.

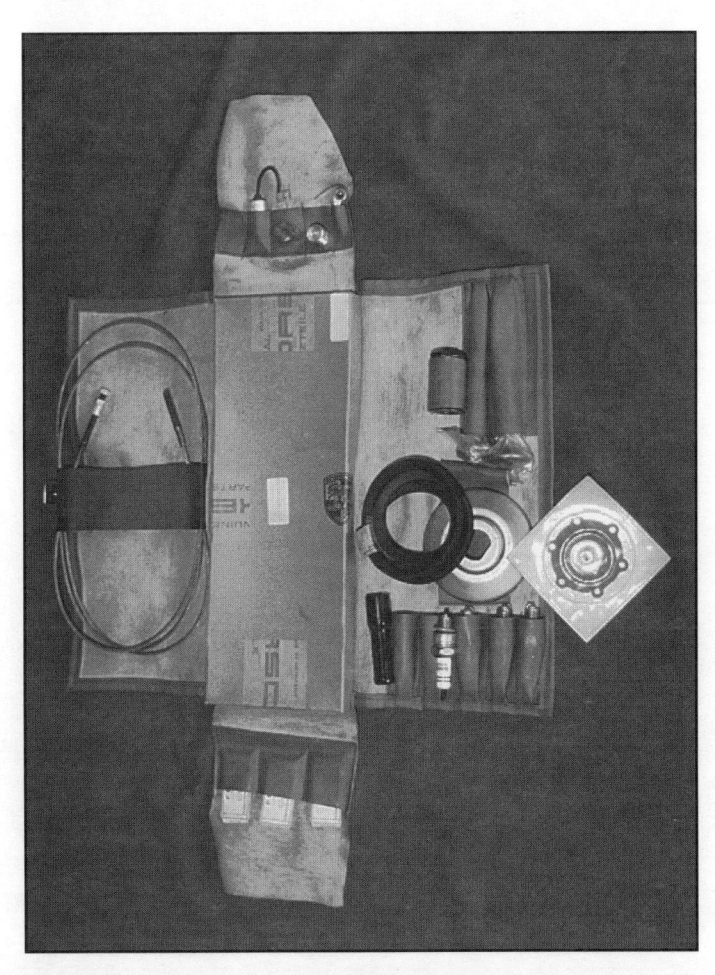

Travel kit contained items to repair the car when on the road.

Chapter 6

Interior

Dashboard

The coupe and cabriolet shared the same dashboard with minor differences. This dashboard made one major change between the 356 and the 356A: the early dashboard in the 356 (through 1955) was removable, with late versions welded in place. The first of the removable dashboards had two defroster vent slits that were approximately three inches long. In late 1951 they were lengthened to approximately six inches.

On coupes, aluminum shims made of flat stock were located between the sides of the dashboard and roof pillars. Cabriolets had an aluminum wire bead rather than a shim.

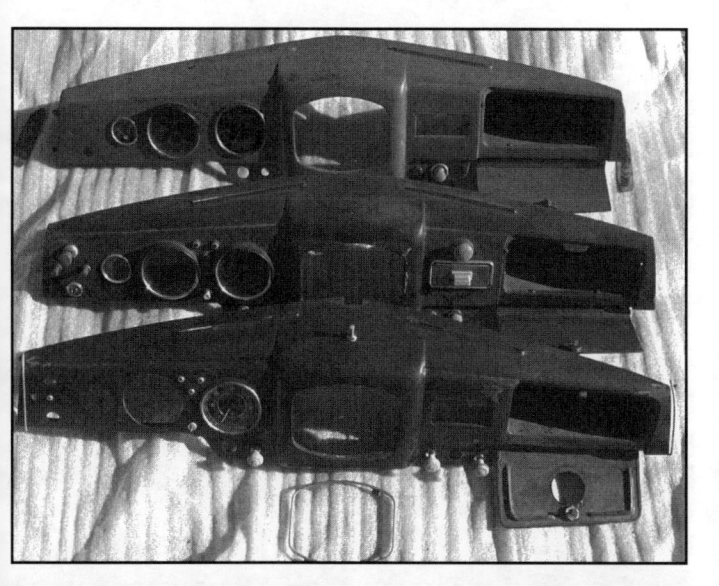

1951 cabriolet with small defroster vent & without oil gauge

Dashboard 1950 or 51 cabriolet; note wire bead on left.

Three early dashboards: The front one is the earliest as can be determined by the central turn signal switch and inner structure on the glove box door. Note also the hole where the mechanical clock was mounted. The second one, a cabriolet, has a map light above the ash tray.

1954 cabriolet dashboard with Porsche knobs; note instrument hoods, VDO speedometer and factory installed Beck fuel gauge. Horn rings were nearly always painted.

87

Dashboard, early 356A with central ash tray

Dashboard T 2 356A with ashtray below the radio

The 356B had different control placement and black plastics.

The major change for the T 6 was the central vent control.

Revised glove box and ashtray surround on the 356C

Carrera 2 instrument arrangement; note tach.

The dashboard in Speedsters, Convertible Ds, and Roadsters were distinctly different from the coupe and cabriolet. An upholstered "eyebrow" covered the three gauges. A minor change occurred with the introduction of the 356A, when three gauges of equal size were used. Convertible Ds and Roadsters had piping between the eyebrow and the dashboard; Speedsters did not.

Early Speedster dashboard

356A Speedster dashboard

Convertible D dashboard

The Roadster dashboard resembled the Speedster but had black plastics and altered controls.

Speedometer

The 1953 parts book listed three speedometers. The first was the 160-km black and white Veigel unit with convex glass used on the first cars. Second was a 200-km unit with trip odometer listed as available from May 1952 (Model 52). The final instrument is a 120-mph speedometer with trip odometer. The 1955 parts book showed only the latter two; these are the deep-faced, black with green lettering instruments which generally say VDO or Veigel in small green letters. The change occurred between November 1953 and June 1954 with later cars saying VDO. The owner's survey had the last Veigel at coupe 52473 and the first VDO at 52619.

The glass covering the faces also changed – early cars were dished, later cars were flat – in late-1954 (Speedster 80155 from survey results). Early gauges had a flexible cable to reset the trip odometer rather than the straight rod found on later units. They also had straight rather than angled output drives.

The 356A speedometer was much different. For one thing, the face of the gauge was closer to the glass. All had black faces with green lettering. Six different speedometers were used for the A model, two for run-of-the-mill 356s, four for Carreras. U.S. units read up to 120-mph, the European units up to 200-kph. Carrera speedometers read to 160-mph and 250-kph. Carreras with 12-volt electrical systems had slightly different speedometers due to the different voltage of the warning lights.

356Bs had basically the same style speedometer as the 356A but with new part numbers. There was no "12-volt" speedometer, but pushrod and Carrera units had the same speed ranges as the 356A unit.

No additional changes were made with the exception of a 6 and 12-volt option in the T 6 356B non-Carrera models.

Early black and white Veigel speedometer

Black and green Veigel speedometer

Standard 356A/356B speedometer

160 mph Carrera speedometer

356C speedometer

A change in position of the green lines on the T 6 speedometer occurred between cabriolet 156414 and 156533. On the early cars the green lines started at 25 mph, late cars started at 30 mph corresponding to a mid-1962 change. The purpose of the green lines was to give the driver a quick reference of typical "city" speeds.

Model	Highest Calibration	Green Lines Start	Stop
356			
U.S.	120		
Euro	200km/hr		
356A			
U.S.	120	25	40
Euro	200km/hr	40	60
1500GS	250km/hr	50	80
1500GS	250km/hr	40	60
1500GT	160	25	40
356B			
U.S.	120	25	40
Euro	200km/hr	40	60
T 6	120	30	40
(62 running change)			
2000GS	160	30	40
356C			
U.S.	120	30	40
Euro	200km/hr	50	60

Tachometer

Changes in the tachometer were more numerous than in the speedometer. Most early cars had clocks rather than tachs, but by the Model 52, the tachometer was standard. Two earlier tachometers are listed in the 1953 parts book. These were black and white Veigel gauges with no indicated red lines optional from April 1951. The parts book indicated no tachometer for 1.1-liter cars and one each for 1.3 and 1.5 cars for the "from May 1952" tachometers. These were the black/green, deep-faced gauges. The 1955 parts book listed different part numbers. There was again a brand

Early black and white Veigel tachometer

Black and green Veigel tachometer

Tachometer, 1500 GS/GT

change, Veigel to VDO, as with the speedometer. No warning lights were used on tachometers through 1955.

The 356A shallower tach was quite different. The 1300 and 1600 Normal shared a tachometer with 4500-5000-rpm red area. The 1300S and 1600S had a 5000-5500-rpm red area. Carreras came with 8000 rpm gauges in both 6 and 12-volt versions (all cable-driven). A red turn signal indicator light was present as was a blue high beam light.

Tachometer, 356B 1600 Super

The T 6 tachometer had turn signal indicator arrows at the bottom center.

Electric tachs appeared in May of 1964

The 356B had a similar tachometer, but there was a third version for the Super 90 engine with a red band between 5500 and 6000 rpm. Carreras had a 8000 rpm limit gauge with red area between 6000 and 7500. Warning lights were the same as on the 356A.

For the T 6, the turn signal indicator light moved to the bottom of the gauge. The high beam indicator light remained in the same location and color. A green parking light indicator was in the former location of the turn signal indicator; this change is not noted in the T 6 parts book.

Electric tachometers replaced the mechanical variety in May 1964. External appearance was altered by a change in the red line. On the early tach red "rings" replaced green ones at the red line. On the later tach the red line was a smaller 200 rpm wide mark. The parts book gave the engine numbers for the first installations: S models started at 731968 and 713689, with SCs 820997 and 812145. The owners' survey places this change as follows:

	Cabriolet	Karmann Coupe	Reutter Coupe
Mechanical	159575	217578	126785
Electrical	160588	218381	129476

Tach Calibrations

Model	Engine Type	Highest Calibration	Red Starts	Red Stops	Green Starts	Green Stops
356						
	1500	6000	4500	5000	Black/white gauge	
	1500N (1952)	6000	4500	5500	2500	4500
	1500N (1955)	6000	4500	5000	2500	4500
	1500S	6000	4500	5500	3000	4500
356A						
	1600	6000	4500	5000	2500	4500
	1600S	6000	5000	5500	3000	5000
	1500GS/GT	8000	6000	7500	4000	6000
	*	8000	7000	7500	4000	7000
356B						
	1600	6000	4500	5000	2500	4500
	1600S	6000	5000	5500	3000	5000
	1600S90	6000	5500	6000	3000	5500
	S90GT	8000	6000	7500	4000	6000
	2000GS	8000	6200	7000	2200	6200
356C						
Mechanical Tach						
	1600 C	6000	5000	5500	2500	4500
	1600 C	6000	5000	5500	3000	5000
	1600 SC	7000	5500	6000	3000	5500
	1600 SC **	7000	5500	6000	2500	5500
Electric Tach						
	1600 C	6000	5200	5500	–	–
	1600 SC	7000	6000	6200	–	–

* Early - green/red lights were flat, not rounded. Possibly this tachometer could have been locally converted to Carrera with VDO factory face.

** 1963 European Police Car

The mechanical Veigel clock

Other Instruments

The earliest cars had only two large gauges, a speedometer and a tachometer or clock. Two clocks were listed in the first parts book, an early clock and a "from May 1952" (Model 52) clock. As with the speedometer and tachometer, the second was a black/green gauge, while the early one was black/white. Only the late clock was listed in the 1955 parts book followed by the words "upon request." There was also an eight day clock described in the 356A accessories book. This clock was not electric and was shown on the glove box door. The photo shows the non-locking glove box knob used in 1954 and 1955. The car illustrated was definitely a 356A, making the clock installation likely very early in 1956, before the locking glove box knob was standard. These clocks were always mounted to the glove box door. A 1957 price list made note of the "radium dial."

By the 1958 T 2 change, an electric clock replaced the manual one. It was on the dashboard, dead center below the interior light. The setting knob was at the bottom center of the clock.

Clocks remained optional on T 5 356Bs with 6 and 12-volt available. There was a change in part number at the T 6 356B when the hand adjustment was moved

356A electric clock with adjuster at bottom center

The T 6 clock had revised adjustment position.

from the bottom to the center of the face. This clock was also used on the 356C (although the 356B clock had a sweep second hand not on the 356C) as standard equipment. Post-1960 clocks were generally in the center of the dashboard, but if other instruments were fitted, such as an inside/outside thermometer, the position was such that symmetry was achieved.

The oil temperature gauge was the only other instrument in early cars. The first type, made by MotoMeter, was available with either a single Fahrenheit or Celsius scale. They were first installed in early 1951. In May 1952, the black/green Störk instrument was introduced. These early temperature gauges had a capillary tube that ran all the way from the sender in

Eight-day clocks were mounted in the glove box door on 356s and early 356As.

The early MotoMeter oil temperature gauge

Early Störk gauge in a 1953 coupe

Late Störk gauge

Factory fitted Beck fuel gauge; note instrument hoods.

Pneumatic pump for Beck fuel gauge

the engine compartment to the instrument. On early cars the sender was incorporated with the dipstick. When the three-piece case was introduced in November 1954, the temperature gauge sender screwed into the engine case at the flywheel end, forward of the oil cooler. While it was possible that a dipstick sender could be used in a three-piece case motor despite the cable length difference required, the fact that the screw-in bulb type sender was part number 539.07. 714 indicated it was for use in a three-piece (type 539) engine.

The 1955 parts catalog listed a "System Beck" mechanical fuel gauge. The sender in the tank was not the float-actuated lever-type which moved a rheostat, but was a small inverted brass cup at the end of a metal tube. There were actually two tubes, one inside the other. At the other end, one tube connected to the pump, the other to the gauge. By pressing a dash-mounted pump button (if it worked) air was injected into the tank, and that air vented into the inverted cup. To actuate the pump more than once, it was necessary for the operator to take his finger off the button each time to permit more air to enter the pump. After doing this a few times (if you listen closely without the engine running, you can hear the bubbles) the cup is full

of air; additional air will bubble to the top and out the vent. At this point the pressure on the air trapped in the cup was proportional to the height of gasoline above it; the fuel gauge was calibrated to read this pressure as gallons since the size of the tank was known.

In the early 1950s an aftermarket kit was available from Beck for retrofitting earlier cars without fuel gauges. That gauge read $1/4$ through 1 rather than 2 through 14, as on gauges fitted as original equipment. The gauge was shown in a bracket attached to the steering column. Presumably the small push-button air pump was dash-mounted. The kit application was listed for coupes after chassis 11361 and cabriolets after 11271 (should have read chassis 10271), which put it in May 1952 at the introduction of the Model 52 indicated in the early parts book as the time when the other gauges changed.

Aftermarket Beck fuel gauge with calibrations in quarters

The small VDO fuel gauge was used in 1955 only.

The dashboard picture in the 1953 parts book did not show a hole or space for a gas gauge, and a 1951-1952 difference was implied by two different part numbers for these models. The 1955 parts book showed a dashboard with a hole for a fuel gauge, 356.70.135, as listed for 1954 and later coupes. The 1955 parts book also noted dashboard part number 356.70.015 for coupe chassis 11779-52029 (1953 model year), and dashboard part number 356.70.010 for coupes 5001-11778 (up to the Model 52). There is some confusion here, as the same part number was given for coupe and cabriolet dash while the illustration for the cabriolet showed a notch in front for the tension rod and a locking glove box.

To conclude, the fuel gauge hole appeared at coupe 52030 (1954 model year) and the VDO electric gauge started at coupe 53527 and cabriolet 60816 (early-1955), with those before having the System Beck gauge.

Speedsters didn't fare so well, getting fuel gauges only after the 1956 356A model change. The fuel gauge in pre-A non-Speedster cars was to the left of the oil temperature gauge.

For 1956, the 356A combination gauge included the fuel gauge, the oil temperature gauge and a variety of warning lights. The 1956 through mid-1957 cars had a temperature gauge with numbered calibrations. Late 1957 through 1959 cars had a graded scale with only a green and red area. Regrettably this change was never recorded in the 356A parts book. The only two listings are for the 6 and 12-volt units. Information from the owner's survey is as follows:

	Speedster	Coupe	Cabriolet
Numbered Scale	83498	101502	
Non-numbered Scale	83532		150153

No change was listed for T 5 356B models. These instruments had red generator indicator lights on the left and green oil pressure warning lights on the right.

Early 356A combination gauge with numbered scale

Late combination instrument without numbered scale was used on late 356As and T 5 356Bs.

A change was noted for both 6 and 12-volt units in the T 6 356B parts book; this version had an "O" to the left of the "R" on the fuel gauge. Also, a note indicated that right-hand-drive cars did not get this modification. The T 6 bottom-sender gauge had the "R" almost in the center of the indicator, while on the top sending gauge, it was far to the left.

356Cs had two more warning lights from the two on earlier instruments. They were, left to right, generator (red), oil pressure (green), blank (green) and parking brake (red). No fewer than six varieties of this gauge existed. The first two were the 6 and 12-volt variety for 52 and 70-liter tanks, the next two for 110-liter tanks and the final two for right-hand steering models with 52-liter tanks.

The T 6 bottom sender combination instrument

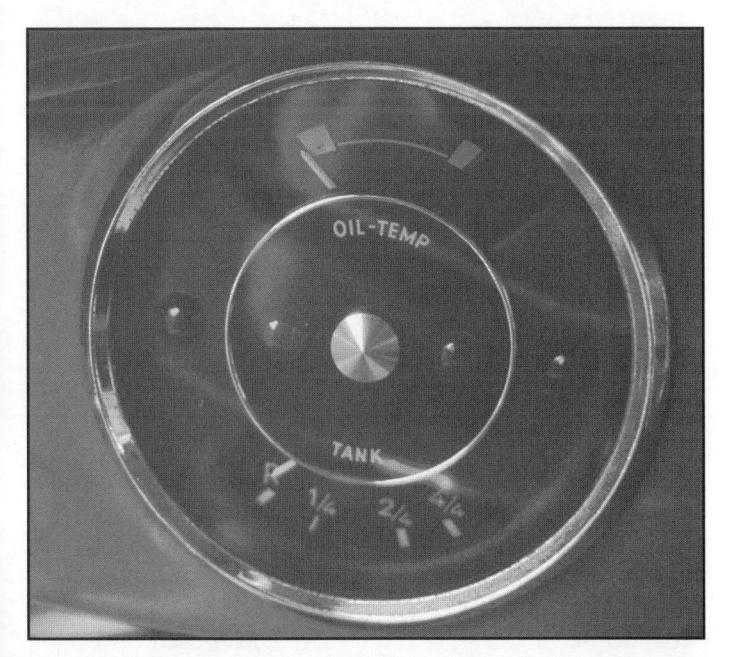

The 356C combination gauge with additional warning lights

The only other instrument fitted optionally was the MotoMeter inside/outside air thermometer mentioned earlier. It was available on the T 6 356B where it was place in the clock's location. If a clock was also fitted, it was to the right of the glove box. On the 356C the temperature gauge was to the right of the clock.

An instrument-related item was the individual instrument hood on 356 cars. It was illustrated in the 1953 parts book, although it was unclear when they were first installed. They were optional during the Model 51 production and became standard by the Model 52. Their use continued through 1955 models, although they were not used on Speedsters. Small hoods over fuel and oil temperature gauges were used as well. The small hoods were available after the introduction of the 1954 models.

Placement

Cars with two gauges positioned the speedometer on the left with the tachometer or clock on the right.

Early 356As had the speedometer on the left, tachometer in the center and cluster gauge on the right. At the T 2 body change, the cluster gauge has moved to the left and the speedometer to the right. This arrangement remained unaltered through the 356C model.

Warning Lights

These wonderful items were first installed on chassis number 5000. The green one was for oil pressure, the blue one for turn signal and the red one was for the generator. There was also a blue high beam light over by the headlight switch. This last light was only used through mid-1951. After this point the blue light in the center cluster became the high beam indicator and the turn signal flashed on the generator light. The SWF flashing column turn signal lever eliminated the necessity for this double duty.

Larger warning lights were first installed on coupe 11361 and cabriolet 10271 (introduction of the Model 52) per the factory parts manual. These were used from that point to the end of the 1955 model year. At the introduction of the 356A, warning lights were incorporated into various other instruments, although their colors remained the same.

Early small warning lights

Larger warning lights used from mid-1951 through 1955

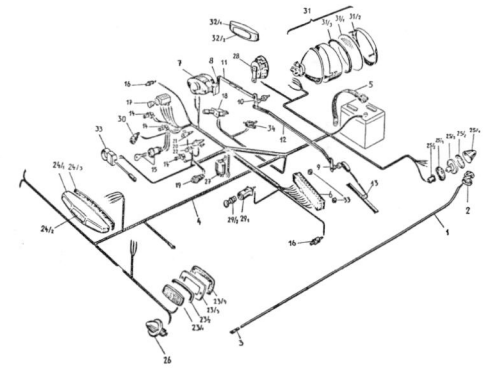

Illustration 22, 1953 Parts Book

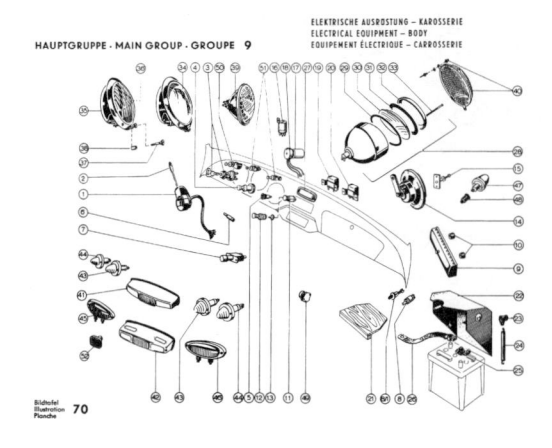

Illustration 70, 356A Parts Book

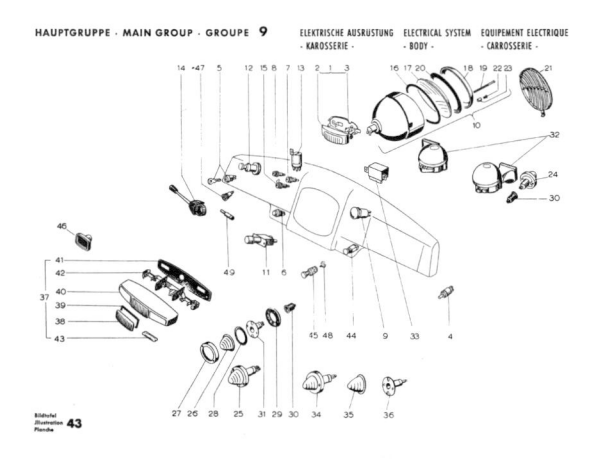

Illustration 43, 1955 Parts Book

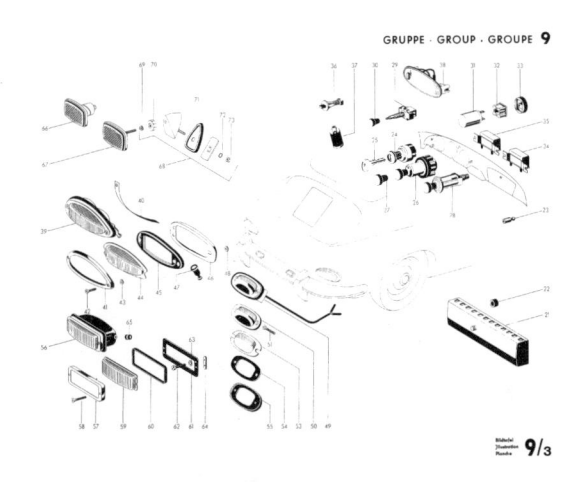

Illustration 9/3, T 5 Parts Book

VW knobs, 1951 coupe

Porsche knobs, 1954 coupe

Knobs

The first 356s used ivory-colored plastic for all dashboard knobs, window cranks and escutcheons (the circular rings behind the inner door handle and window crank). Many of these had Volkswagen parentage.

Most 1954 - 1959 356 and 356As had these combinations:

Upholstery	Knobs and Steering Wheel
Red	Beige
Brown/Tan	Ivory
Black/Grey	Grey

No participants in the owner's survey disagreed with these combinations. The knobs always matched the steering wheel color (wood not included) and always matched the window crank knobs, escutcheons, and shift knob. There was also a correlation between top frame color and knob color in Speedsters; the early cars tended to have black frames, and no ivory frames were made. Grey frames generally went with grey knobs, and tan frames with beige and ivory knobs. Frames on later cars (including Convertible Ds and Roadsters) were tan only. In 1960, or very late 1959 by some accounts, all plastic components went black.

Early rotating headlight switch

Headlight Switch

A rotating lever type headlight switch was used on the earliest 356s, left of the speedometer. Somewhere around coupe 10531 and cabriolet 10001 (Model 51), this was replaced by the pull-type headlight switch common to later cars. The earliest cars had a ribbed-back ivory knob found on VWs of similar vintage. This changed at coupe 52030 and cabriolet 60550 (1954 model year) to the Porsche-style knobs in ivory, beige and grey. All headlight switches had a similar exterior appearance from this point on, which coincidentally was when the panel light rheostat was combined into the switch.

Mid-356A wire connectors to the headlight switch were changed from screw-in to press-in. Owner survey information on this was not entirely conclusive, but the approximate time was shortly after the T 2 body change.

Speedster	Coupe	Cabriolet
83378 screw	102457 screw	150153 press
83836 press	102908 press	
84294 screw		
84400 press		

The 356B manual gave the switch a new number due to additional terminal holes. The black knob was also first used at this time. No additional changes were noted.

The first pull-type switch was on the left side of the dashboard, high above the ignition switch. After the fuel gauge was added, it remained in essentially the same area, but was now between the oil and fuel gauges. On 356As the headlight switch was on the lower dashboard between the two left-most gauges. On Speedsters it was left of the instrument cluster.

On T 5 356B coupes and cabriolets, the headlight switch was between the tachometer and the cluster gauge, on the upper part of the dashboard. On Roadsters it was right of the instruments, where it remained throughout Roadster production. T 6 356B non-Roadsters had the light switch high on the dashboard between the tachometer and speedometer. It moved again, this time to the right of the speedometer, for the 356C.

Wiper Switch

Early 356s used a VW wiper switch. The knob was dished and always ivory in color. A similar switch was used for instrument and interior lights.

The Porsche-style knob adopted in 1954 was much smaller than the medium-sized headlight knob. Changes in wipers were detailed earlier. Changes in the switch paralleled changes in the different wiper types. 356A wiper switches were identical to those of late 356s.

356B switches were similar, with the exception of their black knobs. A similar switch for electric washers was optional. The T 6 switch was larger (headlight switch size), adjustable and available in either 6 or 12-volt. It was right of the center line, immediately left of the glove box. The same switch was used on the 356C on the left side of the console that surrounded the ash tray.

Later VW knobs: headlight above, wiper and interior light switches below

Porsche medium knobs were used for both headlights and wipers on the T 6 356B.

Dash top turn signal switch

356Bs and 356Cs had this type of turn signal switch.

Turn Signal Switch

Early cars had a centrally located dash-top toggle switch for the turn signal lights. This changed at coupe 11361 and cabriolet 10271 (Model 52) to a column-mounted turn signal lever, which had a dark red plastic knob with SWF embossed on the end. The entire knob flashed when the indicators were on. SWF was responsible for all later turn signal switches. The 356A type had a round shaft and teardrop-shaped, color coded knob. The switch shared by 356B and 356C models had a flattened shaft with a flattened black knob; this switch controlled turn signals and headlight dimmer functions.

Starter Button

Directly to the right of the steering wheel was the starter button on 356 coupes and cabriolets. On Speedsters it was above the ignition switch. Mention was made in the 1953 parts book, and an illustration and description were in the 1955 parts books. With a few exceptions in very early cars (which had black buttons) starter button color matched the color of the other knobs and steering wheel.

Starter buttons were discontinued when the 356A gained a combination ignition/starter switch. This was at or very close to the 356 – 356A model change.

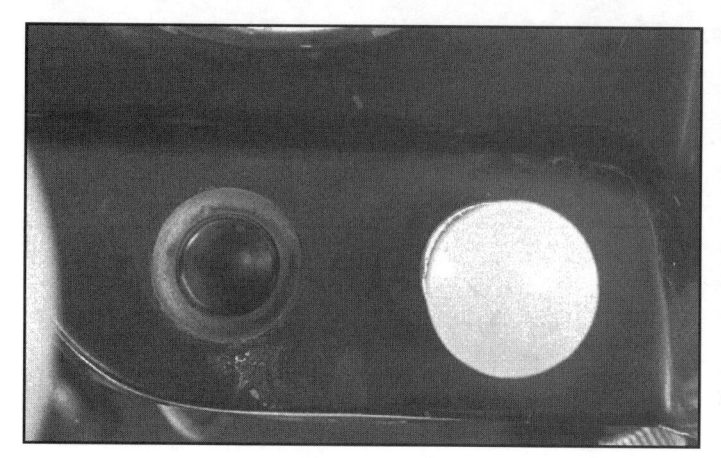

The first column mounted turn signal switches had a red flashing knob.

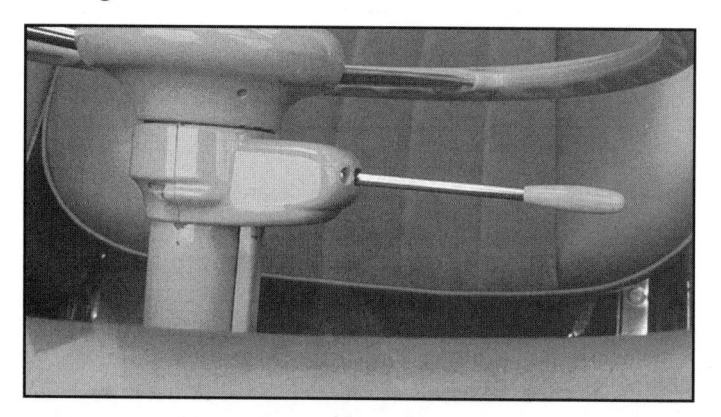

Early black starter button; to the right was the choke control.

356A turn signal lever

Later starter buttons were color matched.

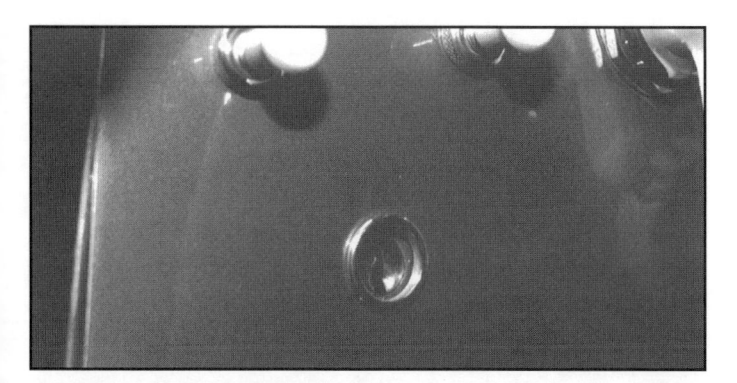

The first style of ignition switch

Early 356A ignition switch

Later 356 ignition switch with aluminum ring

The final type of ignition switch, T 2 on

Ignition Switch

As alluded to on the previous page, ignition switches were just that on 1950 through 1955 356s. The first cars had a depressed switch surrounded by a small metal ring. There was no start position.

This was replaced (mid-1952) by a protruding switch with a larger chrome or aluminum ring. This switch was used through 1955. The ignition switch on 356As in 1956 and 1957 looked similar but had a starter function at the key. In 1958 the T 2 had a different style ignition switch with a larger key receptacle; this was used until the T 6 356B, when a lock-out feature was incorporated to prevent engaging the starter while the engine was running.

The ignition switch was always at the lower left of the dashboard, except for Roadsters, Speedsters and Convertible Ds, where it was to the right of the gauge cluster.

Lighter

With the exception of Speedsters, all 356s had cigarette/cigar lighters. The changes in the lighter basically followed model years with the primary difference being the knob: pre-1953 cars had VW-type knobs; 1954 through 1959 cars used the medium sized grey, beige or ivory knob; and post-1959 cars had black medium knobs. Lighters were optional on Convertible Ds and Roadsters.

On 356s the lighter was on the lower dashboard, to the right of the radio. On 356As and 356Bs it was immediately right of the right-side instrument (cluster gauge or speedometer). On Convertible Ds and Roadsters the lighter was farther right, to the left of the dashboard script or clock (when fitted). The lighter on 356Cs was right of the ashtray in the dashboard extension.

The first lighters were in the middle of the 3 switch cluster to the lower right of the radio area.

The lighter on the 356C was located to the right of the ash tray. The switch to the left was the wiper control.

The dome light control was to the right of the identical wiper switch. Between the two larger instruments was a third identical switch that controlled the instrument lights.

Flasher light was located between wiper and dome light switch through mid-1951.

Other Dashboard-Mounted Controls

To the right of the wiper switch on 1950 through late 1953 model year cars (coupe 51958) was an identical switch controlling the interior dome light. From then the switch was on the light itself (see page 104). Through mid-1951 cars with the dashboard-mounted turn signal switch, a flasher light was left of the temperature gauge.

As mentioned on page 93, 1954 and 1955 cars with the System Beck fuel gauges had an air pump; it was on the lower right side of the gauge (see photo page 93).

On cars fitted with electric sunroofs, the sunroof switch was on the bottom of the dashboard, to the left of the ignition switch.

Sunroof switch on lower left of the dashboard

Between the two instruments, starting mid-1951 (coupe 10712 per survey), a switch identical to the wiper/interior light switch was installed to control the dashboard instrument lights. It had no rheostat. This switch was eliminated mid-1954 at coupe 52030 and cabriolet 60550.

356A Carreras had distributor ignition switches above and between the gauges. These two switches were the same as used for the wipers on 356As and had small color-coded knobs.

Dual ignition switches on the 356A Carrera

Through 1953 on the lower dash to the left of the radio and to the right of the starter button was the choke, with an "S" on the knob which stood for *starterzug*. See photo on page 98. This was replaced with a plain knob in 1954.

The 356A hand throttle was on the lower dashboard between the two right side gauges replacing the choke used on the 356. As with the light switch, it moved up on the T 5 356B but remained between the two right instruments. Hand throttles were discontinued with the introduction of the T 6 356B. On Speedsters, Convertible Ds and Roadsters, the hand throttle was to the right of the ignition switch.

In the center of the dashboard of T 6 356B and 356C coupes and cabriolets was the fresh air control, in three varieties. The first, for the standard car, had a

The 356A hand throttle replaced the 356 choke.

Fresh air control for T 6 with optional blower but no gas heater

Fresh air control for T 6 with optional gas heater

single lever that allowed air to be directed up, down or not at all (photo page 105). The second type was for cars with the optional fresh air blower. The lower lever again directed the air flow, while the upper regulated blower speed. The final type was for cars with gas heaters. The last two types had illumination to let those inside know that the blower/heater was on.

The heater control on the first 356s was to the right of the radio, on the lower dashboard left of the lighter. This knob had the letter "H" on it. When the knobs changed in 1954, a large color-coded knob was used. The heater control moved to the floor at coupe 52901 and cabriolet 60708 (early 1955 model year). Floor mounted heat controls are described on page 114.

To the right of the lighter from 1950 through 1953 was the "extra dash button." On some very early cars it was used to control an optional front air vent, but in most cars, it served no purpose but could be used for owner-added accessories. A photo on page 45 of Dirk-Michael Conradt's *Porsche 356, Driving in its Purest Form* shows a car with a vent hole in the nose panel. The knob disappeared mid-1953.

Heater, lighter and extra knob, 1952

Map lights were also mounted on the dashboard; they are described on page 104.

Dashboard Scripts

The 1955 parts book listed a small Porsche script, either chrome or gold. This script was fitted on the cloth covered panel which housed the radio on coupes or cabriolets not equipped with radios or clocks in this location. They were not used on the 356A.

Speedsters, Convertible Ds, and Roadsters featured a silver and gold-plated brass script on the dashboard in front of the passenger. It was a single piece and had the word "Porsche" on it.

The early Porsche dash script

The Speedster through Roadster dash script

Radios

The parts books did not mention the existence of radios but they frequently appeared in 356s. They were always optional, and several varieties were offered each year. The earliest documented data is from 1959.

The 356 models which had that wonderful 1940s dashboard often had a radio in the center. The most popular brands were Blaupunkt and Telefunken. Telefunkens were most frequently seen in the earliest cars, with Blaupunkts taking over later. The vertical push buttons common on early Telefunkens were really spectacular. The size and shape of the radio opening was large enough to house both radio and speaker (common in that era). It is no coincidence that this opening was identical to that in the first VW Beetles.

Early Telefunken radio with vertical push buttons

Early Blaupunkt radio

Very early cars without radios had a dummy gauge in the center of the radio area. It had a chrome rim and the word "Porsche" in the center (photo page 98).

Official documentation:

1959 356A

Blaupunkt

  Bremen: AM/long wave (transistor)
  Stuttgart: AM/long wave/short wave/push-
    button (transistor)
  Frankfurt: AM/FM/long wave/push-button
  Frankfurt: AM/FM/long wave/push-button,
    for U.S.
  Köln: AM/FM/long wave/signal seeking

Becker

  Europa: AM/push-button
  Europa: AM/FM/long wave/push-button
  Europa: AM/FM/long wave/push-button, for
    U.S.
  Mexico: AM/FM/signal seeking
  Mexico: AM/FM/signal seeking, for U.S.

Telefunken radio with the power supply box that lived under the passengers floorboard

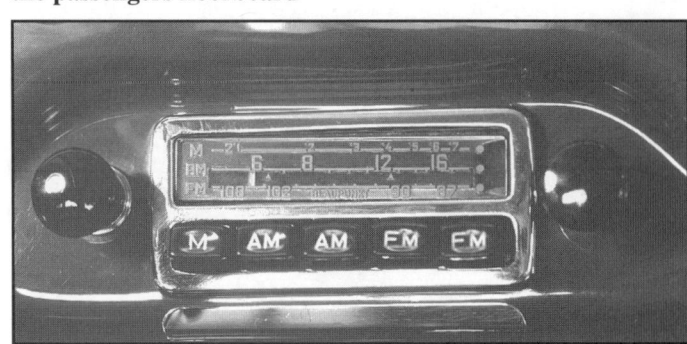

Blaupunkt Frankfurt radio, 356B

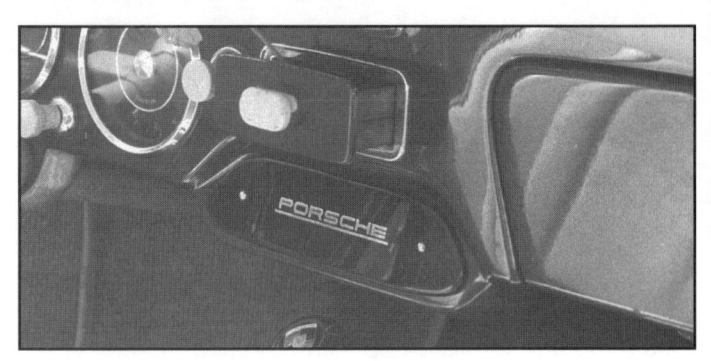

Radio plate, used from 1958 through 1965

356B

Blaupunkt

  Bremen: AM/long wave (transistor)
  Stuttgart: AM/long wave/short wave/push-
    button (transistor)
  Frankfurt: AM/FM/long wave/push-button
  Frankfurt: AM/FM/long wave/push-button,
    for U.S.
  Köln: AM/FM/long wave/signal seeking
  Köln: AM/FM/long wave/signal seeking, for U.S.

Becker

  Europa: AM/push-button
  Europa: AM/FM/long wave/push-button
  Europa:AM/FM/long wave/push-button, for
    U.S.
  Mexico: AM/FM/signal seeking
  Mexico: AM/FM/signal seeking, for U.S.

356C

Blaupunkt

Bremen: AM/long wave (transistor)
Stuttgart: AM/long wave/short wave/push-button (transistor)
Frankfurt: AM/FM/long wave/push-button (transistor)
Frankfurt: AM/FM/long wave/push-button, for U.S. (transistor)
Köln: AM/FM/long wave/signal seeking (transistor)
Köln: AM/FM/long wave/signal seeking, for U.S. (transistor)

Becker

Monte Carlo: AM/long wave
Europa: AM/FM/long wave/push-button
Europa: AM/FM/long wave/push-button, for U.S.
Grand Prix: AM/FM/long wave/signal seeking
Grand Prix: AM/FM/long wave/signal seeking, for U.S.

Non-transistor versions had a power supply box containing vacuum tubes and other things under the floor board on the passenger's side.

From 1956 through 1965, coupes and cabriolets without radios had flat plastic plates with the Porsche script embossed in the back. They were black, grey or beige.

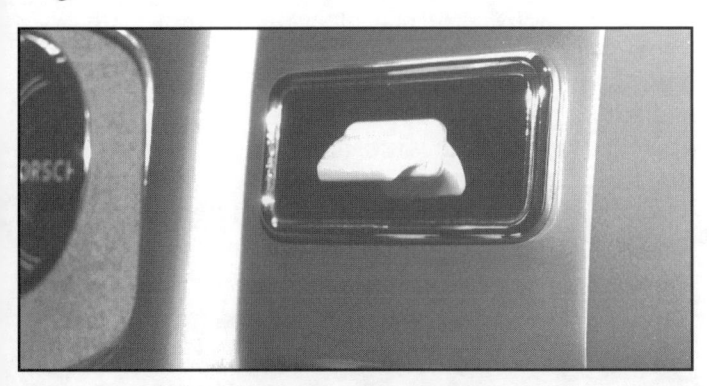

Chrome ash tray on 356 with early knob

Oval knob on painted ash tray, pre-T 2 356A

Ashtray

On the 356 coupe and cabriolet, the ashtray was to the right of the radio. It had an aluminum surround, and the ashtray itself had a chrome-plated cover. The ivory, down-turned knob was used until the other knobs changed in mid-1954. After that a color coded oval shaped knob was used.

Early 356As used a similar but slightly smaller ashtray, whose front panel was painted to match the dashboard. T 2 models had an under-dash chrome-plated ashtray. This ashtray was used throughout the duration of all 356 production. In 356C models it was mounted in the painted dash extension.

Ashtrays were standard on all coupes and cabriolets. They were unavailable on Speedsters until the T 2 body, when they became optional. They were also optional on Convertible Ds and Roadsters.

The chrome ash tray used from T 2 356A through 356C

Glove Compartment

Early cars had a glove compartment on the right side of the dashboard. Through the Model 51 the actual boxes were steel upholstered with fuzzy headliner material, while later cars used flocked fiberboard. The glove compartment door on very early cars had dual wall construction with a fairly elaborate pressed inner panel. Later cars did not have the inner pressing. The

Early glove box showing inner structure

103

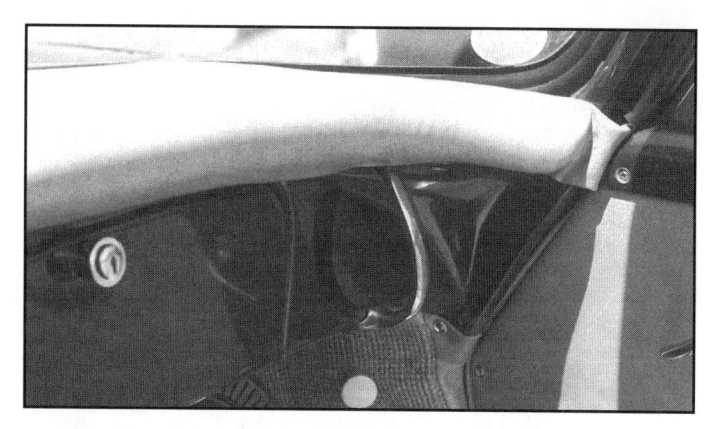

Locking glove box and middle type grab handle

Inner glove box door had an elastic band to hold objects.

knobs were the same as those on the ashtray which made it impossible to lock one's gloves away. A locking knob was available for cabriolets (also found on some 1950 coupes). With the 356A redesign in late 1955, a chrome-plated locking knob was placed on the newly rounded glove box door and inner liner. Speedsters, Convertible Ds and Roadsters had no glove boxes.

The 356C had a slightly altered glove box door with a sculpted hand grip and lock at the upper right. The glove compartment door was held closed by a magnetic catch.

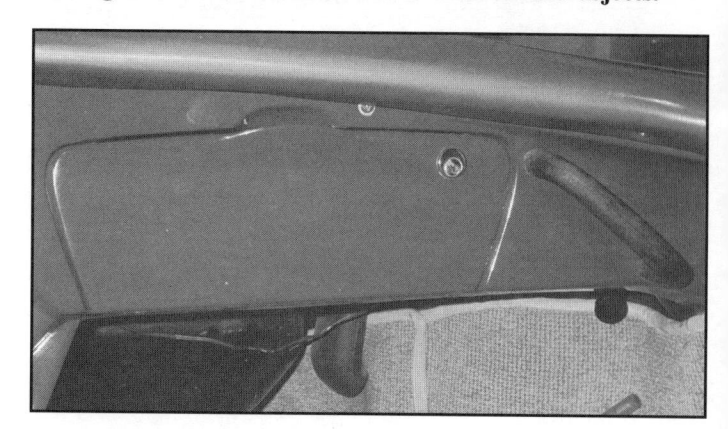

356C glove box and plastic grab handle

Grab Handles

Most very early cars had no grab handle, but some had a white plastic VW type. The earliest car on file with a metal handle is 5447. This 356 grab handle was chrome-plated and mounted right of the glove box. The handle was modified on the 356A and 356B coupes and cabriolets. The lower part mounted with three screws, and the upper part penetrated the dashboard and was secured by a rubber grommet.

Speedsters, Roadsters and Convertible Ds, because of their different dashboards, continued to use the early-style grab handle. The 356C model brought a change in the grab handle from the chrome version above to a black plastic handle.

Interior and Map Light

Starting at coupe 5001 and running through 51957 (late 1953 model), a metal rimmed dome light was mounted between the sun visors; it had a small white plastic oval lens. A larger, clear plastic light with external switch was introduced at this time and was used until the introduction of the 356A. The first cabriolets had a long narrow light below the mirror on the metal plate that divided the windshield halves. Cabriolets from 10271 (Model 52) through the end of the 1955 model year had a large pull-type map light on the dashboard over the ashtray (see photo page 87).

This grab handle was used on Speedsters, Convertible Ds, Roadsters and coupes and cabriolets in 1954 and 1955.

The early metal rimmed dome light was switched on by a dash-mounted control.

1950 - 1951 cabriolet interior light on windshield center post

Late 1954 and all 1955 coupes had this interior light.

356A models had a smaller, rectangular, Hella dash-mounted interior light for 1956 and 1957. In 1958, coupes went to dual oval lights above each door; cabriolets had a single oval light in about the same location as earlier cars. T 5 356Bs were unchanged.

356C coupes had a rocker-type dome light replacing the oval, switch-operated variety. A light on the lower center of the dash pad was also on T 6 356B and 356C coupes and cabriolets.

Speedster, Roadsters, and Convertible Ds were again left out when it came to such luxury features as interior lights.

One 1958 cabriolet had a very original-looking map light to the right of the clock with a chrome plastic knob. It was activated when pulled out and could be turned to direct the beam of light.

356C rocking dome light

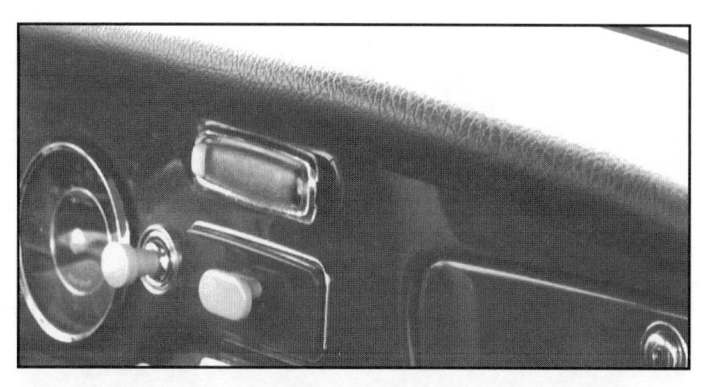

Rectangular dash light used in 1956 and 1957 (T 1)

Oval dash light T 2 cabriolet

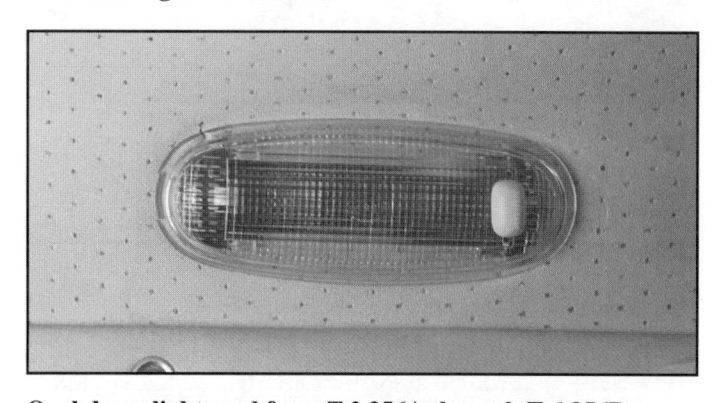

Oval dome light used from T 2 356A through T 6 356B

Dashboard light used on the T 6 356B and 356C

Other Odd Things

An accessory socket on the lower dashboard, left of the steering column accepted 6 or 12-volt accessory items, such as map lights and the like. Early cars had a hex rim on this socket, which was changed mid-1952 to a rounded rim.

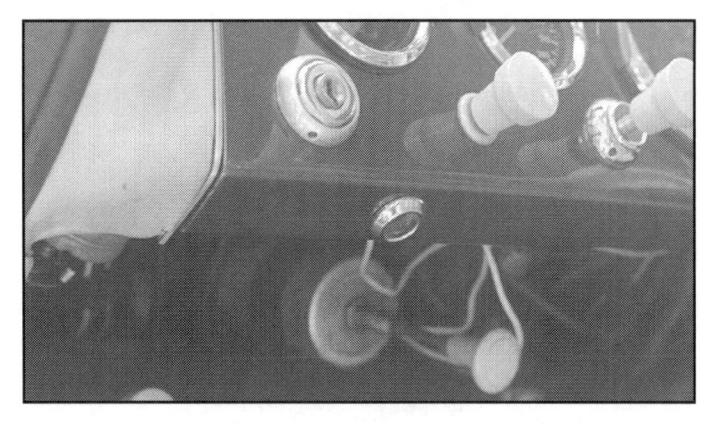

The accessories socket on the bottom of the dashboard

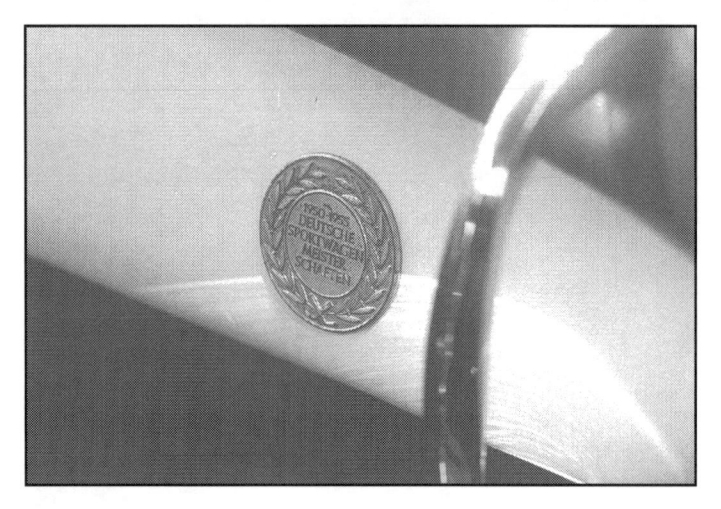

The "Meister Schaften" commemorative badge

A small round plaque commemorating racing wins was found on the dash of most 1956 through mid-1958 models. On 1956 cars the plaque read "1950-1955," on 1957 cars it read "1950-1956," and on 1958 cars it read "1950-1957." Generally, it was on the right side of the dash, left of the glove box except on Speedsters where it was further right. The latest cars on file with this item were coupe 103614 and Speedster 84770 (mid-1958).

Interior Rear View Mirrors

Coupes and cabriolets had different rear view mirrors due to the lack of mounting area in the cabriolet. The 1953 parts book did not illustrate the coupe version but mentioned two cabriolet mirrors, one for Model 51s and one for Model 52s and later. The latter was clamped to a chrome-plated rod via an aluminum block. First use of this type was when the bent windshield was adopted.

Illustration 41 in the 1955 parts books showed both coupe and cabriolet mirrors. The coupe mirror mounted via screws between the visors, was used from the first coupe through the 1956 model year. The illustration also showed two cabriolet versions: one for cars prior to 60405 (mid-1954), one for later models. The clamping block, though, was listed to fit cars later than 10271 (Model 52).

Model 52 cabriolet mirror

An aluminum block attached this Speedster mirror to the tension rod.

This pressed steel bracket allowed the use of the 356A coupe mirror on open cars.

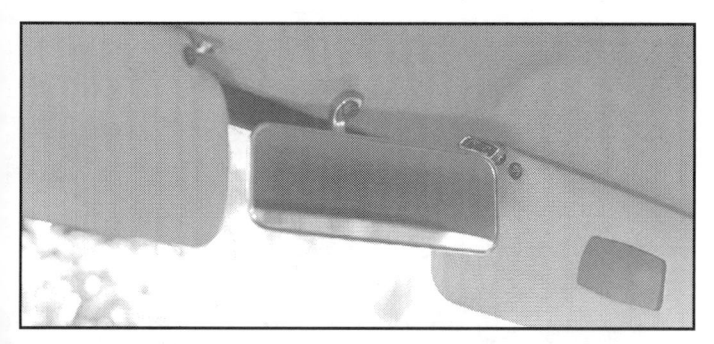

Coupe mirror for 356As appeared mid-1956 and was used through T 5 356Bs.

Breakaway mount coupe mirror

Late coupe mirror with three mounting screws

356C cabriolets finally received day/night mirrors. Note also symmetrical visors.

While a different tension rod was used on Speedsters, the mirror and mounting block were identical to the ones on cabriolets.

356A cabriolets had the same interior mirror as earlier cars, but somewhere around the T 2 change the mounting block changed from aluminum to pressed steel. The mirror also changed to the single allen bolt mirror used in all 356A coupes. This change was not made on Speedsters. Convertible Ds had a different tension rod than the Speedster and used the 356A coupe mirror. This arrangement was unchanged for T 5 356Bs, although the accessories book listed an optional day-night mirror.

The 356B T 6 cabriolet remained the same, but the coupe had a different mirror, of the day-night variety with a breakaway mount. Another mirror was listed for 356C coupes; this coupe mirror was mounted by three screws. The breakaway mount T 6 mirror was used on very early 356C coupes. The latest known cars on file with breakaway mirrors are 126544 and 213720. The 356C cabriolet had a new larger, post-mounted day-night mirror.

Sun visors

The 1953 parts book had no listing for sun visors in early cars. The 1955 book listed only one style for all pre-1956 coupes and cabriolets, but this was incorrect. The visors' general appearance, chrome-plated frame at the top and two sides and dark green plastic visor, were similar, but there are a number of subtle differences.

The earliest sun visors had hex clamp nuts on friction pivot mounts. The translucent plastic was flat and 2mm thick (not $1/16$ or $3/32$ of an inch) and was held by aluminum rivets.

The next style had no clamping device and a down-turned edge on the unsupported edge of the plastic. It was a classic example of two guiding principles in manufacturing: make it cheaper – make it better. The bent lip stiffened the plastic and the new mounts were less expensive.

Early visors had hex nut pivots.

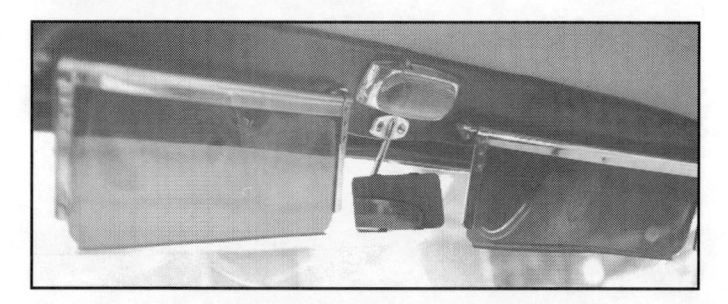

The second variety of visor without hex nuts

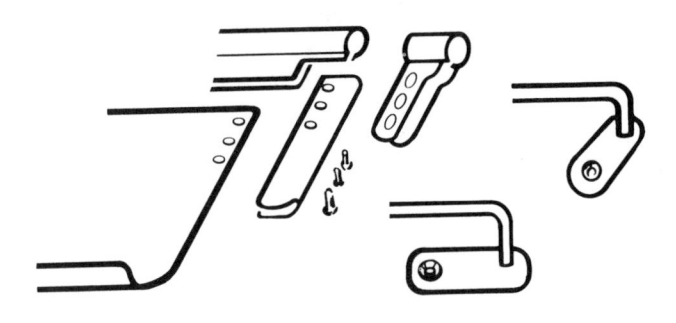

Construction detail of plastic visor. Lower "foot" is 356 type, upper was used on early 356A models.

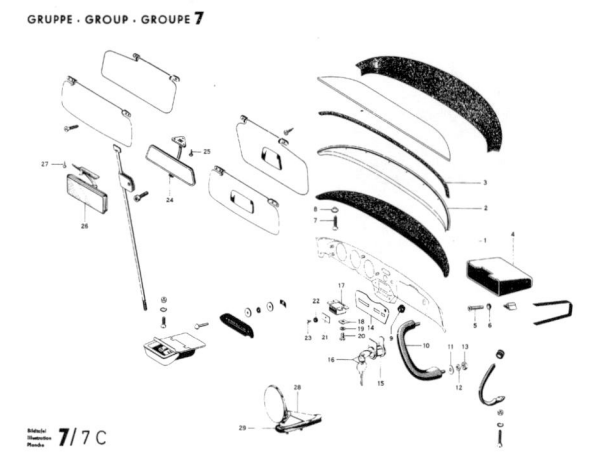

Illustration 7/7C, 356C Parts Book

Plastic 356A visors; note early rear view mirror.

Use of plastic visors in 356A cars brought yet another change. The mounting foot was made smaller and angled to fit the new contoured "headboard" which made the headliner easier to install. The lip on the plastic was not quite as wide as the visor and extended about two cm past the metal side pieces and then bent down about one centimeter at a right angle.

The latest chassis number on file with the hex nut type visor is 51187 (1953). The change from plastic to later padded type visors in 356As was in March 1957 at the time the teardrop taillight change occurred.

In regard to padded visors, the parts book showed the same visor used for left or right in coupes and cabriolets and no vanity mirror was present. Vanity mirrors were optional from at least the T 2. Speedsters did not have sun visors, but Convertibles Ds did, as an option. Roadsters came standard with a single visor on the driver's side; passenger-side visors were optional.

Convertible D with single visor

Lopsided T 6 visors; note vanity mirror.

In any event, the T 5 356B coupe and cabriolet had the same visors listed as the 356A. Also listed was a passenger's visor with vanity mirror. The vinyl was white and had a textured surface.

The T 6 got lopsided sun visors, but the part numbers were the same as the earlier visors. The C parts book illustration 7/7C showed both visors but does not indicate any change having occurred for that particular model.

Standard Steering Wheels

The 1953 parts book illustrated two types of steering wheels. The first had three sets of four aluminum spokes, no horn ring and came in two diameters, 400mm or 425mm (optional). It was ivory in color and used a plain white horn button.

The other type, also ivory and also 400mm, appears to be the one seen in many early cars. Both were manufactured by Petri. This model, the Pealit, had a horn ring with plain white horn button and listed as optional.

The two spoke wheel made by VDM was introduced on the 1953 model. It featured the first use of the newly designed Porsche crest on its center horn button. The wheel was 400mm in diameter and was painted ivory in color. Grey and beige (to match the

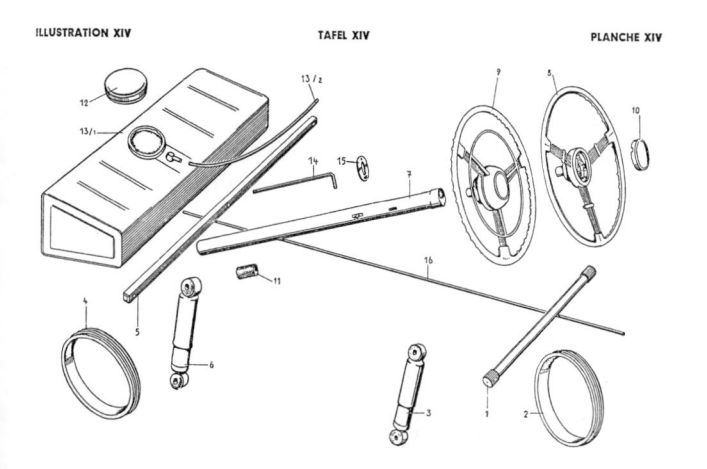

Illustration 14, 1953 Parts Book

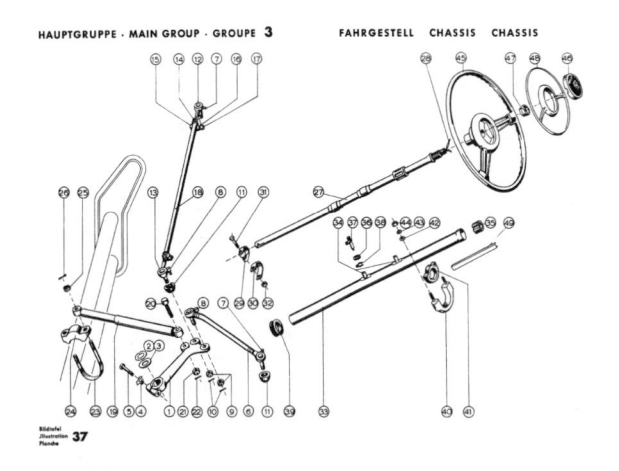

Illustration 37, 356A Parts Book

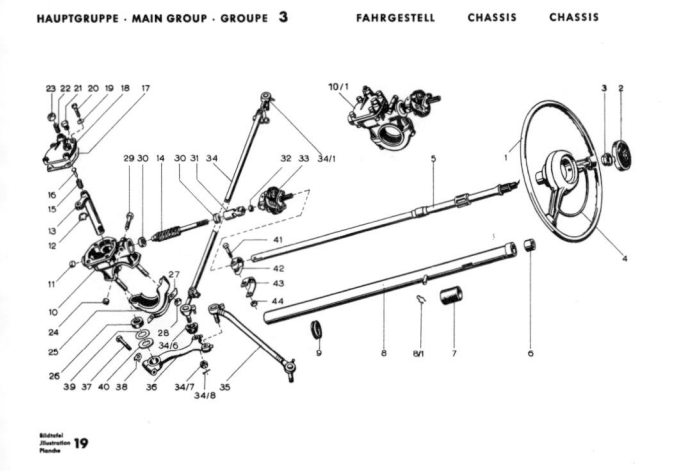

Illustration 19, 1955 Parts Book

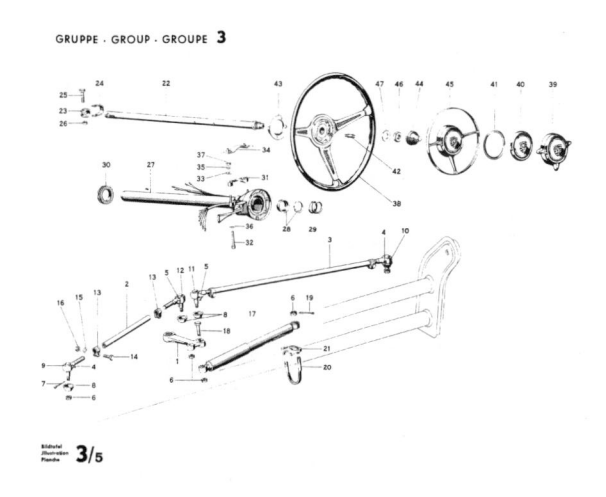

Illustration 3/5, T 5 Parts Book

knobs) were added in 1954 when a lower one-third circle horn ring was standard on all but Speedsters. If the ring was fitted, it would be used to blow the horn. The parts to convert it were listed in the parts book. The ring was generally painted the color of the steering wheel, although a factory photo showed a chrome-plated one (photo page 87).

The 356A parts book confused the issue a bit. The 400mm steering wheel without a horn ring was listed as being used up to coupe 101693, cabriolet 61893 and Speedster 83692 (T 2 change). It then listed a different wheel with the complete circle 230mm horn ring which was changed in conjunction with the steering column change (for the Z-F steering box) at the chassis numbers above. This wheel was available in two diameters, 400mm and 425mm, in the same colors listed before. In fact, the circular horn ring was used from 1956 and was optional on Speedsters, becoming standard in 1958. On cars with the circular horn ring the center button was a headlight flasher.

Standard wheel used through Model 52

Optional Pealit steering wheel

109

Standard VDM wheel with small horn ring

Standard VDM wheel with large horn ring

The 356B featured a different black plastic three-spoke steering wheel made by VDM. It was used through the remainder of 356 production as standard equipment. The November 1959 Factory Accessory List included an optional, extended steering column (30mm), presumably for those who wished to steer with their elbows. There was also an optional horn ring.

VDM wheel used on 356B and 356C with optional horn ring

Wood Steering Wheels

The earliest Porsche wood steering wheel known was manufactured for the factory by VDM, which made a wide variety of plastic and wood wheels for the factory from 1953. The VDM 356A wood wheel has been referred to as an "unsigned Nardi." The spokes closely resemble those of the Nardi wheels made for 356A cars, but the VDM wheel accommodated the factory 356A horn button, where the Nardi did not. The VDM wheel had a pair of black-accented grooves on the wood rim facing the driver, where the Nardi had an ebony inlay and no groove. The VDM wood wheel was supplied as original equipment on most Carrera GT cars from 1957 through 1959. In addition, the "flat" VDM wood wheel was standard issue on Type 550A Spyders.

To distinguish the VDM steering wheel from the Nardi, all Nardis were signed on the upper part of the right-hand spoke. The "flat" Nardis for 356As were definitely factory supplied on some cars, especially 1959 Carrera GS and GS/GT models. Nardis had a funny horn button, somewhat like a broad flat black mushroom growing out of the hub with a tiny Porsche-crested horn button growing out of the center of the mushroom. The separately spring-loaded outer rim of this button was to flash headlights. Certainly, "flat" Nardis were also available on the aftermarket to be fitted to 356A cars. Factory installed Nardis can be distinguished from aftermarket versions by the fact that the latter had the last two digits of the year of manufacture stamped on the back of the middle spoke; the "original" Nardis did not.

One other wheel often seen on 356As was the made-in-England Derrington, distinguished by its flat brass rivets embedded flush with the wood rim, facing the driver. The Derrington wheel was likely never factory installed but was probably added to cars by dealers prior to sale. Anyway, it is also quite attractive and appropriate and "vintage" looking. The "original"

Optional 356A VDM wood wheel

Early flat Nardi steering wheel

356B/C normal spoke VDM wheel with optional horn ring

Early VDM flat spoked wheel

356B/C slotted spoke VDM wheel

Aftermarket Derrington wheel

Aftermarket Nardi dished wheel

111

Derrington can be distinguished from the replica currently available by its machined – as opposed to cast – aluminum hub.

VDM made two distinctly different wood steering wheels for the factory for cars produced from 1960 through 1965. The earlier of the two versions had slotted polished aluminum spokes like the earlier VDM and Nardi for 356As, only in a "dished" shape. The rim was smooth, with no inlays, grooves or rivets, but finger grips were carved into the back. The second, later version, had stainless steel spokes exactly like those on the black plastic wheels, also made by VDM, for standard issue 356B and 356C cars. The wood rim had an ebony inlay around the outside circumference and the customary finger grips at the back. Both these wheels used the factory standard 356B/C horn button.

The final type was the Les Leston (LL) wood wheel. The VDM and LL wheels were the only factory-supplied wood wheels for 1960 through 1965 cars, including Abarth Carreras and 904s. Nice aftermarket wheels of the era were made by Nardi and Derrington and looked like dished versions of the respective flat wheels for 356As.

Pedals

The early 356 pedal assembly was different from the ones used later, distinguishable by the early version's rectangular brake and clutch pedals. This early pedal assembly was installed through 1953, although the point of change to the more familiar type of pedal pads (which continued to be used on 911s) was not documented. The owner's survey listed the change between 51798 and 51984, which corresponds to early 1954 toward the end of the 1953 model year car production. Accelerator pedals were the same on all 356 cars. The rubber cover on the accelerator, originally an Opel part, was identical on all 356s.

Early pedal assembly; note clutch cable.

Late pedal assembly did not require use of false floors.

The pedal assembly was changed completely for the 356A, including addition of a hand-throttle mechanism; as opposed to earlier cars, the entire pedal mechanism was removable. It remained unaltered through 1965 except for the cable attachment on the clutch pedal, which was modified in 1962. The accelerator pedal took a similar progression, changing with the 356A then remaining the same through 1965.

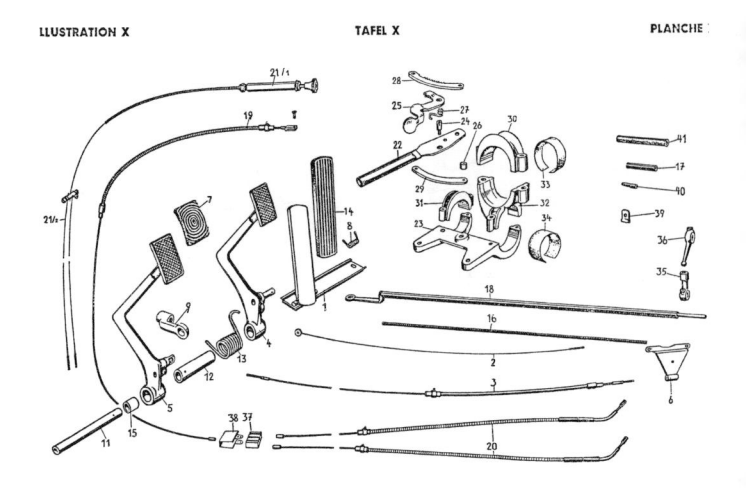

Illustration 10, 1953 Parts Book

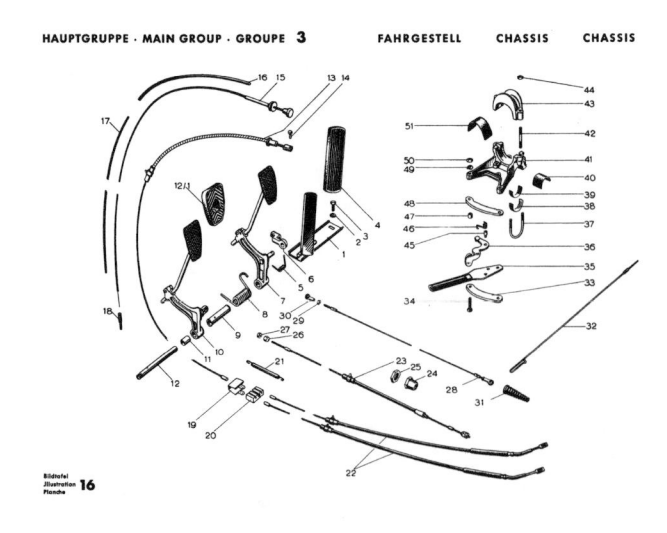

Illustration 16, 1955 Parts Book

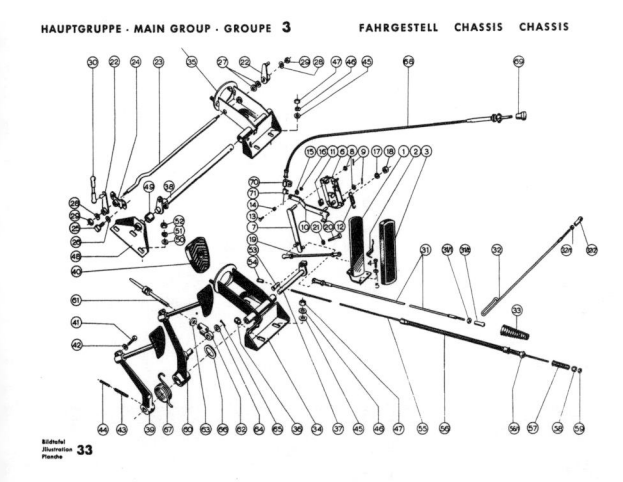

Illustration 33, 356A Parts Book

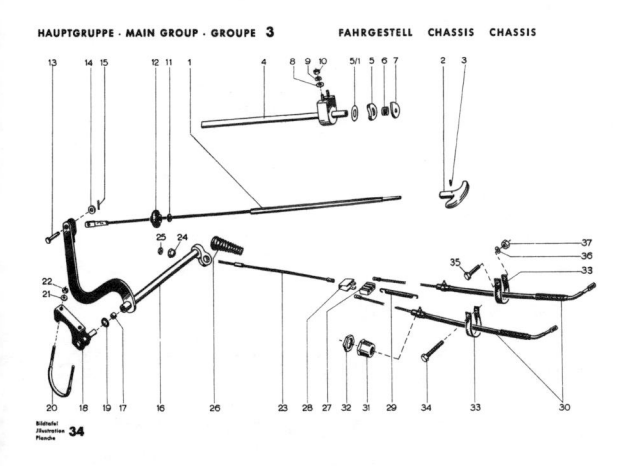

Illustration 34, 356A Parts Book

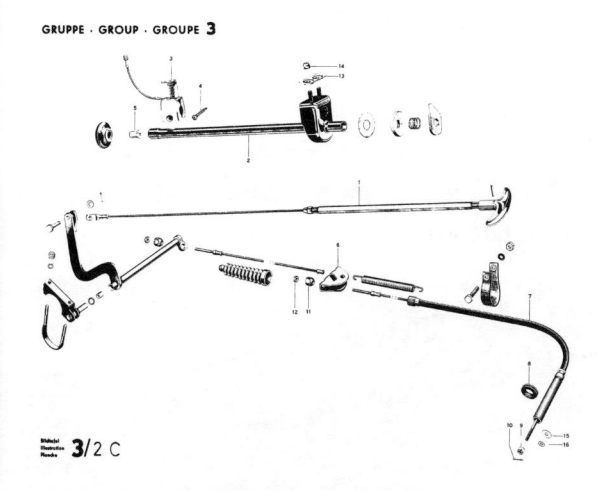

Illustration 3/2C, 356C Parts Book

Handbrake Handle/Assembly

The early 356 had the handbrake assembly mounted to the steering column below the dash. It had a thumb release on the lever with ratchet-like teeth. This general arrangement continued through 1955, but a change may be noted in the base casting between the 1953 and 1955 parts books; the exact point of change was not noted. A hand pump for the windshield wash-

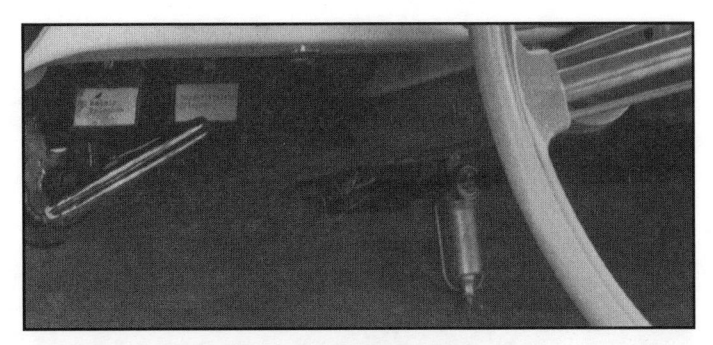

Chrome ribbed 356A handbrake handle

356C dull aluminum handbrake handle

er also bolted to the defroster tube in the handbrake area. The knob had a "W" on it.

The 356A handbrake had a chrome-plated ribbed handle and was mounted to the firewall rather than the steering column. Instead of the ratchet mechanism of the 356, the 356A handbrake was a push/pull affair with a twist release. It was used on all 356As and 356Bs; although 356Bs had a different handle that was not ribbed. The T 6 356B had a dull finished handbrake handle. The 356C handle had a smooth, dull aluminum lever. It also had an electrical switch to advise the driver that the handbrake was on.

Front Kick Panels

Below the dashboard to the left and right of the footwells were the kick panels. With the exception of GTs, these were always covered by carpet which had

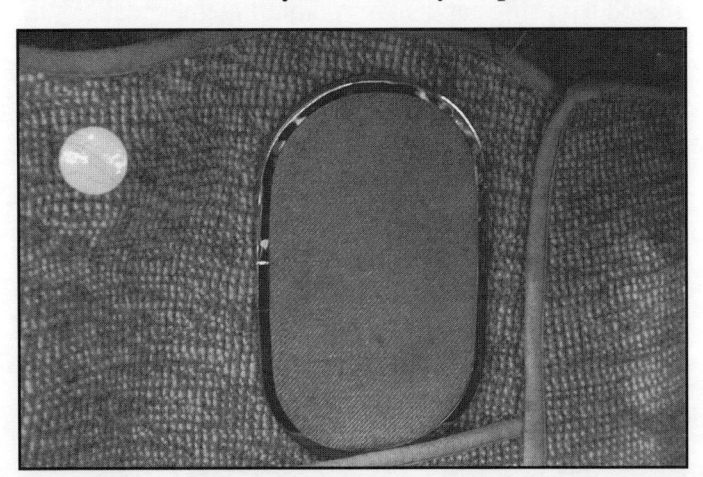

Oval speakers were found in the 356A and 356B kick panels when radios were fitted. Note also vent knob.

113

Early fuse boxes were on the passenger's side kick panel.

The 356A fuse block was mounted above the passenger's side footwell.

a pocket for storing maps and such. In 1952 vent pulls were added. They had ivory-colored ribbed VW-type plain knobs. In 1954 large size Porsche color keyed knobs replaced them. These side vents were deleted on the T 6 356B when the cowl vent was added.

Twin oval radio speakers appeared on both kick panels of 356As equipped with radios. They had chrome plated trim rings and silver painted metal speaker grilles. These were used until the 356C, when a smaller round speaker was introduced.

Through 1953 the fuse block was located on the passenger's side kick panel above the map pocket. It was moved to a more central under-dash location in 1954.

The front lid release was on the driver's side above the kick panel. This was a large white mushroom-shaped knob, also used on the the rear lid pull, which was on the left side behind the driver's seat. By late 1951 the VW type knobs as used on the vent pulls replaced the larger knob. Large color-keyed Porsche knobs replaced the VW ones in 1954. An optional locking release was available from 1960 (356B) for Roadsters and cabriolets.

Gear Shift, Heater Control

The shift lever changed some time in the early 356 years, although the parts manual didn't mention when. The change should be associated with the upgrade from non-synchro to synchro gearbox at coupe 11799 and cabriolets 15051 and 12352 (1953 model year). The early shift lever was straight, and the later version had a bend in the bottom third. There was a modification in the location of the bend prior to the 356A model change. The T 2 356A had a slightly shorter lever.

Straight "crashbox" gear shift

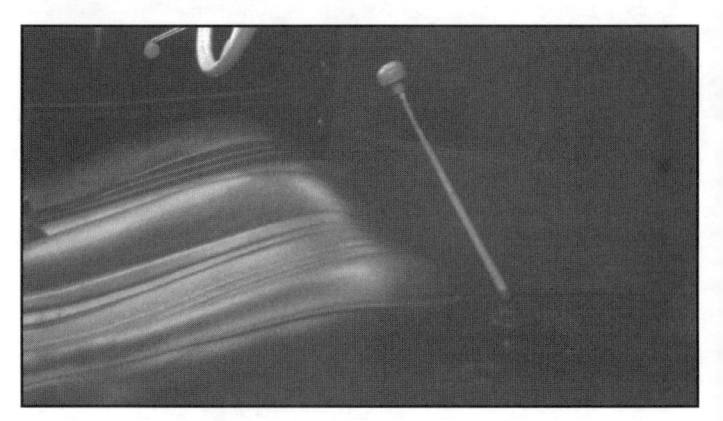

Early low bent shift lever

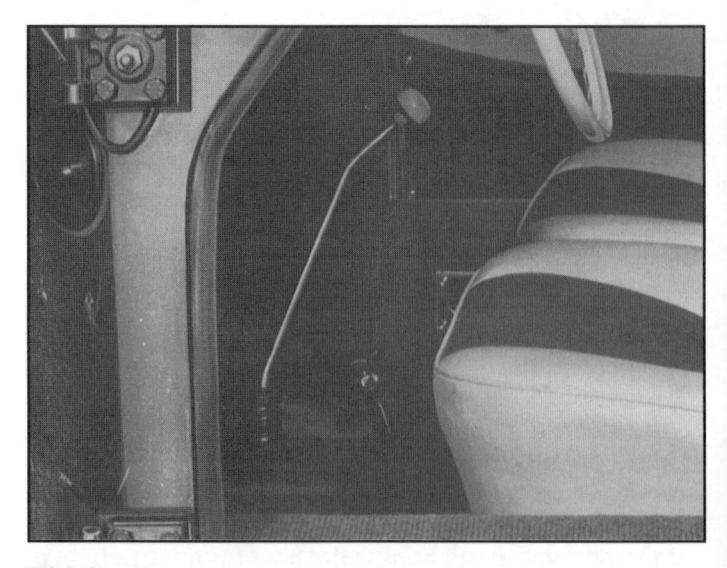

High bent lever

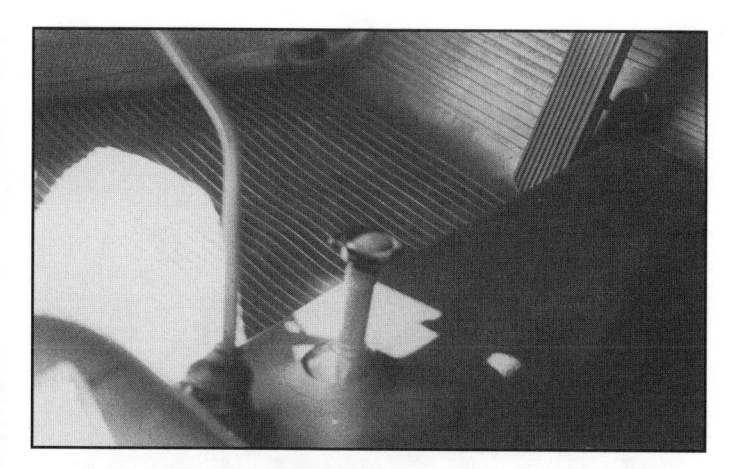

T 2 shift lever; note position of heat knob.

The first floor mounted heat controls appeared late 1954.

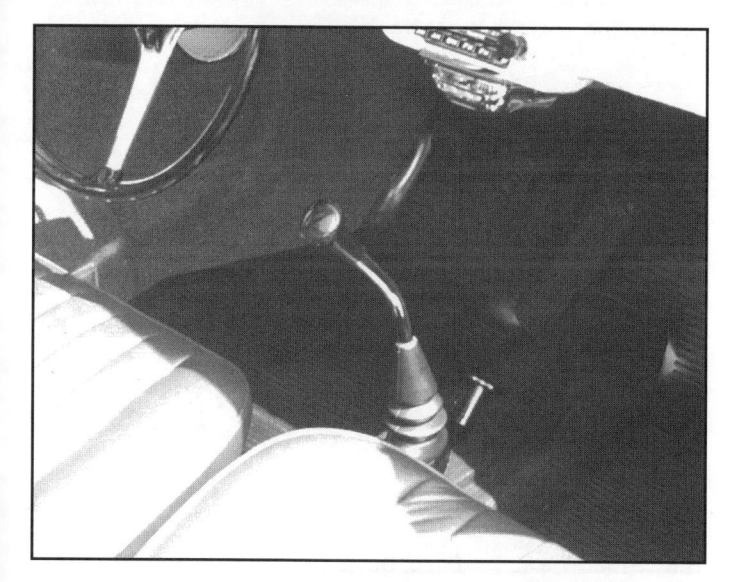

356B/C shift lever with front-mounted heater knob

356C heat lever and transmission lock

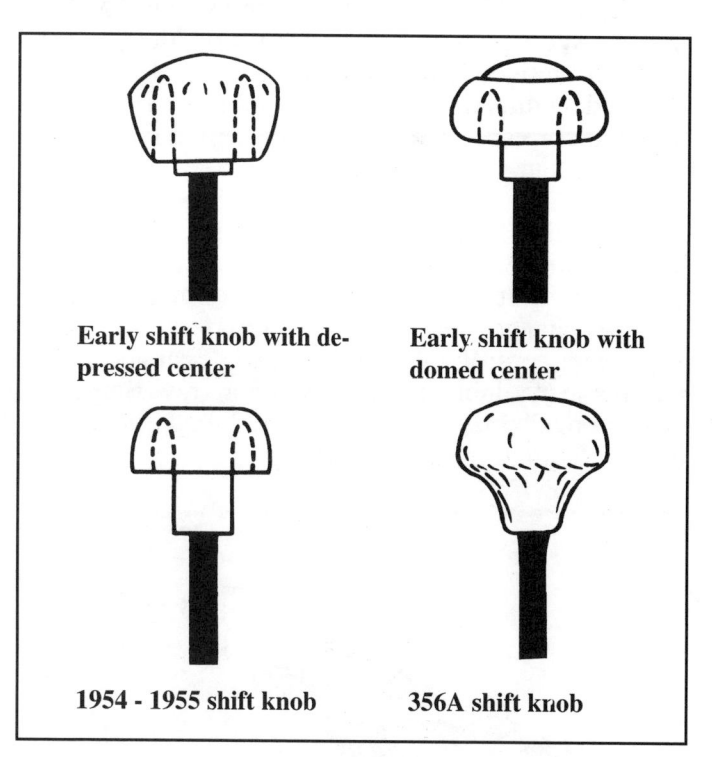

Early shift knob with depressed center

Early shift knob with domed center

1954 - 1955 shift knob

356A shift knob

The 356B's lever, of course, was considerably different, chrome-plated, as opposed to silver painted. At coupe 110407, cabriolet 153023 and Roadster 87492, a change in mechanism occurred, outwardly noticeable by the optional shift lock mechanism. The 356C included another change as the knob-type heat adjuster was replaced by a lever.

The first cars used early VW shift knobs. In 1952 a special Porsche knob with a depressed center was used. 356As had a rounded-top knob, while subsequent cars had the familiar black mushroom. From 1950 through 1959 the color of the shift knob matched other dash knob and steering wheel color.

While floor-mounted heater controls were mentioned previously, the first 356s had them on the dashboard (see page 101). At coupe 52907, cabriolet 60708 and around Speedster 80100 (early 1955 model year), the controls moved to the floor behind the shift lever. In 1958 (T 2) the heater control moved forward of the shift lever. This remained unchanged until 1963. A black twist knob was used from the point that heater controls were moved floorward. This was modified to a lever with the 356C.

Floor Mats

All 356s came with carpet just about everywhere except on the floor, which was instead covered by rubber mats. The earliest cars featured grooved mats, but molded mats followed soon after. 356s with dash-mounted heater controls had a center tunnel mat with

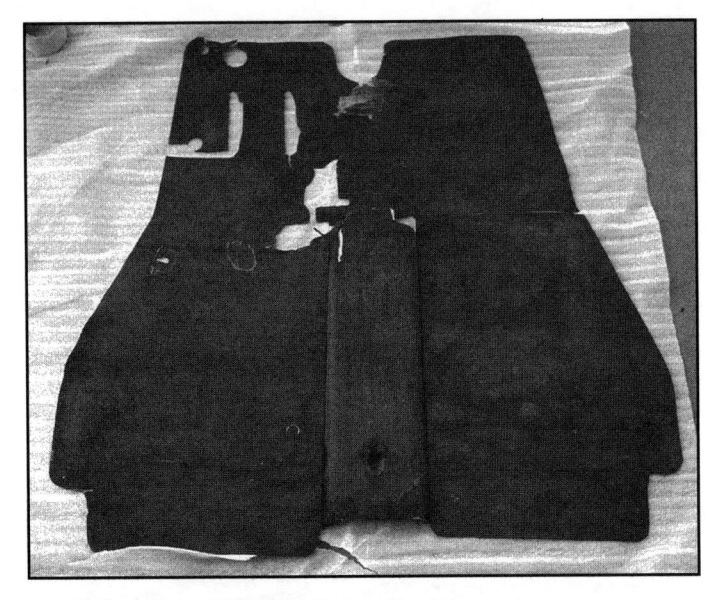

Early fine ribbed floor and tunnel mats

a single hole for the shift lever. This was used until coupe 11778 and cabriolet 15072 (through Model 52). A second-style mat, again for dash-mounted heater controls, was used from that point until coupe 52900 and cabriolet 60707. The difference was the position of the shift lever. The change was due to the conversion from non-synchro to synchro gearboxes. Non-synchro boxes had a distance of 16 inches from the pedal board to the shift lever. Synchros were 13 1/2 inches. At coupe 52901 and cabriolet 60708 the heater control moved to the floor and the tunnel mat changed again. All mats to this point had a ribbed texture that corresponded to the rib pattern in the main floor mat, but at a 90 degree angle.

Although the illustration in the 356A parts book looked like a 356 tunnel mat, the actual mat had a pebble grain. It was available in black only. At the T 2 model change, due to repositioning of the shift lever and heater control, the tunnel mat was changed and was made available in black, beige or grey. Beige mats were slightly thicker and were found only on cars with tan or oatmeal carpeting.

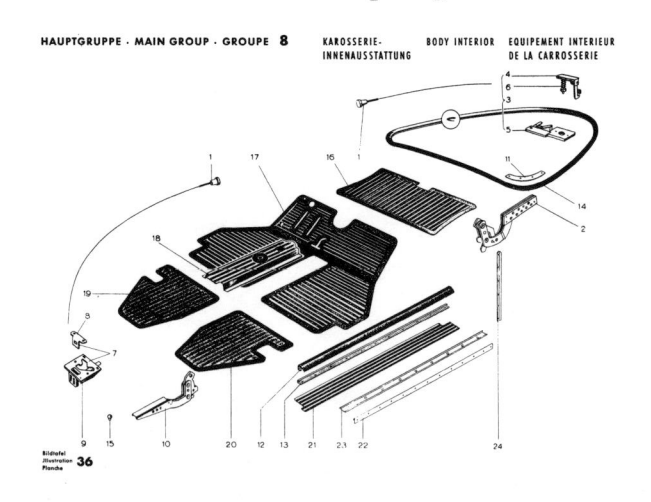

Illustration 36, 1955 Parts Book

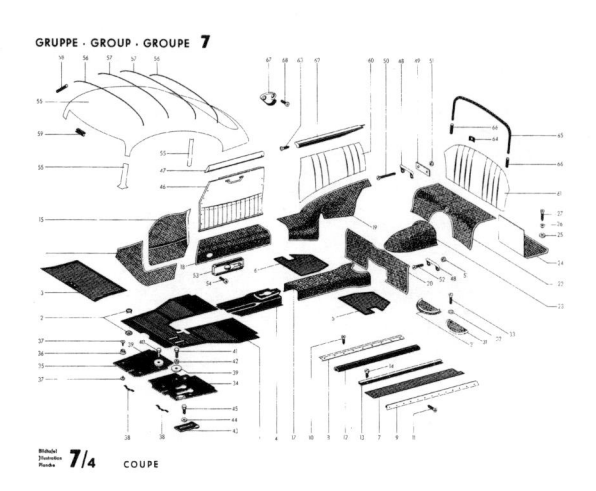

Illustration 7/4, T 5 Parts Book

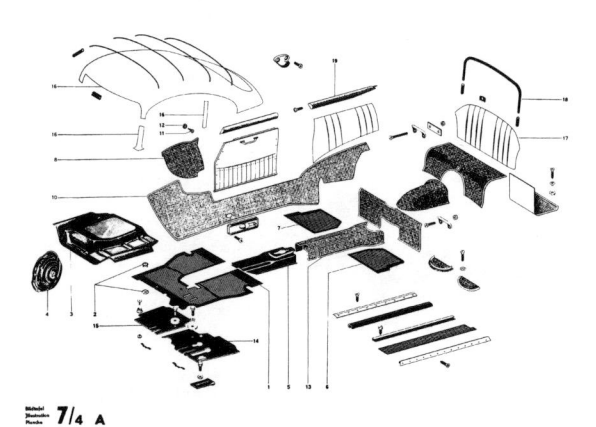

Illustration 7/4A, T 6 Parts Book

The tunnel mat was considerably changed for the 356B. The texture was again pebble-grained. The mat was modified due to the change in the heater control at the 356C model introduction.

The main floor mat changes were fewer. A single mat was used for 356s, and a change was made for the 356A. The main mat, like the tunnel mat, was available in black, beige or grey. The T 5 and T 6 356B had similar mats, the main difference being the height above the pedals due to the change in gas tank. These were only available in black. The 356C was identical to the T 6 356B.

Rear floor mats followed a similar progression with one less mutation. The 356A was identical to the T 5 356B. The change at the T 6 356B model was caused by redesigned seat mounts.

Floor Boards

Wooden floor boards followed model change progression pretty closely. The 356 had a one-piece pedal board and false floors which elevated the floor mat about two inches. The false floors allowed the clutch cable to pass beneath the driver's feet.

From 1956 to March 1957, 356As had a one-piece floor board. This was changed to a two-piece board, which must have been to facilitate servicing, as no difference in shape was noted.

T 5 356B boards were again two-piece and very similar to the 356A except for a block for the foot-operated windshield washer pump in the upper left hand corner. The T 6 356B was different due to the change in gas tank. The 356C was the same as the T 6 356B.

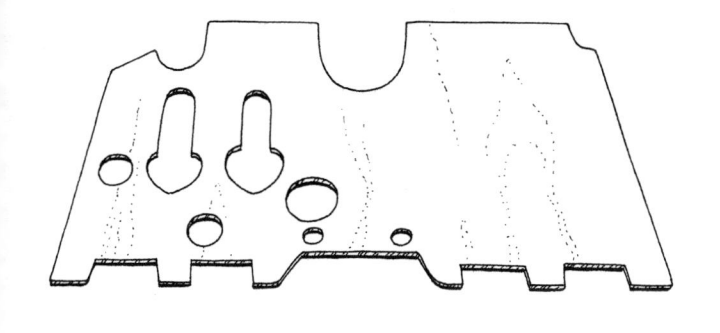

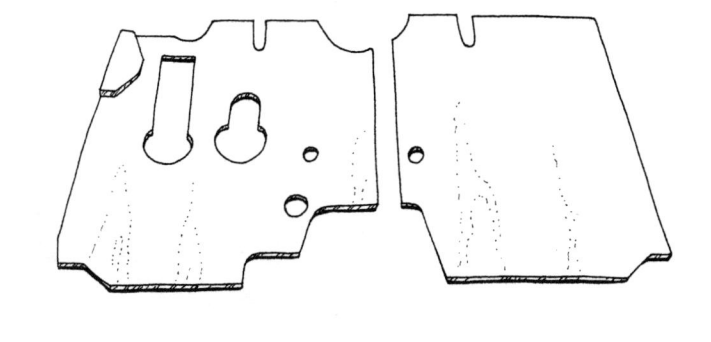

Pedal boards, T 5 356B

Pedal board, 356

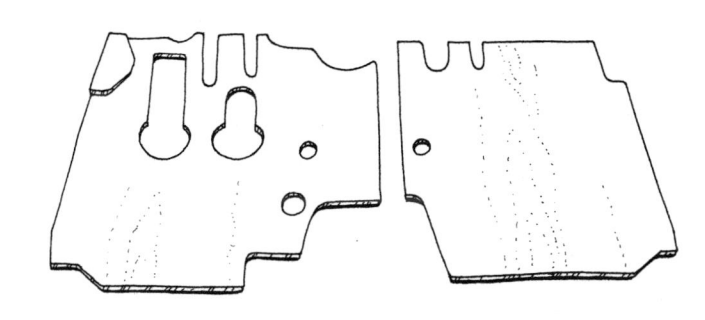

Pedal boards, T 6 356B and 356C

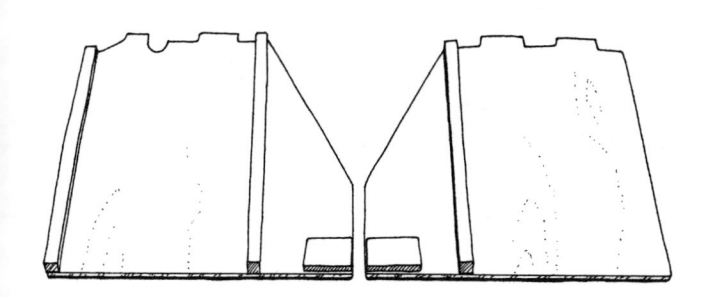

False floors (bottom view), 356

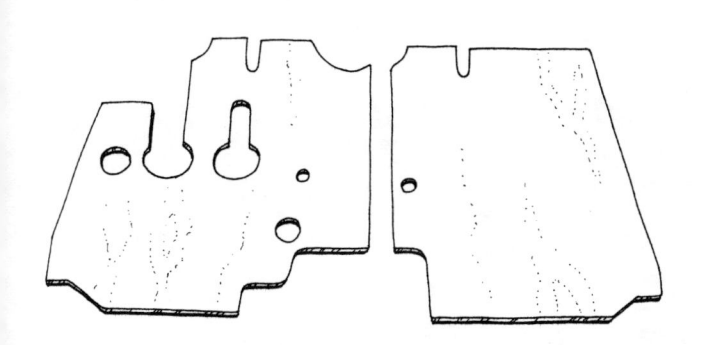

Pedal boards, 356A

Carpet

Carpeting for Porsche 356s from 1950 through 1965 was obtained from a single vendor, which also supplied Mercedes-Benz, VW and probably other German auto manufacturers. Colors available were blue, green, red, charcoal, tan, oatmeal (combination of beige and brown thread in each knot) and also light grey and dark tan.

Generalities? Most early cars seem to have been carpeted in blue and tan. The majority of 356s and 356As were in tan or oatmeal, while 356Bs and 356Cs had good variety, with an emphasis on charcoal.

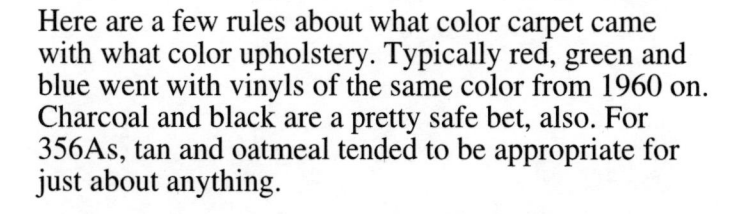

Here are a few rules about what color carpet came with what color upholstery. Typically red, green and blue went with vinyls of the same color from 1960 on. Charcoal and black are a pretty safe bet, also. For 356As, tan and oatmeal tended to be appropriate for just about anything.

Included are illustrations for 356 carpet sets. Some of the sets were quite strange, especially Karmann Hardtop, peculiar by its rolled, non-bound edges rather than the typical vinyl or cloth binding found on other 356 models. There was a choice of binding. Generally, the binding was the same color as the carpet, although early Speedsters often had tan carpet with black vinyl binding. Vinyl binding was typically found on Speedsters, Convertible Ds and some Roadsters. All other models were generally cloth bound. Leather edging was occasionally seen in early cabriolets.

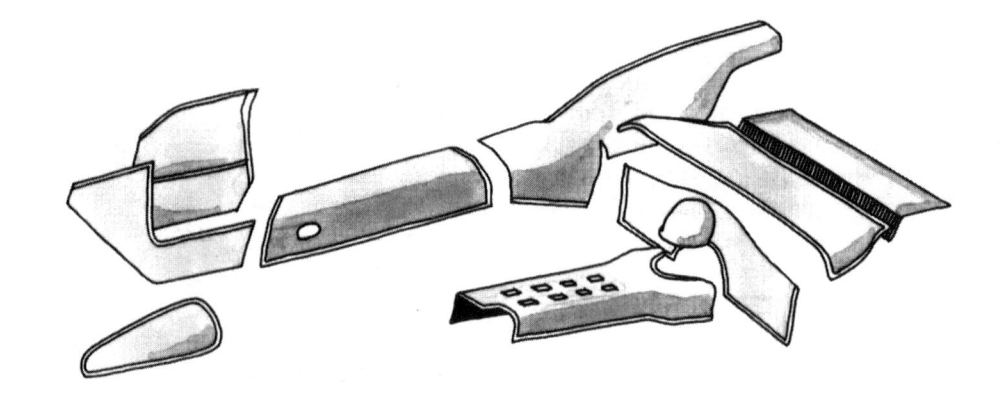

356 coupe

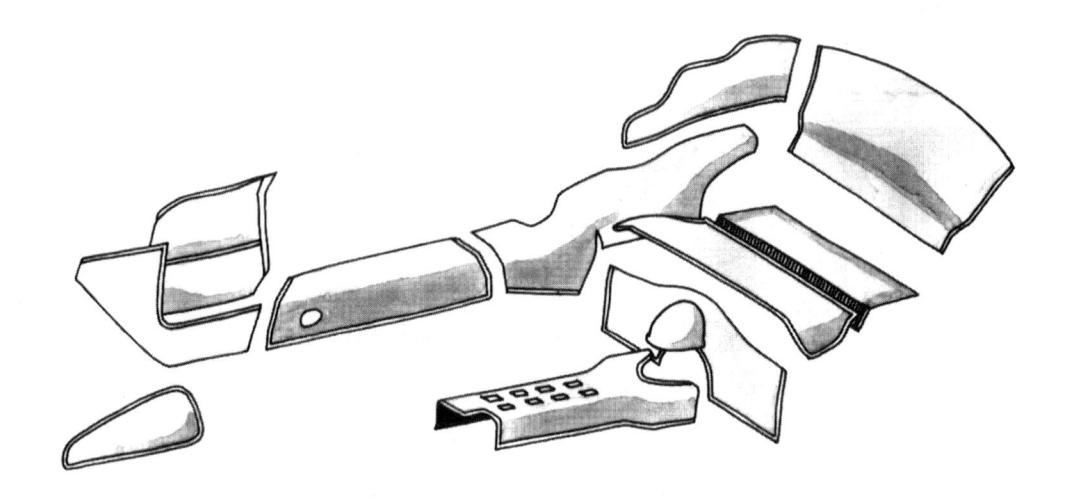

356 cabriolet

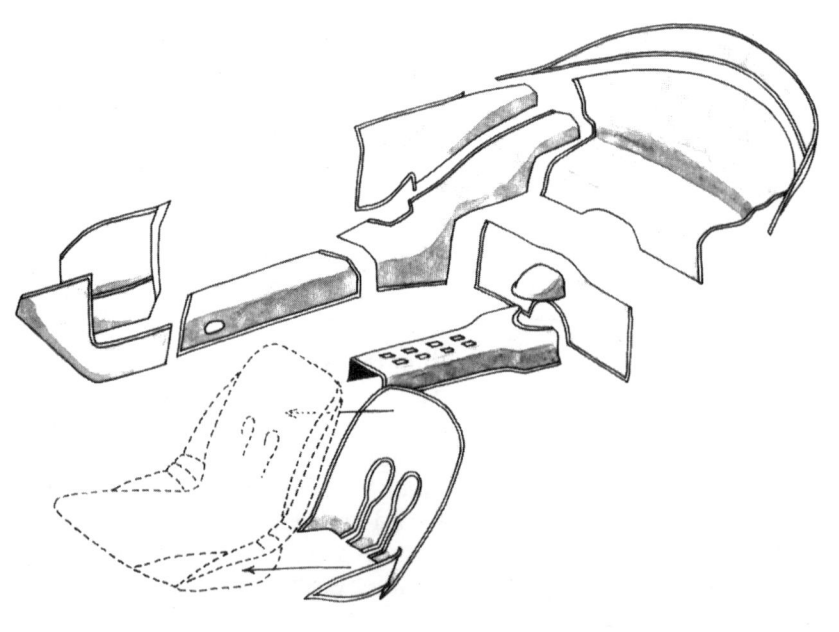

Speedster

Early 356A coupe

Early 356A cabriolet

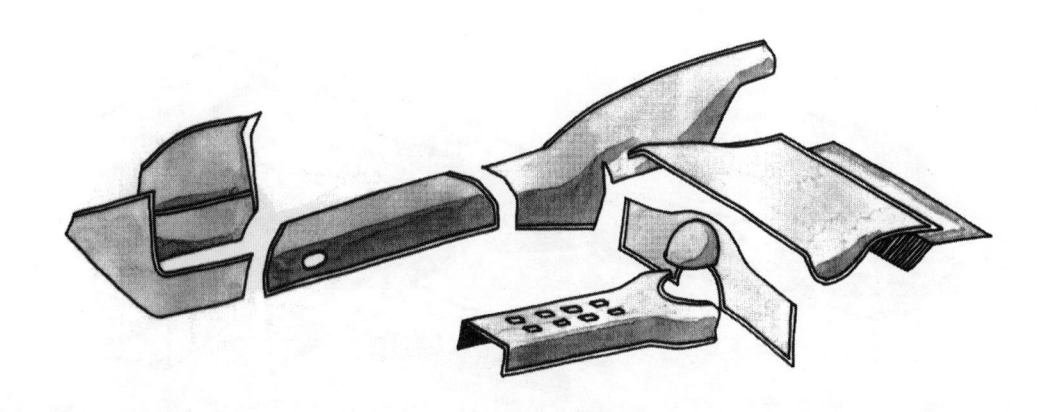

T 2 356A coupe

T 2 356A cabriolet

Convertible D/Roadster

T 5 356B coupe

T 5 356B cabriolet

Karmann Hardtop

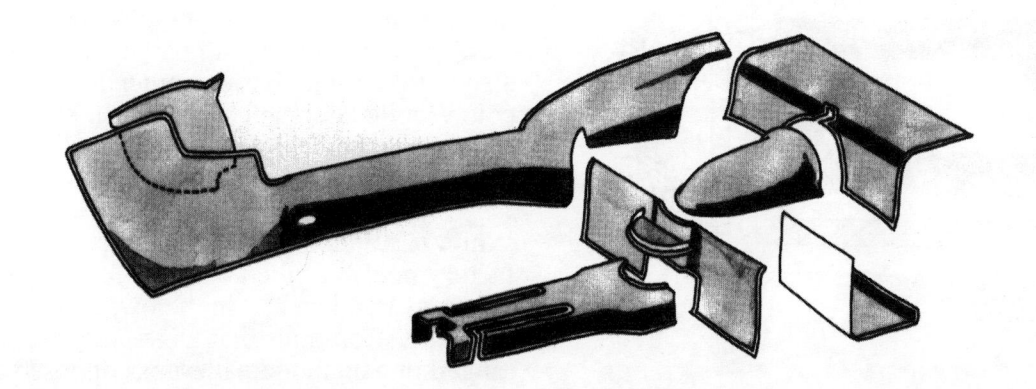

T 6 coupe

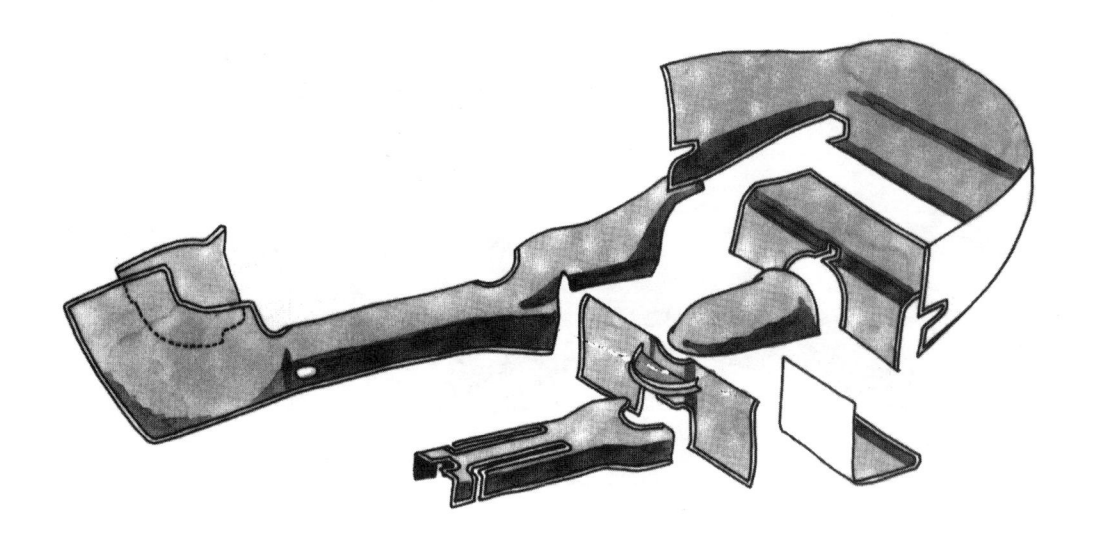

T 6 cabriolet

Careful inspection revealed that original installation was carried out not only with glue, but an occasional screw and a number of tacks which were actually hammered into the sheet metal. There were wood tack strips around the rear seat on some cars. Carpet was also retained in aluminum "grab" strips at the front of the door opening on pre-A coupes and cabriolets and front and back of the door opening on pre-A Speedsters.

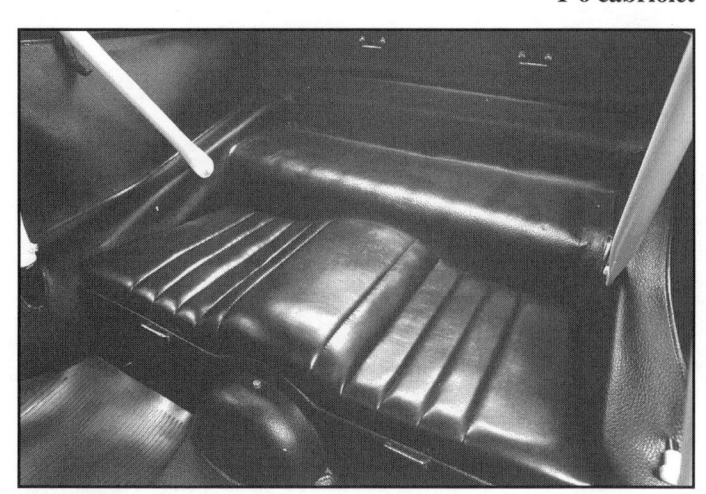

Early Carrera GTs had coarse-grained vinyl, where other models had carpet. Speedster seat backs were carpeted, including the rear seat back. Later cars had vinyl up front and carpet from the door jambs back.

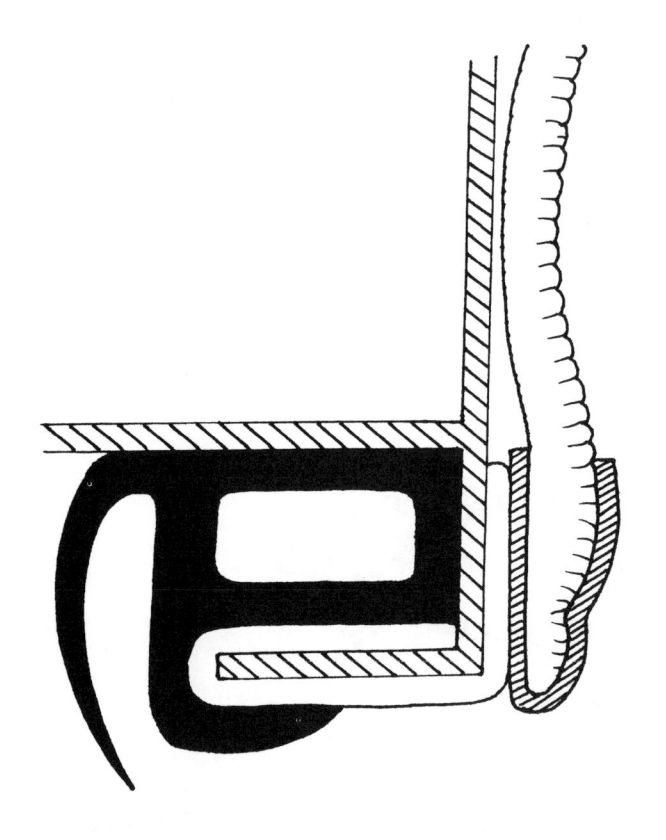

Headliners

It is interesting that both the 1953 and 1955 parts books listed a single headliner for coupes, but this is not the way it was. The 1953 through 1955 headliners were not compatible with earlier cars. Colors were also not the same. Early cars tended to be blue/grey in color, while later cars came in tan, as well. The material was napped cloth similar to that in early American cars.

White perforated vinyl headliners, according to the factory books, arrived with the 356A model change. This was not disputed in the owner's survey. This vinyl had perforations that were pierced and were arranged in a diamond pattern, as opposed to a square pattern. The holes are neither round nor perfectly punched. Perforated white vinyl graced not only the inside roof but the pillars of the roof in the 356.

Cross section through door jamb area on cars with aluminum grab strips

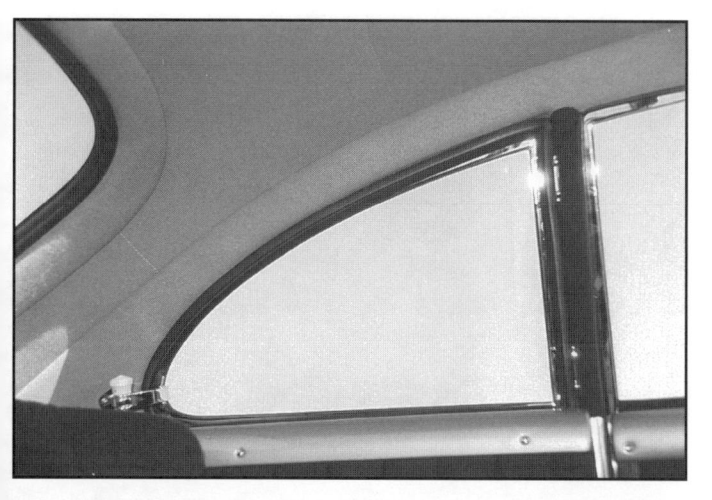

Early cloth headliner, rear

Roadster showing corduroy covered bows and top padding

Early cloth headliner, front

Roadster front bow covered with headliner material

While on the subject of white vinyl headliners, there were four basic types: 1) for 356A and T 5 356B coupes; 2) for 356A and T 5 356B sunroof coupes; 3) for T 6 356B and 356C coupes; 4) for T 6 356B and 356C sunroof coupes with zipper for electric motor access. The change for the sunroof was obvious, and the change from T 5 to T 6 was based on the revised windshield and rear glass.

Speedsters, Roadsters and Convertible Ds were "bottom-of-the-line" vehicles and had no headliner. Cabriolets though, always had a headliner; a single 356 style was mentioned in the 1955 parts book. Moving on to the 356A, the familiar herringbone pattern headliner was adopted. A change in headliners was noted at 15001 (T 2), when the change from the rear wooden tack strip to the removable soft top occurred. There

White vinyl headliner

Padded cabriolet headliner

T 6 sunroof coupe headliner had a zipper for motor access.

was no change in 1960 for the 356B cabriolet or for the T 6 356B nor 356C cabriolets.

A removable hardtop appeared in 1958 with the T 2 model. Its headliner was perforated vinyl like the coupe's. T 6 356Bs had a different part number, which probably has something to do with the opening quarter windows. No additional changes were made. Karmann Hardtops mirrored the changes on hardtops.

Coat Hook

Coat hooks in pre-1957 356 coupes were polished aluminum and were found on the inner B-pillar on both sides. For some curious reason they were illustrated with the bumpers in the 1955 parts book.

Starting with the 1957 356A, coupes (and removable hardtops and Karmann Hardtops) had tan rubber coat hooks. They were not changed from that point until 1969 (being used in early 911 and 912 models). While in most instances the original hooks weathered badly, developing surface cracks, their original color was generally tan. Grey hooks were also made by Porsche, but it is uncertain if these were used during production.

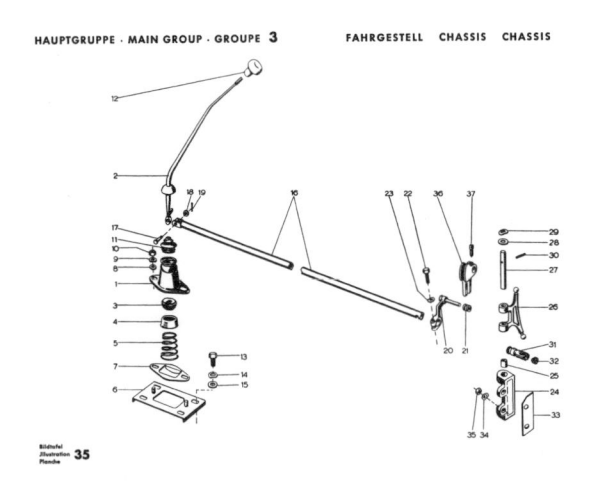

Illustration 35, 356A Parts Book.

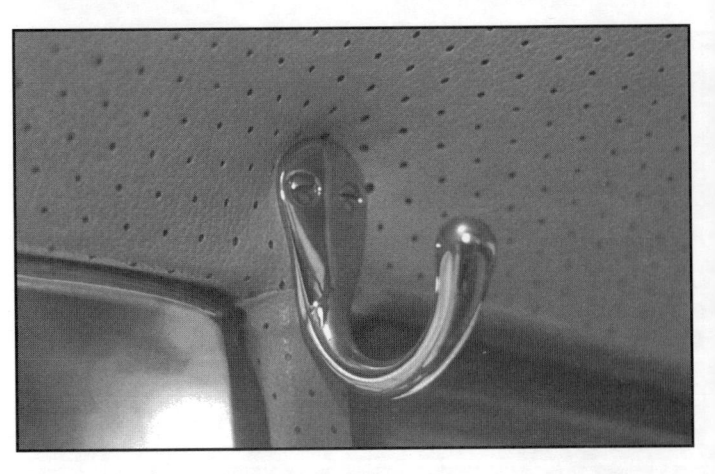

Early metal coat hook.

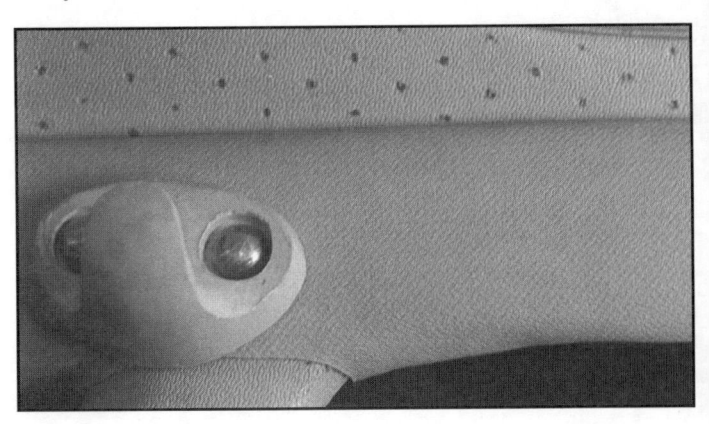

Tan rubber coat hook.

Upholstery

Materials in 356 upholstery ranged from cloth to vinyl to corduroy to leather. Most early cars were upholstered in cloth or leather. 1953 was a good year for corduroy. 1955 through 1965 official colors:

1950-55	1956-59	1960-61	1962-63	1964-65
Light Grey	Red	Red	Green	Red
Black	Beige	Lt. Grey	Black	Black
Red	Brown	Lt. Brown	Grey	Grey
Green	Green	Black	Lt. Brown	Green
Beige	Black	Blue	Blue	Blue
Blue		Dark Grey		
Yellow				
Beige/rose				

Two other generalities: cabriolets usually had leather seats and Roadsters usually had vinyl seats.

The familiar door panel with a pocket at the bottom was on most models. Speedsters and most, if not all, 1953 cars had no pockets. In addition, the early cars varied in the way the pocket was constructed (see photos). The pocket with locking clasp was seen on Convertible D and Roadster models, generally only on the driver's side, although they were optional for the passenger's door. Locking pockets were used because there were no glove boxes on these models.

Early door panel with wood top

Before Model 52 coupes wood was below the quarter window.

1953 corduroy door panel with VW knobs and escutcheons; note "flat" grab handle and lack of lower pocket.

Unusual two-tone treatment on a 1956 356A door with Porsche knobs and escutcheons

Cabriolet and coupe door panels were in all cases identical and interchangeable. The material generally matched that covering the seats, except in the case where leather seats were in otherwise vinyl upholstered cars. Leather seats were standard in cabriolets; however, they were not always present. The option of leather seats in coupes or full leather upholstery was available in all models.

Coupes featured vinyl or leather rear compartment panels; other models were carpeted in this area. Rear quarter panels had upholstery on all models except Speedsters and Roadsters which were carpeted. On cabriolets from T 2, these panels were removable; separate panels for soft top or hard top were used. Karmann hardtops had panels similar, but not identical to coupes.

The very plain Speedster door panel

T 2 through T 5 door panel

125

Convertible Ds and Roadsters had a locking compartment on the driver's side door panel.

Light weight equipment on a 356SC GT

cars and continuing on with 356C cars, this piece was covered in vinyl or leather to match the door panel. On coupes the trim piece over the rear quarter interior panel was similar to the trim molding on the door described above.

Speedsters, due to their side curtains, had a modified door molding. It was vinyl covered, matching the door panels, and had receptacles front and rear for attaching the side curtains. Vinyl covering continued for Convertible Ds and Roadsters.

Door Handles, Window Cranks, Etc.

Interior door handles were of VW origin. The models through T 2 featured a double-ribbed variety as used on similar year VWs. From T 2 on, the handles had a more rounded cross section.

Convertible Ds and Roadsters had either the locking compartment on the passenger's side door panel or just a simple pocket, as above.

The molding at the top of the door panel was wood on 356 coupes through 11360 and cabriolets through 10270 (Model 51). Starting at coupe 11361 and cabriolet 10271, this became a painted metal part. Prior to 356As the paint color matched the dashboard color. On 356A and T 5 356Bs it was a complementary color to the upholstery and matched the inner color of the windshield frame on cabriolets. Starting with T 6

Changes in window cranks followed those in door handles with one additional change. Cars through the 1953 model year had VW window cranks, while 1954 through 1959 cars had Porsche knobs affixed to a VW crank. Colors of knobs: 1950 through 1953, ivory only; 1954 through 1959, ivory, beige, or grey (matches dashboard knobs); and 1960 through 1965, black.

Arm rest used through the T 6; note upholstered door cap.

Combination arm rest and door pull, 356C

The color of escutcheons (those things between door handle/window crank and upholstery) was the same as the knob color. Three different types of escutcheons were used: 1) 1950 - 1953, VW type; 2) 1954 through 1957, large 2 inch diameter, and 3) 1958 (T 2) through 1965, small 1 1/2 inch diameter.

When the wood door-top molding was replaced on the Model 52, a chrome door pull was added to the top of the door panel on all subsequent models except Speedsters and 356Cs. Early ones were flat while later ones were bowed allowing easier grip. The change occurred in late 1958 or early 1959.

Arm rests were standard on 356Cs and were optional as early as 1959. The earlier arm rests fit entirely flush to the door panel, while the ones on 356Cs fit flush only at the ends, with a "finger grip" in the middle. Arm rests with "finger grips" replaced the chrome door pulls as the appropriate way to close the door from the inside.

A final piece of door-related trim was the mirror access plug on each door. These devices made it possible to remove or install door mirrors without removing the interior door panel. They first appeared in May or June 1957 prior to the introduction of the T 2 body style. These first covers were flat plastic with a slightly beveled edge. They were silver in color and held in place by two tabs. At or around the T 6 body change a dished black plastic plug replaced the earlier style.

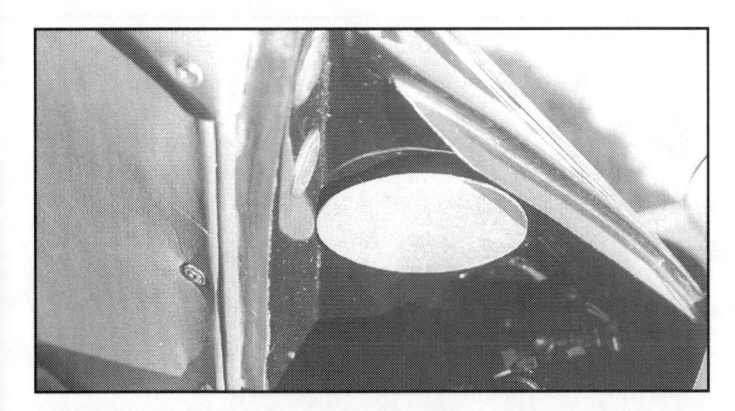

Early silver plastic mirror access plug

Late, dished mirror access plug

T 5 hinge post showing light switch and manufacturer's plate with chassis and paint numbers

Hinge Post

The only item of interest on the hinge post was the switch that turned on the interior light when the door opened. These were in the center of the top door hinge on both driver's and passenger's side doors. Cabriolets and Speedsters did not share this feature through the end of 1955, since they did not have interior lights. 356As had the same switch as the earlier cars. Since cabriolets now had interior lights, they used the same switch arrangement. Speedsters (and subsequent Convertible Ds and Roadsters) still lacked interior lighting.

The switches changed at coupe 100001 and cabriolet 61701 (March 1957, when the tail lights changed). These were used until the final evolution took place at the T 6 356B body introduction.

Also located on the hinge post was the body manufacturer's plate which had the chassis number stamped on it. Paint plates were located below the manufacturer's plate. These did not always have the paint number on them.

Threshold Trim

The body area under the door bottom consisted of two aluminum trim rails, rubber mat, threshold seal and steel channel. The illustration on the following page shows the configuration. No changes were made to these components. The aluminum trim rails were held in place by chrome-plated slotted sheet metal screws until mid-1955 when they were replaced by Phillips-head screws. The steel channel was mounted with slotted sheet metal screws.

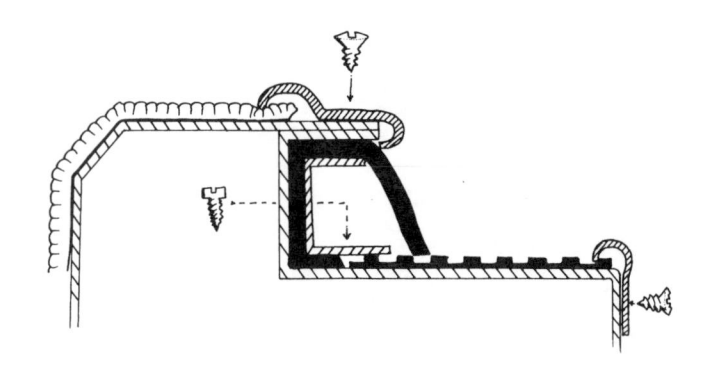

Cross section through the threshold area

Lock Posts

Striker plates, at the back of the door opening, had two basic forms: the five-bolt and three-bolt. A five-bolt striker plate was used the first seven years. The first variety, to coupe 11360 and cabriolet 10269, had a flat inner surface. The second type fit from coupe 11361 to 53288, cabriolet 10270 to 60779 and Speedster 80001 to 82000; it had a small lump at the level of the middle screw hole. The third variety had a substantially smaller cut-out and was used from coupe

The first style of five bolt striker plate

Third type of five bolt striker and aluminum wedge

Three bolt striker plate

53289 through 101692, cabriolet 60780 through 150000 and Speedster 82001 through 83791. These striker plates were held to the door jamb by five slotted screws with a bolt plate at the rear.

All subsequent cars had three-bolt striker plates. These were mounted with Phillips-head screws and had bolt plates similar to the earlier versions. Screw heads on all striker plates were painted black.

The only other occupant of the lock post was the metal guide below the striker plate. The purpose of this item was to direct the door into proper position when closing. A rubber wedge on the door slid into the guide and also helped keep the door from rattling. The guide was made from aluminum though the earliest ones were brass. This item was deleted in 1959. The survey results show the change between coupes 107664 and 107922.

Heat Vents

Down by the front of the seats was a hole in the inner longitudinal member. In the first 356s this was covered by a pivoting carpet flap. No mention of this was made in the parts manual. On the Model 52 the flat aluminum-style heater slide replaced the carpet flap (1951 Gläser cabriolet 5142 had slides) and, with the exception of some early Speedsters, was used from then until the introduction of the 356B.

Carpet flap heat vent

128

Even though pre-A Speedsters had no defroster vents, slides are generally present on restored cars. Several unrestored original cars had an aluminum "kringle" fixed to the carpet over the heater outlet.

The T 5 356B featured a more directional, all-aluminum heater slide. It was mounted by four self-tapping screws. According to the parts book, 356Cs were unchanged, but that just isn't so: the slide part became black plastic and mounted with six screws.

356 Speedster with "kringle"

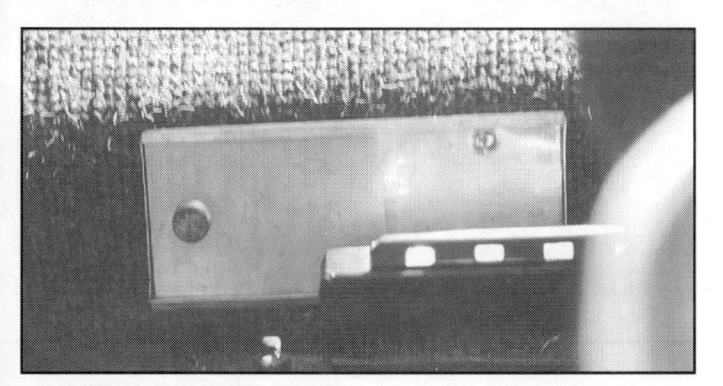

The first style aluminum slide

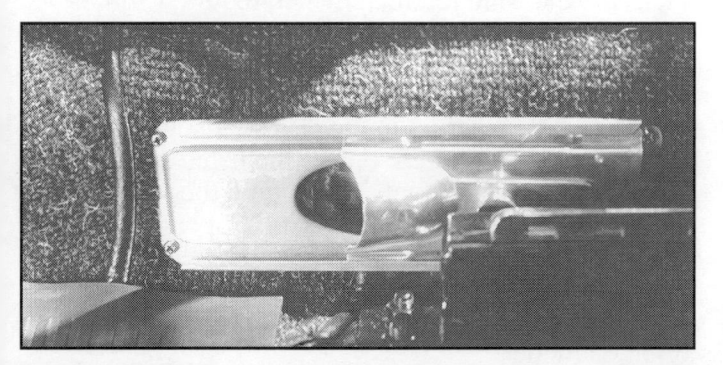

356B heater slide

356C heater slide

Seats

The general configuration of seating in 356 models was two bucket seats in the front with occasional seating in the rear.

Front buckets on the first 356s were non-reclining. According to the parts book, these were used until coupe 52029, and cabriolet 60549 (1953 model year), when reclining seats became standard.

The 1953 parts book distinguished between seats for a Model 51 and Model 52 as shown in the illustration: 356.59.023 and 356.59.024 for the 1951, 356.59.025 and 356.59.026 for the 1952. Differences appear to be that the 1951 (and earlier) had a flatter back, and the top of the side hinge plates were covered by upholstery where they attached to the back. The Model 52 had a slightly curved back, and the boomerang-shaped hinges were mounted externally by screws. Above the hinge was an upholstered extension. Neither of these was a reclining bracket. Since the parts book covered up through 1953, this would infer no recliners until at least the end of 1953 (the 1954 model), but these two non-reclining seats were available.

The early unrevised (i.e. no "644" numbers) January 1955 parts book appeared to pin down the introduc-

The top half of the first seat hinge brackets were covered by the seat upholstery

Second style hinge bracket bolted to the outer seat back

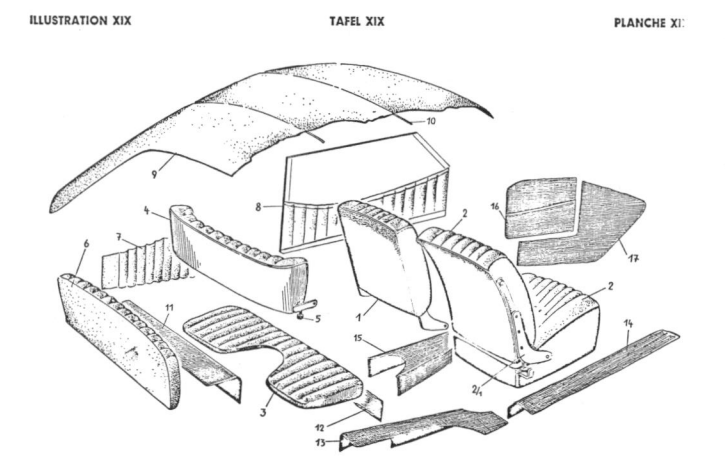

Illustration 19, 1953 Parts Book

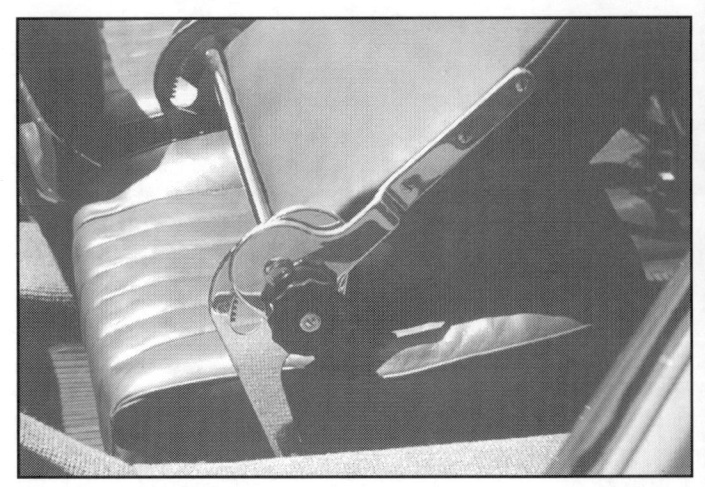

Keiper reclining mechanism

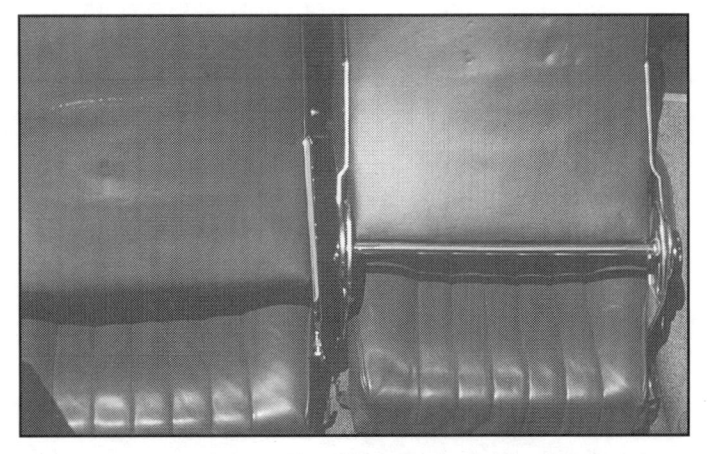

The non-reclining seat back (left) had no bar at bottom.

Recliners with thick seat backs were used from 1953 - 1957.

tion of the recliners but confused things by listing only one type of non-reclining seat and one reclining seat using new numbers. According to this source, the recliners were introduced at coupe 52010 and cabriolet 60550, which was in 1954. From the parts book, seats were available in genuine leather, artificial leather and artificial leather/corduroy combination.

Why were the 1951 and 1952 model seat part numbers deleted? A guess is that there was a new seat design offered in both reclining and non-reclining versions (for the older cars). Notice that the recliner seat bracket is part number 356.59.027 (and 028) in the original part number sequence and that the "standard" (non-reclining) hinge part numbers were the same in both books, 356.59.159 and 160, and were also listed as fitting chassis 5001-52029 and 5015-60549. From this one may conclude that the reclining and non-reclining hinges were interchangeable and that early cars could be retrofitted. There is evidence that reclining seats were optional despite the parts books info. The Kardex information on 1951 cabriolet 10158 mentions "reclaining seats." This car was also painted with a non-standard color, metallic green (number 232), leather interior, horn ring, slotted wheels and window washing system. Factory photos as early as 1951 also show Keiper recliners.

Further support for the absence of recliners on most early cars (at least up to about 1954) is given in advertisements from *Road and Track*, September 1954: Jack McAfee sold recliners which required "no changes to the Porsche seat" for installation. The units pictured were of German Keiper manufacture and were often found on early Mercedes-Benz and early Porsches. The other ad in the classifieds was for a 1953 1500 Super, where one of the listed selling points was reclining seat. These were the standard Recaro recliners that were fitted to all Supers on U.S. specification cars from the 1953 model year. On those with Normal engines reclining seats were optional. This was the Hoffman inspired "America" budget-oriented model.

Strange permutations out there? Of course. Chassis number 11994 had a reclining driver's seat with fixed passenger's seat; 51984 had a fixed driver's seat with reclining passenger's seat. Either could have been updated.

Bench seats are not listed, but a non-reclining one has been reported in a 1952 car; authenticity though is uncertain. The bench seat was listed as an option in the 1955 accessory catalog. It had individual reclining backs and used the same recliner mechanism as individual buckets.

130

Bench seat with individually reclining seat backs

T 2 through T 5 reclining seats

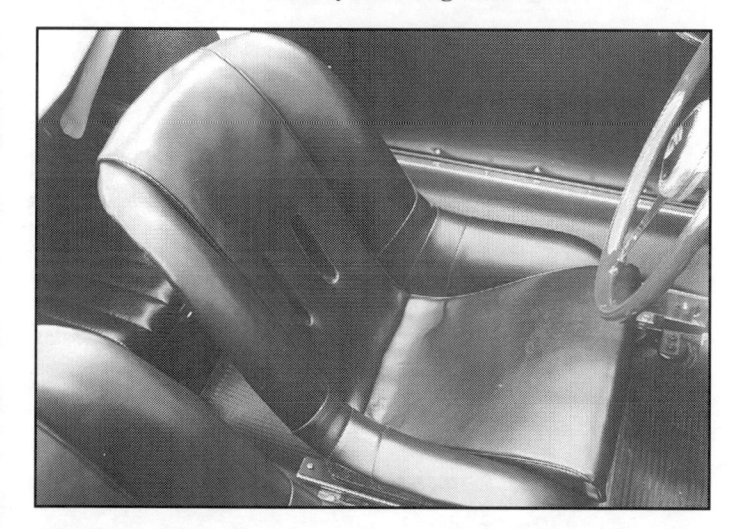

Speedster seat

Headrest that was used on 356s

According to the 356A parts book, the same reclining seat was used from coupe 55001-101692, cabriolet 61001-150000 and Speedster (optional) 82001-83791. These were wood-framed. The ending numbers in this series corresponds to the T 2 body change; the beginning numbers were likely incorrect. The earlier parts book was probably correct. The change at the T 2 body resulted in a thinner, lighter, less expensive seat with a pressed steel frame. Recliners were shorter, although overall appearance was similar.

The T 5 356B seat was identical to the late 356A's. A non-reclining seat was again available, this time on the Roadster, although reclining seats were optional. The T 6 was different; the main change was in the seat bottom, which was changed to accommodate the T 6 seat rails. The recliner mechanism was modified by adding a locking seat back function on the passenger's seat. 356Cs had a different cushion on the lower part of the seat, but no changes were made to the recliner.

Headrests were shown in the 356A accessories books printed in late 1955. They were available from 1953, possibly earlier. Attachment to the seat back was via screw-type brackets. These were available from at least 1953 through 1965.

Then, of course, there were the infamous Speedster seats. Appearing in late 1954, this steel-shelled seat had minimal padding and front mounted hinges (the first hundred or so Speedsters did not have forward hinging seats) on a wooden frame. This seat was standard in Speedsters and occasionally turned up in other models. Late GTs were aluminum rather than steel, for lighter weight. Later seats tended to be a bit wider.

Non-reclining Roadster seat

356C reclining seat; note flat sided recliner.

Rear seats in early 356s were often just lumps in the carpet. 1951 coupe 5430 had two square hog's hair pads that are under the carpet. There was also a bench-type rear seat covered in carpet, as well as vinyl/leather covered cushions, all seemingly quite authentic. Many very early cars had no rear seats at all.

There were three different hinged rear seat backs used between 1950 and 1959. Only one was mentioned in the parts book. One was used from 1953 through 1955 and while similar to the later one they were not interchangeable. From 1956 through 1959 they were essentially the same except that in 1958 the pleating changed. Before that, an unmentioned taller and narrower seat back was used on cabriolets. There was a central latch on some cars; in conjunction with this seat back, a full-width vinyl/leather-covered seat cushion was used.

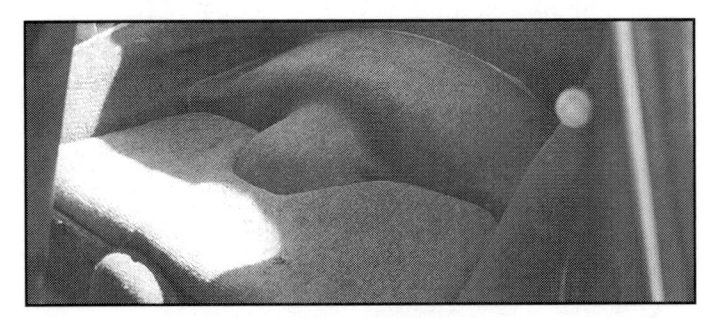

Early rear seat area; note lack of flat rear parcel shelf area.

Early cabriolet seat back

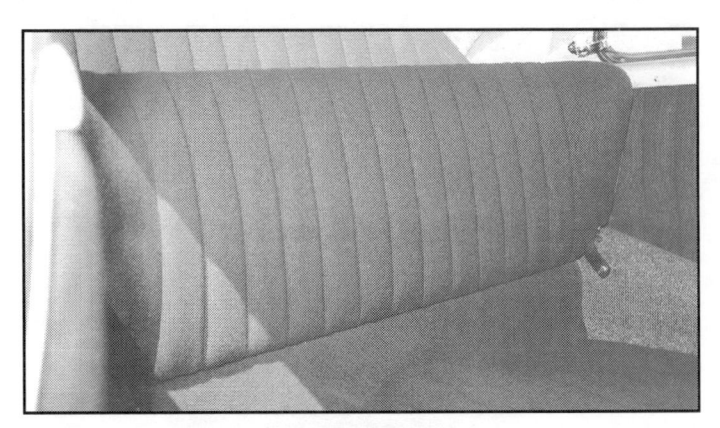

1952 coupe with early pleat pattern

This pleat pattern was used from 1953 through 1957.

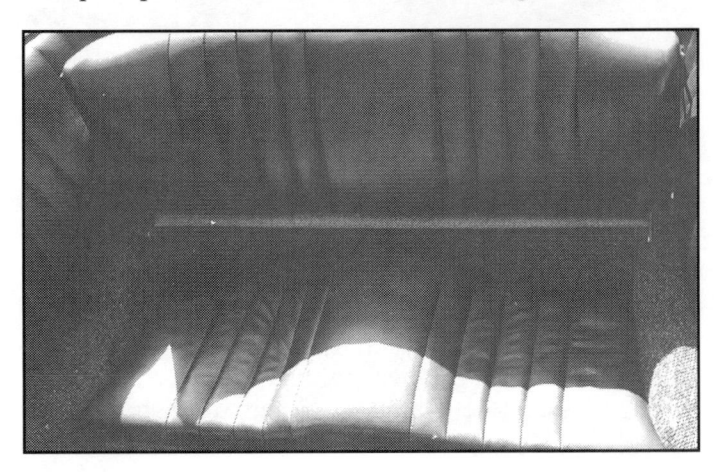

The pleat pattern used on T 2 seat backs

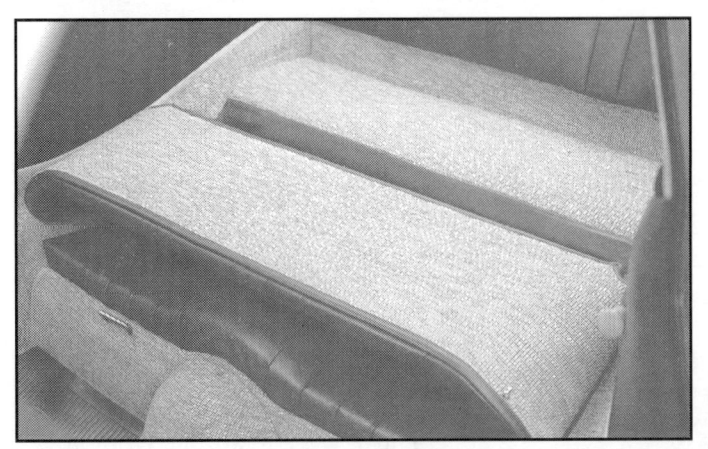

Seat back folded showing flat parcel shelf area behind

132

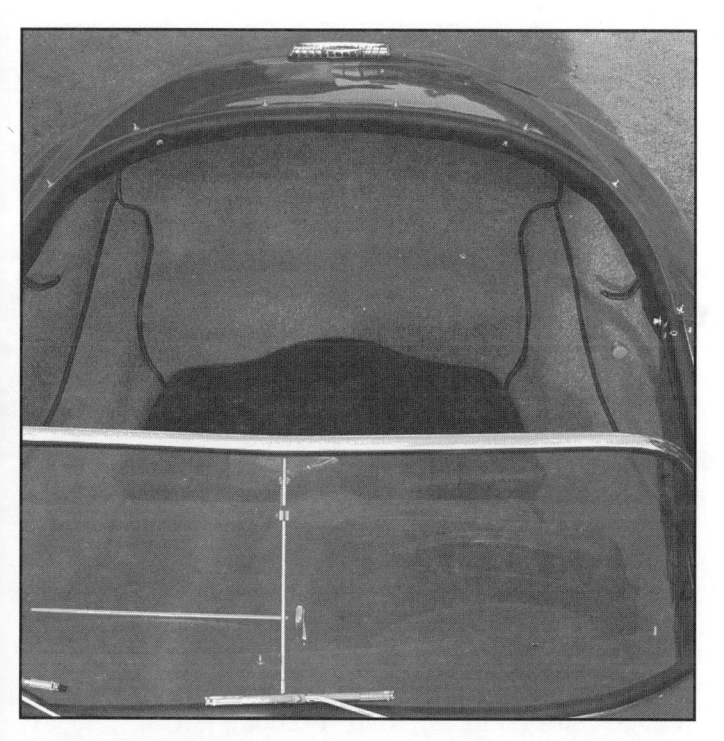

Standard Speedster rear seat area

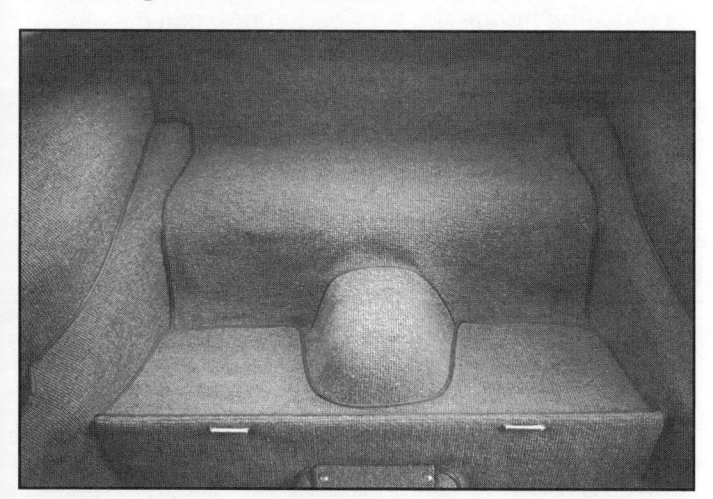

The Roadster rear compartment had no seat cushion or back, though a one-piece cushion was a rare option.

Bungee cord showing holding clip

356C rear seat area

Seat backs down with optional luggage straps

The unusual rear area of the Karmann Hardtop

All 356B cars had individual cushions. T 5 356Bs and T 6 356Bs were the same; however, 356Cs had shorter seat backs with a small up-turned edge at the top. Exceptions to rear seat back/cushion combinations:

1. Early 356s: variety of configurations.
2. Speedsters: cushion present, back optional, generally absent.
3. Convertible D: cushion absent, back absent.
4. Roadster: cushion optional, back absent.

One final note: bungee cords, generally white with tan hounds-tooth pattern, were supplied to hold seat backs upright from 1953 through 1959.

Appendicies:

Color Charts

The following color charts are the most accurate and complete available. They are substantially more detailed in the first few years than previously presented. This information has been procured from dealer color listings and factory documentation. There is a lack of consistency in format during the evolution of the 356, but this should not be surprising. With the exception of Speedsters, 1950 - 1955 cars were painted with nitrocellulose lacquer. Speedsters and all 1956 - 1966 cars had enamel finishes. Most of the exterior colors, including the very early ones, can be obtained from suppliers that carry BASF paint.

As a rule, most cabriolets had leather seat upholstery. Other models had vinyl with leather optional. Other upholstery, door panels, rear seats etc. were occasionally leather trimmed, as well. U.S. specification cars generally had vinyl inserts on the front seats, while in most other markets cloth/corduroy was predominantly used. Exceptions to this include 1950 - 1952 cars which commonly had cloth seats and door panels, though the storage pockets were vinyl, and the 1953 America series coupes, most of which had simplified corduroy interiors.

1950 - 1952 356

Records of the first few years of production at Porsche are a bit sketchy when it comes to color information. The following is the most recent "accumulation" of the codes and colors for the first three years. Much of this has been assembled by the 356 Porsche Split-Windscreen Register.

The numbers associated with these color listings were in some cases assigned by the coachbuilders, Reutter and Gläser. The duplication of colors may be due to this. It is likely that exterior and fabric colors and upholstery materials may have varied over time and between suppliers, as well as between the two coachbuilders.

Exterior Colors, Reutter

#	Color
501*	Black
502	Dark Blue
503	Maroon
504*	Ivory
505*	Fish Silver-Grey
506	Moor Green
509	Adria Blue
510*	Radium Green
511*	Light Grey
522*	Azure Blue
523*	Pascha Red
524*	Strawberry Red
526*	Palm Green
527*	Sand Grey
530	Penicillin White (Green?)
531*	Fashion Grey

Exterior Colors, Gläser

The following exterior colors used on Gläser cabriolets and America Roadsters were not used on Reutter cars. The numbers in the Reutter section to the left followed by an asterisk were also used on Gläser cars. All exterior paint used during this time period was lacquer.

White
Flame Red
Rosede Green
Red (#946 Glasso)
Sand Beige
Persian Blue

Standard Exterior Colors (Reutter July 1951)

Coupe

#	Color
501	Black
503	Maroon
504	Ivory
505	Fish Silver-Grey
506	Moor Green
509	Adria Blue
510	Radium Green

Cabriolet

#	Color
501	Black
522	Azure Blue
523	Pascha Red
524	Strawberry Red
526	Palm Green
527	Sand Grey
531	Fashion Grey

Upholstery – Cloth

Generally, this was corduroy or other textured cloth. It may have been used in combination with other cloth or vinyl.

3287	Green
3323	Beige-Rosé
3325	Brown
3326	Blue
3328	Blue
3361	Grey
3362	Beige
3363	Maroon
5287	Russ Green
?	Olive Green

Additionally, various plaid and checked cloths were offered.

Upholstery – Vinyl (leatherette)

145	Yellow Earth, ochre
309	Dark Blue
310	Blue-Grey
319	?
325	Grey-Green "leather"
335	Red (special)
356	Red
357	Green
358	Brown "textured"
359	Brown "leather"
365	Grey
366	Light Beige
368	Grey
378	Red, Rosanil brand
3090	Blue

Upholstery – Leather

2150	Red
2152	Blue
2153	Hound's Tooth (light grey w/ black highlights)
2154	Light Beige
2155	Dark Green
2161	Grey
2164	Beige
2169	Brown
2180	Beige-Rosé

Headliner & Side Upholstery

511	Beige
512	Blue-Grey
3256	Brown?
3292	Black?
3288	Green
3360	Tan/Beige
3364	Blue-Grey, napped cloth
3365	Tan, napped cloth
3366	Brown?
3367	?

Carpet – Velour

685	Blue
691	Green
692	Tan/Brown

Carpet – Square Weave, Bouclé

678	Blue
679	Light Grey
680	Green
687	?
695	Beige
697	Dark Tan
803	?

Top & Tonneau, Cabriolet

100	Beige
110	Beige-Rosé
521	Grey-Blue
5101	Black
5102	Dark Blue
5106	Grey
5108	Beige
5109	Brown
5111	Blue-Grey
6325	Gray-Green

1953

The following information was collected from an undated dealer sample book. Based on the limited selections, we have surmised that it is from 1953, although other combinations from the previous page are potentially correct for this model year. With the exception of the exterior color names, which are the actual Porsche/Reutter names, the other colors are descriptive, based on their appearance in the sample book. No color numbers were listed other than color package number listed at the left.

Coupe

Reutter #	Color	Vinyl	Cloth
R501CS	Black	tan textured vinyl speckled w/ brown dots	tan corduroy
R501B	Black	reddish brown vinyl	no cloth
R501C	Black	medium dark green textured vinyl	no cloth
R504A	Ivory	reddish brown vinyl	no cloth
R504B	Ivory	medium dark green textured vinyl	no cloth
R510 CS	Radium Green	tan textured vinyl speckled w/ brown dots	tan corduroy
R523CS	Pascha Red	tan textured vinyl speckled w/ brown dots	tan corduroy
R523B	Pascha Red	grey heavily textured vinyl	no cloth
R526CS	Palm Green	tan textured vinyl speckled w/ brown dots	tan corduroy
R526B	Palm Green	"oyster" white heavily textured vinyl	no cloth
R531CS	Fashion Grey	grey textured vinyl speckled w/ grey dots	grey corduroy

Cabriolet

Reutter #	Color	Interior (leather)	Top
C501A	Black	reddish brown	tan
C501B	Black	medium dark green	tan
C501C	Black	light tan	tan
C522A	Azure Blue	light tan	tan
C522B	Azure Blue	grey	grey
C523A	Pascha Red	light tan	tan
C524A	Strawberry Red	light tan	tan
C524B	Strawberry Red	black	grey
C526A	Palm Green	light tan	tan
C527A	Sand Grey	reddish brown	mahogany
C531A	Fashion Grey	grey/blue	dark blue
C531B	Fashion Grey	reddish brown	black

Optional leather:

2150 reddish brown   2152 grey/blue   2153 grey
2154 light tan   2155 med dark green

1954 - 1955 356

Porsche #	Reutter #	Exterior Color *	**Coupe** Upholstery (leatherette)	Knobs	**Cabriolet** Upholstery (leather)	Carpet	Lugg. comp.	Headliner	Top/Boot
5401	501	Black	A beige w/ cord. inserts B red or green	beige beige	A red Rosanil 378 B green 2155 C beige	beige 2505 green beige	red vinyl green vinyl beige vinyl	beige rosé 3360 green beige	beige 5108 beige 5108 beige 5108
5402	538	Turkish Red	A beige w/ beige cord. B yellow	beige beige	beige rosé 2180	beige	beige vinyl	beige rosé	beige 5108 beige rosé 110
5403	537	Graphite Metallic	A beige w/ beige cord. B yellow	beige beige	beige 2164	beige	beige vinyl	beige	beige 5108
5404	504	Ivory	A green w/ beige cord. B red w/ beige cord. *also red or green*	beige beige beige					
5405	536	Jade Green Metallic	A yellow w/ beige cord. B yellow	beige beige	beige 2164	beige	beige vinyl	beige	gray/green C 6325
5406	535	Silver Metallic	A red w/ grey cord. B red or green	grey grey	red Rosanil 378	grey 679	red vinyl	grey	black 5101
5407	534	Pearl Grey	A blue w/ grey cord. B red	grey grey	blue 2152	blue 678	blue vinyl	grey	grey/blue 521
5408	522	Azure Blue	A grey w/ grey cord. B yellow	grey beige	grey 2161	grey 679	grey vinyl	grey	grey 5106
5409	533	Terra Cotta	A grey w/ grey cord. B wine red or blue	grey grey	yellow earth 145	terracotta 363	yellow earth	yellow earth	beige 100
(from September 1954) 5410	509	Adria Blue Metallic							

Speedster

Porsche #	Reutter #	Exterior Color *	Upholstery (leatherette)			Carpet			Top
—	601	Signal Red (Fire Red)	Acella bast (basket-weave) cream black			tan dark tan w/ black vinyl binding			tan black
—	602	Speedster Blue (Sky Blue)	Acella bast (basket-weave) cream			tan			tan
—	603	White	black red			dark tan w/ black vinyl binding red			black black

* Coupe and cabriolet exterior paint was nitrocellulose lacquer. Speedster colors were enamel.

1956 356A

Coupe

Porsche #	Reutter #	Exterior Color*	Upholstery (leatherette)	Dashboard Paint	Upholstery
5601	701	Black	A beige w/ beige cord. inserts B red C green	beige beige beige	black black black
5602	604	Polyantha Red	A beige w/ beige cord. inserts B Naturbast beige**	Polyantha Polyantha	dark red dark red
5603	737	Graphite Metallic	beige w/ viscose silk fabric	beige	graphite
5604	605	Sahara Beige	A Carskin 132 beige comb. B red	red beige	dark red dark red
5605	606	Lago Green Metallic	A Carskin 132 beige comb.*** B Carskin 133 beige comb.	Lago Green Lago Green	dark green dark green
5606	608	Silver Metallic	A red B green	silver silver	dark red green
5607	607	Aquamarine Blue Metallic	A red B grey w/ grey cord. inserts	red Aquamarine	dark red blue

Cabriolet

Porsche #	Upholstery (leather)	Dashboard Paint	Upholstery
5601	A beige B green C red	black black black	black green black
5602	beige	Polyantha	dark red
5603	beige	Graphite	graphite
5604	red	red	red
5605	beige	Lago Green	dark green
5606	A red B green	red dark green	red green
5607	A grey B red	blue red	dark blue dark red

* As of the 1956 model year, all exterior paint was enamel
** Available in beige leatherette without charge
*** Viscose silk fabric

1957 - 1959 356A

Porsche #	Reutter #	Exterior Color	Coupe Upholstery (leatherette)	Cabriolet Dashboard	Cabriolet Upholstery (leather seats)	Speedster Top	Speedster Upholstery (leatherette)
5701	701	Black	A red A/C red w/ red cord. inserts B beige B/C beige w/ beige cord. inserts	red	A red	beige	A red
5702	702	Ruby Red	A beige A/C beige w/ beige cord. inserts B brown B/C brown w/ brown cord. inserts	black red	B beige A beige	black black	B beige A tan
5703	703	Meissen Blue	A red A/C red w/ red cord. inserts B brown B/C brown w/ brown cord. inserts	red brown	B brown A red	black black	B black A red
5704	704	Ivory	A red A/C red w/ red cord. inserts B black B/C brown w/ brown cord. inserts	red brown	B brown A red	black black	B black A red
5705	705	Fjord Green	A beige A/C beige w/ beige cord. inserts B brown B/C brown w/ brown cord. inserts	brown brown	B brown A beige	black beige	B black A brown
5706	608	Silver Metallic	A red A/C red w/ red cord. inserts B green B/C green w/ green cord. inserts	red green	A red B green	black	B tan A red
5707	707	Aquamarine Blue	A red A/C red w/ red cord. inserts B brown B/C brown w/ brown cord. inserts	red brown	A red B brown	black	B black A red
							B light brown

SPECIAL PAINTS:

Porsche #	Reutter #	Exterior Color	Coupe Upholstery (leatherette)	Cabriolet Dashboard	Cabriolet Upholstery (leather seats)	Speedster Top	Speedster Upholstery (leatherette)
5710	710	Stone Grey	A red A/C red w/ red cord. inserts B brown B/C brown w/ brown cord. inserts	red brown	A red B brown	black	A red B black
5711	711	Orange	A beige A/C beige w/ beige cord. inserts B black	brown black	A black	black	A light brown
5712	712	Auratium Green	A beige A/C beige w/ beige cord. inserts B brown	brown brown	A beige	beige	B black A beige
5713	713	Glacier White	B/C brown w/ brown cord. inserts B brown B/C green w/ green cord. inserts	brown green	A black B green	black black	B brown B black

1960 - 1961 356B

Coupe & Hardtop
Upholstery (leatherette)

Cabriolet & Roadster
Upholstery (leather seats for cabriolets)

Porsche #	Reutter #	Exterior Color	Coupe & Hardtop Upholstery	Cabriolet & Roadster Upholstery
6001	741	Slate Grey	A red	A red
			A/C red w/ "Bordeaux" cord. inserts	
			D light grey	D light grey
			D/C light grey w/ "Stone" cord. inserts	
			C light brown	C light brown
6002	702	Ruby Red	C/C light brown w/ "Birch" cord. inserts	
			D light grey	D light grey
			D/C light grey w/ "Stone" cord. inserts	
6003	740	Aetna Blue	A red	A red
			A/C red w/ "Bordeaux" cord. inserts	
			D light grey	D light grey
			D/C light grey w/ "Stone" cord. inserts	
6004	738	Ivory	A red	A red
			A/C red w/ "Bordeaux" cord. inserts	
			B black	B black
			B/C black w/ "Mouse" cord. inserts	
6005	705	Fjord Green	C light brown	C light brown
			C/C light brown w/ "Birch" cord. inserts	
			D light grey	D light grey
			D/C light grey w/ "Stone" cord. inserts	
6006	608	Silver Metallic	A red	A red
			A/C red w/ "Bordeaux" cord. inserts	
			F blue	F blue
			F/C blue w/ "Pearl" cord. inserts	
6007	639	Heron Grey	A red	A red
			A/C red w/ "Bordeaux" cord. inserts	
			F blue	F blue
			F/C blue w/ "Pearl" cord. inserts	

SPECIAL PAINTS:

Porsche #	Reutter #	Exterior Color	Coupe & Hardtop Upholstery	Cabriolet & Roadster Upholstery
6010	743	Condor Yellow	B black	B black
			B/C black w/ "Mouse" cord. inserts	
			E dark grey	E dark grey
			E/C dar grey w/ "Stone" cord. inserts	
6011	601	Signal Red	B black	B black
			B/C black w/ "Mouse" cord. inserts	
			D light grey	D light grey
6012	742	Royal Blue	B black	B black
			B/C black w/ "Mouse" cord. inserts	
			D light grey	D light grey
			D/C light grey w/ "Stone" cord. inserts	
6013	701	Black	A red	A red
			A/C red w/ "Bordeaux" cord. inserts	
			C light brown	C light brown
			C/C light brown w/ "Birch" cord. inserts	

1962 - 1963 356B

Porsche #	Reutter #	Exterior Color	Coupe & Hardtop Upholstery (leatherette)	Cabriolet & Roadster Upholstery (leather seats for cabriolets)
6201	741	Slate Grey	A red	A red
			A/C red w/ red cord. inserts	G green
			G green	B black
			G/C green w/ green cord. inserts	D grey
6202	702	Ruby Red	B black	A red
			B/C black w/ Mouse Grey cord. inserts	D grey
			D grey	H brown
			D/C grey w/ Pearl Grey cord. inserts	A red
6203	745	Oslo Blue	A red	G green
			A/C red w/ red cord. inserts	B black
			D grey	A red
			D/C grey w/ Pearl Grey cord. inserts	F blue
6204	738	Ivory	H brown	G green
			H/C brown w/ brown cord. inserts	H brown
			A red	
			A/C red w/ red cord. inserts	
6205	747	Champagne Yellow	G green	H brown
			G/C green w/ green cord. inserts	D grey
			B black	
			B/C black w/ Mouse Grey cord. inserts	
6206	608	Silver Metallic	A red	B black
			A/C red w/ red cord. inserts	D grey
			F blue	
			F/C blue w/ Pearl Grey cord. inserts	
6207	739	Heron Grey	G green	C light brown
			G/C green w/ green cord. inserts	D grey
			H brown	
			H/C brown w/ brown cord. inserts	

SPECIAL PAINTS:

Porsche #	Reutter #	Exterior Color	Coupe & Hardtop	Cabriolet & Roadster
6210	744	Smyrna Green	H brown	A red
			H/C brown w/ brown cord. inserts	G green
			D grey	
			D/C grey w/ Pearl Grey cord. inserts	
6211	601	Signal Red	B black	
			B/C black w/ Mouse Grey cord. inserts	
			D grey	
			D/C grey w/ Pearl Grey cord. inserts	
6212	746	Bali Blue	C light brown	
			C/C light brown w/ light brown cord. inserts	
			D grey	
			D/C grey w/ Pearl Grey cord. inserts	
6213	701	Black	A red	
			A/C red w/ red cord. inserts	
			G green	
			G/C green w/ green cord. inserts	

1964 - 1965 356C

Porsche #	Reutter #	Exterior Color	Coupe Upholstery (leatherette)	Cabriolet Upholstery (leather seats)
6401	—	Slate Grey	A red	A red
			A/C red w/ red cord. inserts	K fawn
			K fawn	
6402	—	Ruby Red	K/C fawn w/ fawn cord. inserts	B black
			B black	D grey
			B/C black w/ Mouse Grey cord. inserts	
6403	—	Sky Blue	D grey	A red
			D/C grey w/ Pearl Grey cord. insrets	K fawn
			A red	
6404	—	Light Ivory	A/C red w/ red cord. inserts	A red
			K fawn	B black
			K/C fawn w/ fawn cord. inserts	
6405	—	Champagne Yellow	A red	G green
			A/C red w/ red cord. inserts	B black
			B black	
			B/C black w/ Mouse Grey cord. inserts	
6406	—	Irish Green	G green	K fawn
			G/C green w/ green cord. inserts	D grey
			B black	
			B/C black w/ Mouse Grey cord. inserts	
6407	—	Signal Red	K fawn	B black
			K/C fawn w/ fawn cord. inserts	D grey
			D grey	
			D/C grey w/ Pearl Grey cord. inserts	
			B black	
			B/C black w/ Mouse Grey cord. inserts	
			D grey	
			D/C grey w/ Pearl Grey cord. insrets	

SPECIAL PAINTS:

Porsche #	Reutter #	Exterior Color	Coupe Upholstery (leatherette)	Cabriolet Upholstery (leather seats)
6410	—	Dolphin Grey	F blue	F blue
			F/C blue w/ Pearl Grey cord. inserts	G green
			G green	
6411	—	Togo Brown	G/C green w/ green cord. inserts	G green
			G green	K fawn
			G/C green w/ green cord. inserts	
			K fawn	
6412	—	Bali Blue	K/C fawn w/ fawn cord. inserts	K fawn
			K fawn	D grey
			K/C fawn w/ fawn cord. inserts	
			D grey	
6413	—	Black	D/C grey w/ Pearl Grey cord. inserts	A red
			A red	G green
			A/C red w/ red cord. inserts	
			G green	
			G/C green w/ green cord. inserts	

Chassis Number List

Chassis numbers can be misleading. The number indicates the order in which the chassis was constructed, but not the order in which the car was completed or sold. Due to damage during assembly or component failures, cars many months out of sequence were completed and potentially fitted with trim and mechanical items that were used on cars being finished along side them. Cars built toward the end of a model year are frequently officially included in the next year's production. When a major change occurred, such as 356 to 356A, some unusual permutations were created. One of which, the 1955 356 Speedster fitted with a 1600 engine, is illustrated in this book. While these cars lead to confusion and controversy, it is not difficult to understand why they exist. It should be noted, however, that they are the exception, not the rule.

Engine numbers are also a bit troubling for some of the same reasons listed above. The numbers on the list should be considered relative. This is especially true at the beginning and end of a model or calendar year. The only way to verify which engine was fitted to which chassis is to examine the original factory records. For a nominal fee, this service is provided to owners of 356s by Porsche Cars North America in Reno, Nevada and Porsche AG in Stuttgart.

For years, the chassis number list that was contained in the *Porsche Spec's* book was the the gospel according to Porsche. In the early 1990s with the help of Olaf Lang at Porche AG and Marco Marinello, the following, more accurate list was compiled. It contains the several additional series of cars, Carrera engine types and exchange chassis numbers. It is interesting to note that some of the latter are duplicates of 1952 cabriolet numbers. A number of gaps in numerical series are not seen in the original Porsche list. Several typographical errors have been corrected, as well.

Year Mfg	Vehicle and Engine Model Designation		Engine Model	Crank-case	Carbu-retors	Stroke/ Bore	Compr. Ratio	HP (DIN) @ RPM	Engine Serial #
1950	**(356)**	356/1100	369	2 PB	32 PBI	64/73.5	7:1	40 @ 4200	0101 - 0411
1951		356/1100	369	2 PB	32 PBI	64/73.5	7:1	40 @ 4200	0412 - 0999
									10001 - 10137
		356/1300	506	2 PB	32 PBI	64/80	6.5:1	44 @ 4200	1001 - 1099
									20001 - 20821
	from Oct.	356/1500	527	2 RB	40 PBIC	74/80	7:1	60 @ 5000	30001 - 30737
1952		356/1100	369	2 PB	32 PBI	64/73.5	7:1	40 @ 4200	10138 - 10151
		356/1300	506	2 PB	32 PBI	64/80	6.5:1	44 @ 4200	20822 - 21297
	until Nov.	356/1500	527	2 RB	40 PBIC	74/80	7:1	60 @ 5000	30738 - 30750
	from Aug.	356/1500	546	2 PB	32 PBI	74/80	7:1	55 @ 4400	30751 - 31025
	from July	356/1500 S	528	2 RB	40 PBIC	74/80	8.2:1	70 @ 5000	40001 - 40117
1953		356/1100	369	2 PB	32 PBI	64/73.5	7:1	40 @ 4200	10152 - 10161
		356/1300	506	2 PB	32 PBI	64/80	6.5:1	44 @ 4200	21298 - 21636
		356/1500	546	2 PB	32 PBI	74/80	7:1	55 @ 4400	31026 - 32569
		356/1500 S	528	2 RB	40 PBIC	74/80	8.2:1	70 @ 5000	40118 - 40685
	from Sept.	356/1300 S	589	2 RB	32 PBI	74/74.5	8.2:1	60 @ 5500	50001 - 50017
1954		356/1100	369	2 PB	32 PBI	64/73.5	7:1	40 @ 4200	10162 - 10199
		356/1300	506	2 PB	32 PBI	64/80	6.5:1	44 @ 4200	21637 - 21780
	until Nov.	356/1300 S	589	2 RB	32 PBI	74/74.5	8.2:1	60 @ 5500	50018 - 50099
	July to Nov.	356/1300 A	506/1	2 PB	32 PBI	74/74.5	6.5:1	44 @ 4200	21781 - 21999
	until Dec.	356/1500	546	2 PB	32 PBI	74/80	7:1	55 @ 4400	32570 - 33899
	until Dec.	356/1500 S	528	2 RB	40 PICB	74/80	8.2:1	70 @ 5000	40686 - 40999
	From Nov.	356/1300	506/2	3 PB	32 PBI	74/74.5	6.5:1	44 @ 4200	22001 - 22021
	From Dec.	356/1300 S	589/2	3 RB	32 PBIC +	74/74.5	7.5:1	60 @ 5500	50101 - 50127
		356/1500	546/2	3 PB	32 PBI	74/80	7:1	55 @ 4400	33901 - 34119
		356/1500 S	528/2	3 RB	40 PICB	74/80	8.2:1	70 @ 5000	41001 - 41048
1955	until Oct.	356/1300	506/2	3 PB	32 PBI	74/74.5	6.5:1	44 @ 4200	22022 - 22245
		356/1300 S	589/2	3 RB	32 PBIC +	74/74.5	7.5:1	60 @ 5500	50101 - 50127
	from July	Carrera 1500	547	RB	40 PII-4	66/85	9.5:1	110 @ 6200	90001 - 90096
		356/1500	546/2	3 PB	32 PBI	74/80	7:1	55 @ 4400	34120 - 35790
		356/1500 S	528/2	3 RB	40 PICB	74/80	8.2:1	70 @ 5000	41049 - 41999
	from Oct.	356A/1300	506/2	3 PB	32 PBI	74/74.5	6.5:1	44 @ 4200	22246 - 22273
	(356A)	356A/1300 S	589/2	3 RB	32 PBIC +	74/74.5	7.5:1	60 @ 5500	50128 - 50135
	from Nov.	Carrera 1500 GS	547/1	RB	40 PII-4	66/85	9.0:1	100 @ 6200	90501 - 90959
		Carrera 1500 GT	547/1	RB	40 PII-4	66/85	9.0:1	110 @ 6200	90501 - 90959
	from Oct.	356A/1600	616/1	3 PB	32 PBIC	74/82.5	7.5:1	60 @ 4500	60001 - 60608
	from Sept.	356A/1600 S	616/2	3 RB	40 PICB	74/82.5	8.5:1	75 @ 5000	80001 - 80110
1956		356A/1300	506/2	3 PB	32 PBI	74/74.5	6.5:1	44 @ 4200	22274 - 22471
		356A/1300 S	589/2	3 RB	32 PBIC +	74/74.5	7.5:1	60 @ 5500	50136 - 50155
		Carrera 1500 GS	547/1	RB	40 PII-4	66/85	9.0:1	100 @ 6200	90501 - 90959
		Carrera 1500 GT	547/1	RB	40 PII-4	66/85	9.0:1	110 @ 6200	90501 - 90959
		356A/1600	616/1	3 PB	32 PBIC	74/82.5	7.5:1	60 @ 4500	60609 - 63926
		356A/1600 S	616/2	3 RB	40 PICB	74/82.5	8.5:1	75 @ 5000	80111 - 80756

Reutter Coupe	Karmann Coupe	Karmann Hardtop	Reutter Cabriolet	Gläser Cabriolet	Speedster		Model Years
5002 - 5013 5017 - 5018 5020 - 5026 5029 - 5032 5034 - 5104 5163 - 5410			5014 - 5015 5033 5115 5131	5001 5019 5027 - 5028 5105 - 5114 5116 - 5130			*1950*
5411 - 5600			5132 - 5138	5139 - 5162			
10531 - 11280			10001 - 10165	10351 - 10432			*Model 51*
11301 - 11360			10166 - 10211 10251 - 10270	10433 - 10469			
11361 - 11778			10271 - 10350 15001 - 15050	12301 - 12387			*Model 52*
11779 - 12084 50001 - 51231			15051 - 15116 60001 - 60394	The two above series include all America Roadsters			*1953 Model*
51232 - 52029			60395 - 60549				
52030 - 52844			60550 - 60693				*1954 Model*
52845 - 53008			60694 - 60722		80001 - 80200 (12223 = 80001)		*1955 Model*
53009 - 54223			60723 - 60923		80201 - 81234		
55001 - 55390			61001 - 61069				
55391 - 58311			61070 - 61499		82001 - 83156		

Year Mfg		Vehicle and Engine Model Designation	Engine Model	Crank-case	Carbu-retors	Stroke/Bore	Compr. Ratio	HP (DIN) @ RPM	Engine Serial #
1957	until Aug.	356A/1300	506/2	3 PB	32 PBI	74/74.5	6.5:1	44 @ 4200	22472 - 22999
		356A/1300 S	589/2	3 RB	32 PBIC +	74/74.5	7.5:1	60 @ 5500	50156 - 50999
		Carrera 1500 GS	547/1	RB	40 PII-4	66/85	9.0:1	100 @ 6200	90501 - 90959
		Carrera 1500 GT	547/1	RB	40 PII-4	66/85	9.0:1	110 @ 6200	90501 - 90959
		356A/1600	616/1	3 PB	32 PBIC	74/82.5	7.5:1	60 @ 4500	63927 - 66999
		356A/1600S	616/2	3 RB	40 PICB	74/82.5	8.5:1	75 @ 5000	80757 - 81199
	from Sept. **(356A T 2)**	Carrera 1500 GS	547/1	RB	40 PII-4	66/85	9.0:1	100 @ 6200	90501 - 90959
		Carrera 1500 GT	547/1	RB	40 PII-4	66/85	9.0:1	110 @ 6200	90501 - 90959
		356A/1600	616/1	3 PB	32 NDIX	74/82.5	7.5:1	60 @ 4500	67001 - 68216
		356A/1600 S	616/2	3 PB	32 NDIX	74/82.5	8.5:1	75 @ 5000	81201 - 81521
1958		356A/1600	616/1	3 PB	32 NDIX	74/82.5	7.5:1	60 @ 4500	68217 - 72468
		356A/1600 S	616/2	3 PB	32 NDIX	74/82.5	8.5:1	75 @ 5000	81522 - 83145
	from May	Carrera 1500 GT	692/0	RB	40 PII-4	66/85	9.0:1	110 @ 6400	91001 - 91037
			692/1	PB	40 PII-4	66/85	9.0:1	110 @ 6400	92001 - 92014
	from Aug.	Carrera 1600 GS	692/2	PB	40 PII-4	66/87.5	9.5:1	105 @ 6500	93001 - 93065
1959	from Feb.	Carrera 1600 GT	692/3	PB	W 40 DCM	66/87.5	9.8:1	115 @ 6500	95001 - 95114
	until Sept.	356A/1600	616/1	3 PB	32 NDIX	74/82.5	7.5:1	60 @ 4500	72469 - 79999
		356A/1600 S	616/2	3 PB	32 NDIX	74/82.5	8.5:1	75 @ 5000	83146 - 84770
	from Sept. **(356B T 5)**	356B/1600	616/1	3 PB	32 NDIX	74/82.5	7.5:1	60 @ 4500	600101 - 601500
		356B/1600 S	616/2	3 PB	32 NDIX	74/82.5	8.5:1	75 @ 5000	84771 - 85550
		356B/1600 S-90	616/7	3 PB	40 PII-4	74/82.5	9:1	90 @ 5500	800101 - 802000
		Carrera 1600 GS	692/2	PB	40 PII-4	66/87.5	9.5:1	105 @ 6500	93101 - 93138
		Carrera 1600 GT	692/3	PB	W 40 DCM	66/87.5	9.8:1	115 @ 6500	95001 - 95114
1960		356B/1600	616/1	3 PB	32 NDIX	74/82.5	7.5:1	60 @ 4500	601501 - 604700
		356B/1600 S	616/2	3 PB	32 NDIX	74/82.5	8.5:1	75 @ 5000	85551 - 88320
		356B/1600 S-90	616/7	3 PB	40 PII-4	74/82.5	9:1	90 @ 5500	800101 - 802000
		Carrera 1600 GT	692/3	PB	W 40 DCM	66/87.5	9.8:1	115 @ 6500	95001 - 95114
			692/3A	PB	44 PII-4	66/87.5	9.8:1	134 @ 7300	96001 - 96050
1961	until Sept.	356B/1600	616/1	3 PB	32 NDIX	74/82.5	7.5:1	60 @ 4500	604701 - 606799
		356B/1600 S	616/2	3 PB	32 NDIX	74/82.5	8.5:1	75 @ 5000	88321 - 89999
									085001 - 085670
		356B/1600 S-90	616/7	3 PB	40 PII-4	74/82.5	9:1	90 @ 5500	802001 - 803999
		Carrera 1600 GT	692/3A	PB	44 PII-4	66/87.5	9.8:1	134 @ 7300	96001 - 96050
	from Sept. from Aug. **(356B T 6)**	356B/1600	616/1	3 PB	32 NDIX	74/82.5	7.5:1	60 @ 4500	606801 - 607750
		356B/1600 S	616/12	3 PB	32 NDIX	74/82.5	8.5:1	75 @ 5000	700001 - 701200
		356B/1600 S-90	616/7	3 PB	40 PII-4	74/82.5	9:1	90 @ 5500	804001 - 804630
1962	until July	356B/1600	616/1	3 PB	32 NDIX	74/82.5	7.5:1	60 @ 4500	607751 - 608900
		356B/1600 S	616/12	3 PB	32 NDIX	74/82.5	8.5:1	75 @ 5000	701201 - 702800
		356B/1600 S-90	616/7	3 PB	40 PII-4	74/82.5	9:1	90 @ 5500	804631 - 805600
		Carrera 2/2000 GS	587/1	PB	40 PII-4	74/92	9.2:1	130 @ 6200	97001 - 97446
	from July	356B/1600	616/1	3 PB	32 NDIX	74/82.5	7.5:1	60 @ 4500	608901 - 610000
		356B/1600 S	616/12	3 PB	32 NDIX	74/82.5	8.5:1	75 @ 5000	702801 - 705050
		356B/1600 S-90	616/7	3 PB	40 PII-4	74/82.5	9:1	90 @ 5500	805601 - 806600

Reutter Coupe	Karmann Coupe	Karmann Hardtop	Reutter Cabriolet	Gläser Cabriolet	Speedster	Convertible D	Roadster
58312 - 59099 100001 - 101692			61500 - 61892		83201 - 83791		
101693 - 102504			150001 - 150149		83792 - 84370		
102505 - 106174			150150 - 151531		84371 - 84922	85501 - 85886	
106175 - 108917			151532 - 152475		84923 - 84954	85887 - 86830	
108918 - 110237			152476 - 152943				86831 - 87391
110238 - 114650			152944 - 154560				87392 - 88920
114651 - 117476		200001 - 201048	154561 - 155569				88921 - 89010 Drauz 89011 - 89483 D'Ieteren
117601 - 118950		201601 - 202200	155601 - 156200				89601 - 89849
118951 - 121099	210001 - 210899	202201 - 202299	156201 - 156999				
121100 - 123042	210900 - 212171		157000 - 157768				

Year Mfg	Vehicle and Engine Model Designation	Engine Model	Crank-case	Carburetors	Stroke/Bore	Compr. Ratio	HP (DIN) @ RPM	Engine Serial #
1963	until July 356B/1600	616/1	3 PB	32 NDIX	74/82.5	7.5:1	60 @ 4500	610001 - 611000 0600501 - 0600600 611001 - 611200*
	356B/1600 S	616/12	3 PB	32 NDIX	74/82.5	8.5:1	75 @ 5000	705051 - 706000 0700501 - 0701200 706001 - 707200*
	356B/1600 S-90	616/7	3 PB	40 PII-4	74/82.5	9:1	90 @ 5500	806601 - 807000 0800501 - 0801000 807001 - 807400*
	Carrera 2/2000 GS	587/1	PB	40 PII-4	74/92	9.2:1	130 @ 6200	97001 - 97446
	Carrera 2/2000 GT	587/2	PB	W 46 IDM/2	74/92	9.8:1	160 @ 6900	98001 - 98032
	from July **(356C)** 356C/1600 C	616/15	3 PB	32 NDIX	74/82.5	8.5:1	75 @ 5200	710001 - 711870 730001 - 731102*
	356C/1600 SC	616/16	3 PB	40 PII-4	74/82.5	9.5:1	95 @ 5800	810001 - 811001 820001 - 820522*
1964	356C/1600 C	616/15	3 PB	32 NDIX	74/82.5	8.5:1	75 @ 5200	711871 - 716804 731103 - 733027*
	356C/1600 SC	616/16	3 PB	40 PII-4	74/82.5	9.5:1	95 @ 5800	811002 - 813562 820523 - 821701*
	Carrera 2/2000 GS	587/1	PB	40 PII-4	74/92	9.2:1	130 @ 6200	97001 - 97446
1965	356C/1600 C	616/15	3 PB	32 NDIX	74/82.5	8.5:1	75 @ 5200	716805 - 717899 733028 - 733197*
	356C/1600 SC	616/16	3 PB	40 PII-4	74/82.5	9.5:1	95 @ 5800	813563 - 813893 821702 - 821855*
1966	March 356C/1600 SC	616/26	3 PB	40 PII-4	74/82.5	9.5:1	95 @ 5800	813894 - 813903

PB: Plain journal bearings
RB: Roller bearings
2: Two-piece crankcase
3: Three-piece crankcase
+ 589/2 1300S engines were also equipped with 40 PICB carburetors
* equipped with new heater system

Reutter Coupe	Karmann Coupe	Karmann Hardtop	Reutter Cabriolet	Gläser Cabriolet	Speedster	Convertible D	Roadster
123043 - 125246	212172 - 214400		157769 - 158700				
126001 - 128104	215001 - 216738		159001 - 159832				
128105 - 131927	216739 - 221482		159833 - 161577				
131928 - 131930	221483 - 222580		161578 - 162165				
			162166 - 162175				

Additionally there were three series of "exchange chassis" for various cars, including race cars, prototypes, damaged customer cars, Abarth vehicles, South African built cabriolets and random production cars. These numbers do not correlate to any particular model or type.

Years Mfg.	Chassis Number
1953 - 1961	12201 - 12376
1958 - 1962	5601 - 5624
1959 - 1965	13001 - 13414

Spotter's Guide

Front

356	1950	Small hood handle without hole. Turn signals below and slightly inboard of the headlights. Integrated bumpers. Split windshield.
	Early 1952	Hood handle with hole. Bent windshield. Aluminum windshield trim. Interim bumpers. Pressed steel bumper guards.
	Late 1952	"A" style bumpers. Pressed steel bumper guards.
	1953	Turn signals directly below headlights.
	Early 1954	Horn grilles added. Low aluminum bumper guards.
	1955	"A" style crested front hood handle. Low chrome windshield frame on Speedster.
356A	1956	Curved windshield.
	Mid-1956	Overrider tubes added on U.S. cars.
	1958	Turn signal mounted on wedge-shaped base. Taller windshield frame on Conv. D than Speedster.
	1959	Higher overrider tube.
356B	1960	Flattened hood. Larger chrome-plated hood handle. Larger/higher bumpers with large chrome-plated bumper guard. Horn grilles above and below the bumper. Last year of front Porsche script.
	1962	Squared-off front hood. Vents on front cowl, except roadster. Gas filler on right front fender, except some RHD cars. Taller windshield on coupe.

Side

356	1950	No trim decos. Coach builder badge on right front fender. Non-hinged rear quarter windows on coupes. No front vent windows. Solid 16" x 3" wheels. Moon hubcaps.
	Mid-1951	Hinged rear quarter windows on coupes. Slotted 16" x 3 1/4" wheels on 1500 cars.
	1954	Speedster features "beltline" aluminum trim. Speedster script on both front fenders. Speedster has aluminum and rubber rocker panel trim.
	1955	"Continental" fender scripts on U.S. spec. coupes and cabriolets.
356A	1956	"European" fender scripts on early coupes and cabriolets. Flattened rocker panels. Rocker panel deco trim on all models. 15" x 4 1/2" wheels.
	Mid-1957	Rear of door handle changed from square to rounded.
	1958 (T-2)	Vent window present on cabriolet. Removable hardtop option on cabriolet. High bow top on Speedster. Roll up windows on Conv. D. Crested "Super" hubcaps optional.
356B	1960	Revised front and rear fender contours. Thinner rocker panel deco trim. Front vent windows on coupes.
	1962 (T-6)	Pop-out rear quarter windows on Karmann Hardtop and removable hardtop.
	1963	Coach builder badges deleted.
356C	1964	Disc brake wheels and flat hubcap.

Rear

356	1950	Vertical taillight placement: rectangular above, round below. Integral bumper. Shine-down license light with brake light in center. Single aluminum grille on rear lid.
	Early 1952	Interim bumper Aluminum rear window trim.
	Late 1952	"A" style bumpers Pressed steel bumper guards Engine designation script added.
	1953	Two round beehive taillights side by side. Center lens on license light clear backup light.
	Early 1954	Low aluminum bumper guards.
356A	Mid-1956	Single overrider tube on U.S. spec. cars.
	Mid-1957	Teardrop taillights. Shine-up license light. Split overrider tube.
	1958 (T-2)	Altered rear cowling on cabriolet. Exhaust routed through bumper guards, except on Carreras.
356B	1960	Larger/higher bumper. Reflectors made by ULO and located either above lights on chrome pods or below bumper. License lights on bumper.
	1962 (T-6)	Larger rear window, coupe. Zip-out rear window, cabriolet. Two vent grilles on rear lid. Larger rear lid, coupe.

Interior

356 / 1950
- Banjo steering wheel.
- Turn signal switch on dashboard.
- Ivory colored VW knobs and escutcheons.
- Two main instruments: black/white speedo and tach or speedo and clock.
- Small oil temperature gauge.
- 3 or more small idiot lights.
- Ash tray in dashboard.
- Black rubber floor mats
- Non-reclining front bucket seats.
- Rear seat area has various configurations.
- Napped cloth headliner.
- Green plastic sun visors.
- Wood door tops.

1952
- Black/green deep faced instruments.
- Turn signal switch moved to steering column.
- Metal door tops.
- Rear seat area standardized with folding back.

1953
- VDM steering wheel with crest in center.
- Larger idiot lights.
- Recaro reclining front seats.
- Most cars have corduroy interiors (1953 only).

1954
- Knobs and steering wheel, ivory, grey or beige.
- Unique dashboard for Speedster with vinyl covered top.
- Larger interior light on coupe.
- Speedster seats.
- Speedster rear seat consists of cushion only.

Mid-1954
- Fuel gauge added.

356A / 1956
- Redesigned dashboard, all models.
- Padded vinyl top on coupe/cabriolet dashboard.
- Three large shallow faced VDO instruments.
- Smaller interior light mounted on dashboard.
- Turn signal switch with chrome stalk.
- Twist release handbrake.
- Perforated vinyl headliner.

1957
- Padded vinyl sun visors.

1958 (T-2)
- Ashtray under dashboard.
- Interior lights in coupe mounted in headliner.
- Beige floor mats used occasionally, 1958-1959.
- Thinner seat back with different pleating pattern.
- No rear seat on Convertible D.
- Window crank and inside door handle repositioned.
- Locking pockets on Convertible D door panel.

356B / 1960
- Black plastic knobs, steering wheel and escutcheons.
- Chrome shift lever with black plastic "mushroom" knob.
- Rear seats with left and right cushions and separate folding backs.
- No rear seats on roadster.

356C / 1964
- Lock on far right of glove box.
- Padded vinyl grab handle.
- Extension below ash tray.

Model Changes

356

Bent or split windshield, two large instruments, 1950-1955.
Black/white instruments, 1950-1951.
Black/green instruments, 1952-1955.
Horn grilles present, 1954-1955.
Hood handle with crest, 1955.

356A

Curved windshield; three large instruments; grey, beige or ivory steering wheel, 1956-1959.
Striker plate with 5 screws, 1956-1957.
Striker plate with 3 screws, 1958-1959.
Ash tray in dash, 1956-1957.
Ash tray under dash, 1958-1959.

356B

Black steering wheel, finned brake drums, 1960-1963.
Gas filler under front hood, 1960-1961.
Gas filler on right front fender, 1962-1963.
One rear grille, 1960-1961.
Two rear grilles, 1962-1963.

356C

Disc brakes, padded grab handle, metal extension under ashtray on dashboard, 1964-1965.

Differentiating Models

Open Cars	Cab	Spd	Conv D	Road
356	*	*		
356A	*	*	*	
356B	*			*
Back seat	*	*		
Roll-up windows	*		*	*
Front vent window	*			
Chrome removable windshield frame		*	*	*

	356	356A	356A T-2	356B T-5	356B T-6	356C
Bent/split windshield	*					
Dual rear grille					*	*
External gas filler					*	*
Disc brakes						*
Vent window, coupe				*	*	*
Vent window, cab			*	*	*	*
16" wheels	*					
Exhaust through bumper guards			*	*	*	*

Index

A

accessories socket 105-106
aerial 60
ash tray 103

B

back up light 73
battery hardware 77-79
battery compartment 9-13, 77-85
battery cover 78
Beck fuel gauge 93-94, 100
Becker radio 102-103
Blaupunkt radio 101-103
blower 79
body panels, exterior 19-44
body panels, internal 9-18
boot 37
bumper brackets 20
bumper trim 45-49
bumpers 19-22

C

carpet 117-122
chassis number chart 143-149
choke control 100
clock 92
closing panel, front 14
closing panel, rear 16
coach builder badges 63-64
coat hook 124
color charts 134-142
combination gauge 94
Continental 62-63
convertible top 31-36
cowl, front 25
cowl, rear 39

D

dashboard 87-88
dashboard scripts 101
diagonal member 14
D'Ieteren badge 64
door handle 65, 126-127
door jamb 37-38, 128
door panel 124-126
door seals 124-126
doors 25-27
Drauz badge 64
driving lights 54

E

engine lid 41-43
engine scripts 70-71
engine shelf 18
escutcheons 126-127
European 62-63

F

fender, front 22-24
fender, rear 40-41
fender brace, front 13-14
fender brace, rear 17-18
fender script 62-63
floor boards 116-117
floor mat 115-116
floor pan 16
fog lights 54
frame struts 14
front body panels 19-25
front chassis 9-13
front lid 23-24
fuel gauge 93-94
fuel tank 12-13, 79-81
fuse block 81

G

gas gauge 93-94
gas heater 18, 79
gas tank 12-13, 79-81
gauges 89-95, 102
gear shift & knob 114-115
Gläser badge 63
glove compartment 103-104
grab handle 104
grille, headlight 51-52
grille, horn 55-56
grille, rear 69
ground strap 77

H

hand throttle 100
handbrake 113
hardtop 33-34, 35
headlight parts 50-53
headlight switch 97
headlights 50-53
headliner 122-124
heat control 100-101, 115
heat vent/slide 128-129
hood 23-24
hood handle 55
hood hinge 82

hood release 81, 114
horn button 108-110
horn grilles 55-56
horn pockets 10
hub caps 75-76

I

idiot lights 95
ignition switch 99
inner nose panel 9-13
inner fender 12-14, 17-18
instruments 89-95, 102
interior 87-133
interior colors/materials 124-125, 134-142
interior light 100, 104-105, 127
interior mirror 106-107

J

jack 80, 83-85
jack spur 15-16

K

Karmann badge 64
knobs 96

L

license light 73
lighter 99
lights 50-54, 71-73, 104-105
lock post 37-38, 128
longitudinal member 14-15
luggage compartment 9-13
luggage mat. 82
luggage rack 70
lug nuts 76

M

manufacturer's I.D. plate 127
map light 104-105
mat, floor 115-116
mat, luggage 82
Meister Schaften badge 106
mirror, interior 106-107
mirror, side 65-66

N

name plates 50, 62-63, 70-71, 101
nose, inner 9-13
nose, outer 22-24

O

oil temperature gauge 92-93

P

paint plate 127
part numbers vi
pedal assembly 112
Porsche script 50, 70, 101
positive terminal 78

Q

quarter panel, inner 17-18
quarter panel. outer 40-41

R

radio 101-103
rear chassis 17-18
rear fender 40-41
rear grille 69
rear lid 41-43
rear quarter window 33-34, 67
rear window 68
reflector 74
Reutter badge 63-64
rocker panel 28
rocker panel trim 64

S

scripts 50, 62-63, 70-71, 101
seat mounts 16
seats 129-133
shift lever & knob 114-115
side mirror 65-66
side molding 64
side windows 66-67
spare tire 9-10, 82-83
speakers 15, 113-114
speedometer 89-90
spotter's guide 150-151
spring plates, bumper 20
starter button 98
steering wheel 108-112
striker plate 128
sun visor 107-108
sunroof 29-30, 100
switches 97-101, 127

T

tachometer 90-91
tail panel 44
taillight 71-72
Telefunken radio 101-102
temperature gauge 92-93
threshold trim 127-128
tire strap 82-83
tonneau cover 37
tool kit 83-85

top boot 37
top, convertible 31-36
top, coupe 28-30
top, hardtop 33-34, 35
top, sunroof 29-30
top brackets 36
towing hook 11
trim 45-76
trunk lid 23-24
turn signal 53-54, 71-72
turn signal switch 98

U

upholstery 117-126, 129-133

V

vent window 66
ventilation system 79, 100-101
VIN plate 127

W

warning lights 95
wheels 74-76
window crank 126-127
windows 33-34, 61-62, 66-68
windshield 61-62
windshield trim 61-62
windshield washer 58-59
windshield wiper 56-58
wiper switch 97
wood steering wheel 110-112